PORTRAIT OF ABERDEEN
AND DEESIDE

Portrait of
ABERDEEN AND
DEESIDE

with Aberdeenshire, Banff
and Kincardine

CUTHBERT GRAHAM

ROBERT HALE · LONDON

© *Cuthbert Graham 1972 and 1980*
First published in Great Britain 1972
Reprinted with revisions 1974
Second edition 1980

ISBN 0 7091 8578 2

Robert Hale Limited
Clerkenwell House
Clerkenwell Green
London EC1R 0HT

PRINTED IN GREAT BRITAIN BY
LOWE AND BRYDONE PRINTERS LTD, THETFORD, NORFOLK

CONTENTS

ILLUSTRATIONS

facing page

7

Pictures provided by Aberdeen Journals Ltd., Ian Hardie and Gordon Bissett

MAPS

FOREWORD

THIS book aims to portray Aberdeen and Deeside, not in isolation, but in their true setting within the region which Scots—though somewhat to the embarrassment of the English—call simply 'the North-East', meaning the knuckle or corner of the country between the North Esk and the Spey.

This corner of Scotland, since 1975 an upper-tier local government division called the Grampian Region, has a unity bestowed not merely by the facts of physical geography but also by human history and economic interdependence. The new-found prosperity enjoyed by Aberdeen and Peterhead, as key ports in the supply and servicing of the offshore oil industry operating in the North Sea, has not altered this underlying reality.

Before the oil boom and the reorganization of local government had boosted the population of the Aberdeen City District to 205,000, John R. Allan, speaking for the region as a whole, remarked: "At a time when big towns seem an infliction on the country around them, Aberdeen remains a necessary condition of our lives. Take away Aberdeen, and the north-east would be a poor dismembered thing. It is the sum of our best qualities; it is our capital. How can a town of nearly two hundred thousand people live so far north? Because it is completely relevant to the country it lives in."

A common stock, mutual achievement over many centuries, has created a deep sense of identity between the Aberdonians and their country cousins—and the phrase 'country cousins' is more than a euphemism. Statistics show that throughout the past two centuries the great majority of settlers in Aberdeen have been migrants from its own rural hinterland, and that kinship with those still tilling the land is extremely common.

What has happened to that land itself is a source of perennial pride. Writing in 1838, and with a certain amount of exaggeration, Lord Cockburn confided in his diary: "I know no part of Scotland so much and so visibly improved within thirty years as Aberdeenshire. At the beginning of that time, the country between Keith and Stonehaven was little else than a hopeless region of stones and moss. There were places of many miles where, literally, there was nothing but large white stones of half a ton to ten tons weight to be seen. A stranger to the character of the people would have supposed that despair would have held back their hands from even attempting to remove them. However, they began, and year after year have been going on making dikes and drains, and filling up holes with these materials, till at last they have created a country which, when the rain happens to cease, and the sun to shine, is really very endurable."

This then, was the Poor Man's Country, which in the nineteenth century was cultivated by such a balance of small, medium and large farmers, that it was still possible for the peasant with the soil in his blood to aspire to a 'placie' of his own. This folk dream has been the inspiration of the imaginative literature of the region for over a century, triggering off a succession of novels from William Alexander's *Johnny Gibb of Gushetneuk* through Lewis Grassic Gibbon's *Sunset Song* to David Toulmin's *Blown Seed* and enriching such a masterpiece of colourful reminiscence as John R. Allan's *Farmer's Boy*.

Royal Deeside, as the holiday home of six successive sovereigns, enjoys a special place in popular esteem and demands special attention. I have described its castles and their relation to that unique phenomenon, the Aberdeenshire School of castle-building. I have quoted ballads. I have drawn on tales and legends, and while this is not a systematic history, I have told as much of local annals as might be needful to explain the background of things seen on the way.

I am much indebted to the writings of the late Dr W. Douglas Simpson, Fenton Wyness and Alexander Keith. I have quoted briefly from the expert opinions in Stewart Cruden's book *The Scottish Castle* (1960). Poets whose lines I have quoted include the late C. C. Abbott, Sir Alexander Gray, Charles Murray, John C. Milne and Rachel Annand Taylor, and among the living George Bruce, Flora Garry, Dr Ken Morrice and Iain Crichton Smith. To Margaret Johnston I am grateful for quotations from *Ninety Wonderful Years* and to W. A. S. Keir for a passage from *The Collected Poems of Burns Singer* (Secker and Warburg). I would like to thank Mr K. J. Peters, Managing Director of Aberdeen Journals Ltd and Messrs J. C. Grant and Peter Watson, successive editors of *The Press and Journal* for kind encouragement. The City Librarian of Aberdeen (Mr Peter Grant) and Reference Librarian, Miss Moira Wilkie, gave unstinting aid. To all my photographer colleagues I am grateful, and especially to Mr Ian Hardie and Mr David Sutherland, while my wife Enid has tracked down errors with relentless hand.

TO THE KINDLY FOLK OF
NORTH-EAST SCOTLAND

And in particular to the 'city folk and country folk'
farmers and fishermen, lairds, ministers and dominies,
bairns at school and veterans in every parish from Esk
to Spey who have guided my steps and who share the
sentiment, 'This is my country.'

I

ABERDEEN: THE FACE OF THE CITY

Mica glittered from the white stone.
Town of the pure crystal,
I learnt Latin in your sparkling cage,
I loved your brilliant streets.

Iain Crichton Smith "Aberdeen"

On the threshold of the 1970s Aberdeen, the third city of Scotland, unexpectedly acquired a new role. It became, almost at the drop of a hat, 'the offshore capital of Europe'. In 1967 Shell Expro approached the city corporation for five acres of land. But at that time oil had not been discovered in quantity in the North Sea and no great significance was attached to the deal. Much more concern was felt about the results of a survey by Professor Maxwell Gaskin of the Chair of Political Economy at Aberdeen University which revealed a substantial outward migration, and the symptoms of decline, along with the falling manpower requirements of the basic industries of farming and fishing.

The Gaskin Report to the Scottish Office saw hope in the identification of "growth areas" on an axis along the surviving rail line between Aberdeen and Elgin, en route to Inverness. But in a short time it became clear that major growth would come on the coast facing the North Sea, where oil was soon being tapped in plenty, and there was an urgent need for supply and servicing facilities to feed the exploratory oil rigs and eventual construction platforms. In the first eight years of the new decade 533 new companies offering services to the offshore oil industry were set up in the city, and at the same time 20,000 new jobs, directly attributable to North Sea oil had been created, with 7,000 to 10,000 more in the back-up category. The need for offshore experts to base themselves upon Aberdeen brought into the city an American colony of about 3,500 and a Dutch colony of 800, both being catered for by their own educational and social organizations.

13

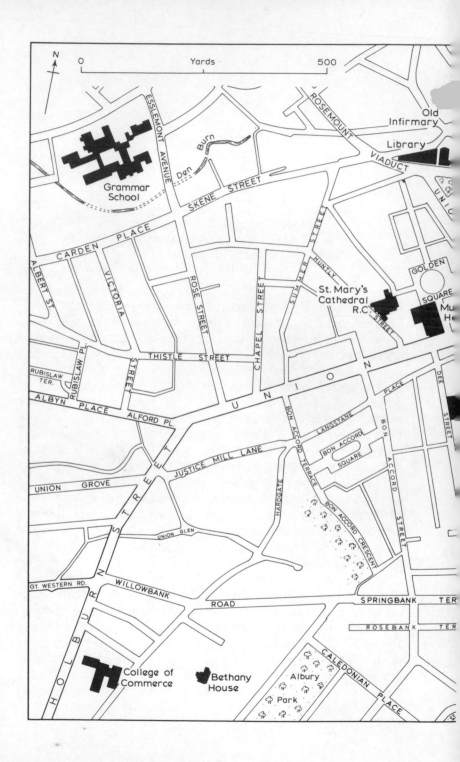

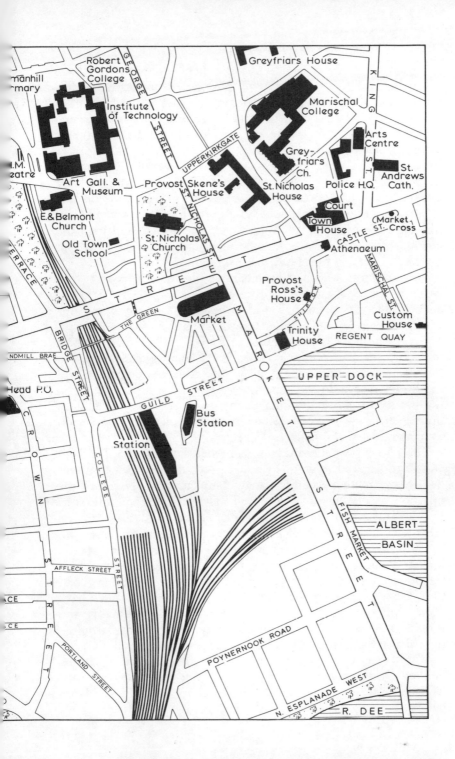

In the early stages of this development Aberdeen did have potential rivals for the new oil business. Dundee, Scotland's fourth city, was also within reasonable distance of the North Sea oilfields, but Aberdeen Airport and Aberdeen Harbour became decisive factors in the competition. The airport at Dyce, apart from its passenger plane services soon acquired two helicopter bases which became indispensable for the day-and-night urgent traffic from shore to offshore installations, while the harbour underwent a rapid transformation at a cost of over £15,000,000, to provide berthage for supply vessels which could be used at any state of the tide. So by the mid-1970s Aberdeen found itself the most prosperous and the most envied city in Scotland. Rapid growth inevitably brought acute problems.

Pressures for new development, at almost any cost to the environment, sent land and house values soaring. But Aberdeen, after 1,000 years of history, had an identity as rugged and immovable as its native granite. It welcomed the oil men, but on its own conditions, which included rigorous planning regulations, respect for its many designated conservation areas and machinery for hammering out problems arising between the newcomers and the indigenous industry. The strength of Aberdeen's character, the beauty of its surrounding countryside, and the riches of its historic heritage made it attractive to the oil men, who soon found it a delightful place to live in.

The North Sea oil industry's maintenance market has been put at an annual sales value of around £400,000,000. But however big a share of that Aberdeen may claim, it can only regard the oil boom as a bonus or addition to its pre-existing economic role. Peel away the outer skin of oil-related activity and you come on Aberdeen as the third fishing port of the United Kingdom. Underneath that again you uncover the monumental granite industry and a small but still vital ship-building sector which remains viable when there is a world-wide ship-building recession. Under that again are textiles and papermaking which have been with the city since the eighteenth century. Finally, and forever is the land—"the country lying quiet and full of farms"— to which Aberdeen is linked by the deepest bonds of all.

"One detests Aberdeen" wrote the novelist Lewis Grassic Gibbon "with the detestation of a thwarted lover. It is the one haunting and exasperatingly lovable city in Scotland—its fascination as unescapable as its shining mail." Another novelist,

Naomi Mitchison, after visiting each of the Scottish university cities commented: "I liked Aberdeen the best, the almost white nights of midsummer reminding me of Leningrad." At a distance of 540 miles from London, Aberdeen is in fact on the same latitude as Leningrad, and its architecture, though perhaps less spectacular, has something of the neo-classic stateliness of Peter the Great's city.

The usual and the most dramatic approach to the city is by the trunk road, largely now a dual carriageway, from Stonehaven and the south. As it crosses the Highland Boundary Fault and traverses, almost imperceptibly the seaward scrag-end of the Grampian mountain range, more properly the Mounth, it yields glimpses of the Spartan Scotland delineated by Sir Alexander Gray:

> Here in the uplands
> The soil is ungrateful;
> The fields, red with sorrel,
> Are stony and bare.
> A few trees, wind-twisted—
> Or are they but bushes?—
> Stand stubbornly guarding
> A home here and there.

Then quite suddenly Aberdeen signals its approach by the appearance, poking up over the brow of a ridge, of a spiky corona of skyscrapers. Some forty of these modern multi-storey blocks, mostly for municipal housing, have broken up the once-unitary image of the distant city—yet the oldest of them dates only from 1961. They may be the first thing about Aberdeen to catch the eye, but they need not hold it for long.

As the highway swings down to the seven-arched Bridge of Dee, built in the first quarter of the sixteenth century, you will see before you a wide spreading silver-veined city arising from a river's brim. The Dee brings a flood of light from its long valley stretching far into the west. On your left as you descend you will glimpse fertile fields and richly wooded slopes and a succession of hills that rise in height to the far-off serrated ridge of Lochnagar and the outriders of the Cairngorms; on your right steep lawns and flowerbeds backed by grey stone houses high on the slope— for this is Kincorth, the earliest of Aberdeen's post-war civic satellites. It was designed on lines suggested by an international competition in 1938, though not implemented until the end of the Second World War. A large proportion of the houses are faced with granite, for it was conceived in an age when Aberdeen was still 'the Granite City' and any other building material for a show-place housing scheme was unthinkable.

On this approach to the town its close and intimate relation to the surrounding countryside is still comfortingly apparent. Green hills and woods on the south-west rise up and dominate the scene. Time was when you could climb to a vantage point anywhere in the centre of the city and see similar open country—or the blue of the ocean—whichever way you looked. Today it is not so easy. The old compactness of the burgh has been somewhat eroded. At its seaward end the city occupies two miles of undulating land between the mouths of its two rivers, the Dee and the Don. It extends inland from a wide sandy bay for three to upwards of half a dozen miles, and on north and south it overspreads its old river-marked bounds into a new suburbia in communities like Dyce, Bridge of Don and Altens, which are largely the children of the oil-boom. Long before that happened it had embraced what were once three quite independent or distinct burghs or local authorities: 'New' Aberdeen, originally a fishing and trading settlement at the point where the small stream called the Den Burn entered the sprawling Dee estuary; Old Aberdeen, a cathedral and university 'village', a short distance from the mouth of the Don, and Woodside, an eighteenth-century mill-town a mile or so higher up the Don valley.

As all are now completely assimilated within the modern city let us look first at the centre of attraction, the force of gravity which holds them together. This is Union Street, a sort of granite canyon 70 feet wide and a mile long, running from east to west, which we may now approach by crossing the river and entering the city by the modern King George VI Bridge, or by the sixteenth-century Bridge of Dee and Holburn Street, leading directly to the western end of Union Street. From there we must move east to its beginning, both in time and place, at Castle Street, traditionally called the Castlegate, for this is the historic kernel out of which it sprouts.

The Castlegate, formerly spelt Castlegait, and meaning simply the 'gait' or 'way' to the castle, is a square of very ancient origin. It has been the official centre of Aberdeen since the thirteenth, and very probably the twelfth century, when the centre of gravity of the town moved up thither via the Shiprow (which we shall shortly explore) from the original collection of rude huts inhabited by fishermen and traders on the waterfront, where the creek of the Den Burn entered the Dee estuary and formed a crude harbour.

The castle to which the 'gait' led was the centre of royal authority, a place of strength, probably an enclosure or courtyard castle, from at least 1249 until the first decade of the fourteenth century. In 1264 it was repaired by one Richard Cementarius—'Richard the Mason'—Aberdeen's first recorded Provost or Chief Magistrate, who also carried out other important building work which we shall meet with in due course. But during the Wars of Independence it was manned by an English garrison in the name of Edward I, the hated 'Hammer of the Scots', and this was enough to seal its doom. When the cause of Robert the Bruce and Scottish independence triumphed the castle was destroyed and never rebuilt. In its place, actually it is said within the courtyard of the old stronghold, the citizens built a chapel which they dedicated to St Ninian. Ironically enough the next and only other occasion when this site was fortified occurred during the only other 'English occupation,' that of Oliver Cromwell, when his soldiers built a bastion of which a fragment still remains on the east side of the Castlehill. It was, however, in modern times, the site of a barracks, and is now occupied by two towering multistorey blocks of flats—nine-storey Virginia Court and eighteenstorey Marischal Court.

In front of these 'skyscrapers' and facing the east side of the Castlegate stands the Salvation Army Citadel, built in a grandiose neo-baronial or castellated style to designs by James Souttar in 1896. The tower of this 'citadel' affords a splendid vantage point. Let us climb it and look down.

The view extends, not merely over the Castlegate itself, but along the entire length of Union Street beyond. Beginning with the immediate foreground, we see exactly the same area (though far from the same architecture) which James Gordon, the Parson of Rothiemay, described in 1661 as "a squair about 100 walking paces in breadth and twyce as much in lenthe", adding "nor can Scotland show such another".

Only one prominent feature of the view remains unaltered since the goodly parson, Aberdeen's first map-maker, wrote his

"Description of the two Towns of Aberdeen". This is the nearer and shorter of the two prominent steeples which you can see on the north or right-hand side of the Castlegate—the lead-covered steeple of the Old Tolbooth, the tower of which was built in 1622 and the lead-covered spire added in 1629. They replaced a much earlier structure built in 1394. A 'tolbooth', it should be explained, is a prison, the municipal lock-up which was from the beginning a necessary adjunct of the authority of an ancient Scottish royal burgh (and Aberdeen was a royal burgh from the time it received its first charter from King William the Lion in the year 1179). In time, however, it became much more than a mere jail. Room had to be found in it for the safe-keeping of documents and treasures. The town clerk had a cubby-hole in it where he could labour at his letters, and eventually the town council itself might meet there in a chamber provided for the purpose; it was then in the full sense of the word the 'Town House'.

Aberdeen's Old Tolbooth is called 'Old' because it is now only an outlying appanage of the Town House proper, a modern building, also in the neo-baronial style (designed by Peddie and Kinnear and built in 1871), whose much taller and bulkier steeple rises up to the west of the Old Tolbooth and overtops it. But to my mind the old steeple is the more beautiful of the two and the tower which it crowns still houses some relics of its ancient predecessor. Among these was 'the maiden', the Scottish variety of the guillotine, employed in 1562 to behead Sir John Gordon, who aspired to marry Mary Queen of Scots, and was the son of the rebellious Earl of Huntly who fell from his horse and died in the Battle of Corrichie.

The Castlegate had a nickname. It was called 'The Plainstanes', after a spacious raised pavement in the centre of the square upon which "of old used many of the inhabitants to pass an hour or two in walking before dinner, bracing their nerves in the free air and discussing the politics of the day".

I seldom hear the name without recalling the proud and passionate cripple child of 8 who haunted the Plainstanes in the last decade of the eighteenth century. He was the future poet George Gordon (not yet Lord) Byron, who was, he tells us, even at that early age "the bondsman of love". In her house in the Castlegate he played at courting, Mary Duff, the daughter of his godfather. "We were", he wrote, "the merest children. . . . I have been attached fifty times since, yet I recollect all we said to each other, all our caresses, her features, my restlessness, my sleep-lessness, my tormenting my mother's maid to write for me to her, which she did at last to quiet me. Hearing of her marriage years after was like a thunderstroke."

One or two houses such as Byron's little sweetheart lived in still survive in the Castlegate. One of them, No. 17 Castle Street, now the Horseshoe Bar, stands on the north side of the square. Built around 1760 it is a typical 'lodging' of the period and its finely-moulded rain-water head is one of the few examples of early lead-work extant.

Immediately opposite No. 17, in the centre of the square, is the picturesque Market Cross of Aberdeen, possibly the finest example of a burgh cross in Scotland. Built for a total cost of £100 in 1686 by John Montgomery, master mason of Old Rayne, it is a hexagonal structure of six open arches. The en-tablature above the arches carries carved portrait medallions of ten Stuart sovereigns beginning with James I of Scotland, and this portrait sequence is unique. Above them from the centre of the cross rises a slender shaft bearing a unicorn rampant.

Even in Byron's day the great change which was to transform the Castlegate from a leisurely residential *place* and market stance, emporium for all the rural produce of the province, into the busy transport hub of a great city was in the making. If you had been able to look down on the Castlegate of the 1790's you would have seen little farther than the square itself, for Aberdeen consisted of a tightly packed little town concentrated mainly around the ancient St Katherine's Hill, and separated from the country to the west by two defiles. These were the watercourses of two streams: the Putachie Burn draining an ancient marsh, which passed down the western side of St Katherine's Hill and had marked for centuries the western limit of the built-up area; and the much larger valley of the Den Burn, some distance farther west still. The old road into the town from south and west dipped down tortuously into both these defiles, then reached the Castlegate by the curving and steep brae or slope of the Shiprow round the southern and eastern side of St Katherine's Hill.

The difficulty of the approach hampered development, and in 1796, Charles Abercrombie, a surveyor who had planned turn-pike roads for Aberdeenshire, proposed that the Aberdeen authorities should open up a new street, through the west end of the Castlegate, across the sliced-off top of St Katherine's Hill, and over the Den Burn valley by means of a bridge and a viaduct "so as to form a communication with the extensive plain to the west of the town".

All this involved a massive engineering operation. Looking along Union Street from our vantage point on the tower of the Citadel today, one can scarcely realize the obstacles that had to be overcome. One can see however, that, after leaving the Castlegate, Union Street dips down gently for the first quarter of its length to the St Nicholas Street-Market Street intersection. This is the western slope of St Katherine's Hill. The Putachie Burn is nowhere to be seen. It now runs in a culvert underground. After this first section Union Street rises, equally gently on its dead-straight course to the west. But what one cannot see from this elevated viewpoint is that this gentle ascent does not follow the natural contours of the land but is sustained on a long viaduct, a succession of blind arches carried high above the ancient approach, the street called the Green on the left or south side of the new thoroughfare.

When it reaches the deep chasm of the Den Burn, Union Street is carried over it by Union Bridge, a single-span structure designed by Thomas Fletcher. The whole of this mighty work was accomplished in the first decade of the nineteenth century, and the street itself, begun in 1800, was named Union Street in commemoration of the Parliamentary Union of Great Britain and Ireland. As if this were not enough the New Streets Commissioners of the town council also opened up a new thoroughfare to the north of the city, beginning from the Castlegate, and called it King Street. Thus at one blow, so to speak, Aberdeen made itself anew—and it made itself of granite, the hardest building stone in the world.

Since the great age of granite building in Aberdeen is now definitely a thing of the past, it is possible to be quite objective about this highly emotive subject. Granite has always had its admirers and its detractors. The case against granite has been very well put by Mr W. A. S. Keir in his introduction to *The Collected Poems of Burns Singer*. Granite, he says, "is a material which has many qualities such as solidity and strength, but one which does not lend itself easily to vitality or elegance, let alone colour or gaiety. Primarily, in fact, it is ideal for building banks and tombs".

On the other hand it must be said that this extremely hard, embarrassingly durable and sometimes very beautiful stone, which derives its scintillating gleam from the 'glitter of mica' among the crystals of quartz and felspar of which it is composed, has its own special genius, a genius which requires the sympathy and talent of a gifted architect to bring it forth. When this is forthcoming—and it was abundantly forthcoming in nineteenth-century Aberdeen—the result can be something so virginally pure, so haunting in its austerity that it is not quite of this world.

Used with mastery by the ancient Egyptians, employed by Philip II of Spain to build the Escorial, granite—in the form of surface boulders—had been widely used in Aberdeen in the Middle Ages, when it was employed in building part of the Cathedral of St Machar. But the first actual granite *quarry* in the Aberdeen area had been opened in 1604 for supplying window sills and lintels and other large stones. Two more followed in 1730 and 1740, but it was not until the end of the eighteenth century that large-scale production commenced.

This was at Rubislaw, where for close on two centuries the fine blue-grey granite was extracted from the "biggest granite hole in Britain", a hole out of which, it used to be said, "the best half of Aberdeen has come". Until around a decade ago it was still being hewed out of Rubislaw's mighty quarry—465 feet deep, 900 feet long and 750 feet wide. In the mid-sixties of this century it was being used to build Leeds University extension, the Halls of Justice at Swindon, the Bannockburn memorial and Dumbarton's municipal buildings. But in 1970 it was announced that no more granite would come from Rubislaw, the economically viable vein of stone having been exhausted.

There are, of course, other granite quarries not far from Aberdeen, which will always be an important granite-producing area. The brute facts of geology have ensured that, and the special skills learned in many generations, have built up in Aberdeen a major monumental granite industry which operates with granites from all over the world. But the days when granite could be, and was, used for every kind of building, domestic and public, humble and grandiose are now over.

Before we descend from our perch on the Citadel and explore Union Street itself, it is time to see what the Granite Age did for the Castlegate. The opening off the Castlegate on the right (or north) in the foreground is King Street, and at the Castlegate-

King Street corner stands the regional headquarters of the Clydesdale, formerly the North of Scotland, Bank, with its semi-circular classical portico. On the flat top of the pediment of this portico you can just make out a seated figure in coloured terra-cotta. It looks rather like the familiar figure of Britannia on the back of an old penny. But it is not Britannia. It is Ceres—whom the Greeks knew as Demeter. Ceres, the Goddess of Plenty. Just fancy! Ceres with her cornucopia in the heart of this Spartan province, where the land is so often stony and recalcitrant, where life has always been frugal and plenty seems like a miracle. This Ceres pleases me mightily. She is the work of a self-made man called James Giles (1801–70) who proved that it was possible to live and even to prosper in Aberdeen as a portrait painter, though he turned his hand to other things and designed decorative table linen for Queen Victoria, whose mind, incidentally he helped to make up on the important question of coming to live on Deeside. On the centenary of his death there was a special exhibition of his work, not only in Aberdeen, but also in the Ashmolean Museum in Oxford.

Giles was a friend of the architect of the bank, Archibald Simpson (1790–1847), to whom central Aberdeen owes much. He was the son of a merchant burgess of the city, and in the period of its great expansion he was at hand to design a dozen public buildings, two fine squares and a plain but impressive crescent that would not dishonour Bath or Brighton. The bank was built in 1840, but a much earlier and simpler example of Simpson's work is the building directly facing us on the west side of the Castlegate with its deep first-floor windows flanked by pillars. This is part of a large block extending some way west up Union Street and known as Union Buildings, begun in 1818 and completed in 1822. The front facing the Castlegate was designed as the Athenaeum News Room run in conjunction with a private circulating library, but this venture did not pay and for a century it has been a restaurant.

The earliest of the new-style dressed granite buildings in the Castlegate, on the south side of the square, was the fine Aberdeen Bank building designed by James Burn of Haddington in 1801, and taken over by the Union Bank in 1849.

Moving west from the Castlegate, as we will now do, the short street to the south of the Athenaeum, giving access to the Shiprow, is called Exchequer Row and takes its name from the

Mint set up there in the twelfth century by King William the Lion. Needless to say, only the name remains today, so we pass on to the Shiprow itself. Here there is one significant survival. Facing a twentieth-century supermarket and multi-storey car park is Provost Ross's House, the second oldest remaining domestic dwelling in 'New' Aberdeen. The house as originally constructed consisted of a rectangular main block with two projecting towers, front and back, both of which are finished with simple well-proportioned gables. It was built in 1593 and along with the adjoining two houses, Nos. 48 and 50 Shiprow, was restored from a state of near collapse and ruin after a national campaign by preservationists in 1952, to which Queen Elizabeth, the Queen Mother, lent her powerful advocacy.

Now made available to the Aberdeen City District Art Gallery and Museums department for use as a maritime museum, by its owner the National Trust for Scotland, Ross's House is thought to have been built by Andrew Jamesone (the father of George Jamesone, Scotland's first notable portrait painter) for Robert Watson, wright, and his wife Margaret Collie, whose initials have been found on the spur stones. It was a century later that Provost John Ross of Arnage acquired the house and altered it, inserting a new front door on the east front—so that he could survey his trading ships in the harbour. Perhaps I may be indulged if I tell the rest of the story in ballad form:

> The Provost stood at the door of his house
>   And he counted his ships on the tide,
> And he sailed on a barque to the Low Countrie,
>   And in Amsterdam he died.

> But the house that he bought and plenished so fine
>   Lived on when he was dead,
> And McGibbon and Ross admired its line,
>   "In some respects unique," they said,
> And that was all very fine.

> But a graceless age took little care
>   Of the house on the Shiprow brae;
> And what with its years and its wear and tear
>   It fell on an evil day.

And the Council met to decide its fate:
"Let's preserve it for the town"
Said some, but some said, "That's too late,
    With a tug it will all come down."

The shades of the Provost and his ships
    Came home from the Low Countrie,
And they stirred the wavering hearts and hopes
    Of the townsfolk by the Dee.

And a well-loved Queen took up the plea
    For the house on the Shiprow brae.
It was built anew by a mason true
    And saved for posterity.

And the shades of the Provost and his ships
    Rejoice in their silent way
That the house they knew is a haven true
    For our guests from over the sea.

In its present form the Shiprow affords a beguiling view of the
harbour of Aberdeen and its shipping, while looking up and
north in the other direction, it shows the contrast to be found in
the centre of the city between ancient and modern. A pedestrian
way leads back to Union Street at its intersection with Broad
Street. Here on the one hand we have the neo-baronial Town
House of 1871 and on the opposite side of Broad Street the
fourteen-storey tower of St Nicholas House, built in the last few
years of the 'sixties, which houses most of the municipal depart-
ments.

Tucked away in the courtyard of this twentieth-century
skyscraper is another fascinating survival, the restored Provost
Skene's House, which as it survives today is largely a seventeenth-
century creation. The title deeds of the property, however, go
back to 1545—so, in a sense it is even older than Ross's House.
It is also much larger, consisting of an L-plan mansion with an
oblong main block, and tall stair turrets at both ends, from which a
square tower projects at the south-east angle. Sir George Skene
of Rubislaw, a wealthy merchant who traded in Danzig acquired
the house in 1669, adding the east wing or tower with its decorated doorway (surmounted by his coat of arms) and the two
stair turrets. An additional small wing had been added to the
west end about 1800. The house is now being used as a period

domestic museum under the care of Aberdeen's Art Gallery Committee.

The building, restored by the town council in 1951 contains among other treasures a remarkable cycle of religious paintings in tempera on the timber vault of the long gallery. Hidden for 300 years under plaster, they are believed to date from 1622. Panels illustrate the Annunciation, the Adoration of the Shepherds and the Crucifixion, while other decoration shows how medieval religious motifs persisted in the strongly episcopalian north-east of Scotland long after the Reformation. The two withdrawing rooms on a lower floor have oak panelling of Provost Skene's day and there are several handsomely decorated plaster ceilings.

It is almost an anti-climax to mention that in the first half of this century this fine old house was a model lodging house and was universally known as Cumberland House. It had been occupied for six weeks in the spring of 1746 by H.R.H. the Duke of Cumberland on his way north to defeat Bonnie Prince Charlie's Highlanders at the Battle of Culloden. The 'Butcher' Cumberland, detested in Scotland for the barbarity of his reprisals after that melancholy fray, was equally unpopular in Aberdeen, but for another reason. While in residence at Provost Skene's House the Duke and his officers made free with the stocks of provisions, coals, candles, ales and other liquors in the cellars. They even milked the cow, they spoiled the bed and table linen and robbed the thrifty Aberdeen housewife of her store of sugar.

Immediately facing the north end of St Nicholas House, on the east side of Broad Street, is the elaborate neo-Gothic façade of Marischal College, the most remarkable but not always the most admired granite building in Aberdeen. The college was founded as a specifically Protestant second university for Aberdeen by George Keith, fifth Earl Marischal, in 1593, in the old buildings of the Greyfriars Monastery. It is one of the major anomalies of Aberdeen that for over two and a half centuries it had *two* universities, as many as there were in the whole of England during the same period! The clash of Catholic and Protestant does not explain this. Even at the time when Marischal College and University was founded, the University of Aberdeen at King's College, little over a mile to the north in Old Aberdeen, was indubitably a Reformed institution. But the Earl Marischal had travelled widely on the Continent and he was an ardent supporter of the new learning of the Renaissance. He expected and hoped that his new university would be superior in its curriculum and system of instruction to the older university, where the coming of new concepts had been somewhat delayed. Once in being, however, the second university developed a strong individuality of its own and the final 'fusion' of the two institutions did not take place until 1860—after much heartburning and lamentation.

A plain eighteenth-century building supplanted the old mon-astery in 1741. Then in 1837–44 Archibald Simpson designed a new set of buildings forming three sides of a quadrangle. For the next half century they remained screened from the vulgar gaze by the pre-existing domestic houses on the east side of Broad Street, one of which was the boyhood home of Lord Byron. Then at the end of the nineteenth century a major scheme of extensions got under way. The Mitchell Tower and the Mitchell Hall (where all Aberdeen University graduation ceremonies now take place) were added to Archibald Simpson's Marischal College, while the old houses on the east side of Broad Street were swept away along with the medieval monastery kirk of Greyfriars, and the present Marischal College frontage, forming the fourth side of the quadrangle, took their place. The new building, designed by A. Marshall Mackenzie, was opened by King Edward VII in 1906. At the time of its erection it was the second-largest granite building in the world—the largest being the Escorial.

The perpendicular Gothic style chosen by the architect gave scope to the granite industry in Aberdeen for the most intricate sculpturing of granite ever attempted. The fretted pinnacles of this gleaming white architectural *tour-de-force* have been criticized by purists for their over-elaboration. Marischal College to me—and to most Aberdonians and visitors—is self-justifying rhetoric in stone: highfalutin certainly, but highfalutin in a way that comes off. It is all of a piece with the Aberdeen temperament, a temperament that, while it is plodding and pedestrian in the main, does have its high flights of passion and self-asserting rhodo-montade. It was an Aberdeen poet after all, Rachel Annand Taylor, who wrote:

> Poverty wears a scarlet cloke
> In my land.

There is little of the scarlet cloak about Union Street, to which we will now return. The keynote of Union Street is dignified and, yes, sometimes elegant simplicity. It has a basic style consisting of plain Regency houses of three or four storeys and an attic, the one block linked to the other in perfect uniformity, and this uniformity is only broken sufficiently often to give a little relief to the eye. A street a mile long of this character would become somewhat monotonous, but geography and inheritance from the past have ensured the necessary relief.

Beyond the slight dip down to the Market Street–St Nicholas Street intersection already mentioned, Union Street in its gentle ascent passes on the right or north the ancient City Kirkyard of St Nicholas. This is bounded by a façade of twelve Doric columns with an arched gateway in the middle. In summer trees cast the green flourish of their branches over the pediment of this neo-classic feature and invite the passer-by to enter the kirkyard itself, where he will find plentiful seats appropriate for a picnic lunch or a pause for reflection. The Church of St Nicholas repays inspection.

Aberdeen is not unique in having chosen St Nicholas, the friend of sailors, as its patron saint. He is the patron saint also of Newcastle and Berwick, Amsterdam, Hamburg and Kiel, all North Sea trading communities. But it is exceptional in that its burgh church stood in the Middle Ages apart and outside the burgh boundaries on the west side of the declivity formed by the Burn of the Loch. The town's church (divided since the Reformation into two separate places of worship, the East and West Churches) was in olden times the largest parochial church in Scotland with a length of 256 feet.

While it has been very much altered down the years it still retains, particularly in the north transept, some of the original Norman work. The church was first mentioned in a papal bull of 1157, and as originally built was a complete Norman edifice, consisting of nave and aisles, transepts, an aisled chancel of three bays with semi-circular apse, and a central tower. The two churches of the present day are separated from each other by the arches of the steeple and the walls of the transepts.

In the north transept, known as Collison's Aisle, there is a window above which is a unique lead apron or tracery. The south transept or Drum's Aisle, rebuilt in the nineteenth century, contains a stone effigy of Sir Alexander Irvine of Drum, who died in 1457, along with a monumental brass. The West Church, originally the nave, was rebuilt in the middle of the eighteenth century by James Gibbs (1682–1754), a famous son of Aberdeen who became the architect of Christ's College, Cambridge, the Radcliffe Library, Oxford and St Martin-in-the-Fields in London. The lovely medieval crypt of the East Church, now called St Mary's Chapel, has been well restored.

Two more features of the City Kirk must be mentioned. In the West Church are preserved four tapestries of Biblical themes, the work of Mary Jamesone, the daughter of George Jamesone and grand-daughter of the architect of Ross's House. The belfry of St Nicholas houses a carillon of forty-eight bells which regularly peal out psalm tunes that can be heard above the clamour of the city's traffic.

The next break in the continuity of Union Street is provided by the deep and wide valley of the Den Burn spanned by Fletcher's Union Bridge. On the south side the bridge is now lined with shops which conceal the railway station in the valley below, but on the north side it remains open giving a delightful view over Union Terrace Gardens, a much-frequented public park laid out in grassy slopes and flower beds alongside the railway line to the north,—much in the same way as Princes Street Gardens utilise the former bed of the Nor' Loch in Edinburgh.

Wherever it is possible in Aberdeen the austerities of the granite are relieved by trees and flowers. It is doubtless for this reason that on many occasions the city won the national Britain-in-Bloom contest. The Aberdonian is a countryman at heart. The sound of a mighty colony of rooks rearing its young at the busy traffic junction of Union Street and Union Terrace, which overlooks the Gardens, is music in his ears—however unwelcome the rooks are as thieves of the cornfields. On the far side of Union Terrace Gardens the view is closed by a fine range of buildings along the line of Schoolhill Viaduct. These are the Central Public Library, St Mark's Church and His Majesty's Theatre, the trio being nicknamed of old 'Education, Salvation and Damnation'.

St Mark's Church has a massive and the theatre has a miniature dome, and this theme of gaily painted domes (usually a bright green) is repeated farther along the line of Schoolhill and the area just behind it, by the dome of Archibald Simpson's extremely handsome neoclassical Old Infirmary building (now in use as an outpatient department) and by the dome of the Cowdray Hall, the war memorial and the art gallery, which form a single continuous block. The perspective of these buildings, all in granite either grey or pink, is completed by and contrasted with Archibald Simpson's splendid brick spire of the Triple Kirks, copied from Marburg Cathedral. This whole complex of buildings, which the eye can take in at a single sweep from the north side of Union Bridge, is a striking answer to those who complain of the severity of the granite as a building material. Properly spaced out and distanced, relieved by the greenery of tree, lawn and flower this is an architectural composition which can lift up the heart in the exhilaration of a sunny day.

This part of the town is also a Valhalla of the famous. Among the procession of statues there is a granite King Edward VII, a bronze of Robert Burns addressing that "wee crimson-tipped" flower the daisy (which is so often removed by vandals that the city authorities have given up trying to replace it), a bronze Prince Consort and in front of the theatre, to which he seems to be pointing, a colossal bronze of Sir William Wallace by W. Grant Stevenson, which is quite the most remarkable monument to the Liberator that Scotland can boast.

Aberdeen has been stigmatized from time to time as being indifferent, if not hostile, to the arts. Yet the art gallery in Schoolhill is one of the finest in Britain. This is due to very generous endowment which has enabled it to amass a catholic and up-to-date collection. There are not many Old Masters, but very well represented is the Scottish School, from George Jamesone (1588–1644) to Sir William MacTaggart, John Maxwell and many others of our own day. Jamesone of course lived and worked in Schoolhill in a picturesque old house which survived into last century, but did not escape the developer's demolition squad. He left to Aberdeen its first public park, the Four-neukit Garden at Woolmanhill, now recreated and centred by the Well of Spa near the Denburn high flats. Not until the early nineteenth century was he followed by any significant Aberdeen painters, but in those stirring days there was a veritable renaissance. James Giles we have already mentioned. He was followed by William Dyce and John ('Spanish') Philip, and it was in thinking of this distinguished trio that James Cassie, another prominent Aberdeen artist gave voice to the most familiar Aberdonian boast of all time. At a dinner with fellow Scottish artists, when competing claims were made, he remarked in the broad patois of the region: "There's Jamesone, Dyce and Philip—tak' awa' Aberdeen an' twal' mile roon an' far are ye? [Take away Aberdeen and twelve miles round and where are you?]"

But there is nothing insular in the Aberdeen Art Gallery collection. The French Impressionists and Post-Impressionists and the modern English school are finely represented with notable works by Monet, Sisley, Augustus John, W. R. Sickert, Degas, Jack Yeats, Wyndham Lewis and Ben Nicolson, while the sculpture includes several works by Epstein and Henry Moore. Besides the permanent collection there are normally up to five visiting exhibitions on view simultaneously at the gallery and concerts are frequently held there.

Schoolhill takes its name from the ancient grammar school of the burgh, founded at least as long ago as the fifteenth century which formerly stood there, but moved west to Carden Place in 1863. This famous school, at which Byron toiled at his Latin, lost its old name and its selective status on being converted into a 'neighbourhood comprehensive' by Aberdeen Education Committee, who renamed it Rubislaw Academy, but it is once again being called Aberdeen Grammar School and treasures its ancient traditions, and many heirlooms. Byron's statue, a notable work by the sculptor-poet Pittendrigh MacGillivray, stands guard before the building designed for the school by James Matthews, apprentice and successor of Archibald Simpson.

Although they are represented on its Board of Governors the civic fathers cannot interfere with such drastic effect in the destinies of the other great school in Schoolhill. This is Robert Gordon's College, approached through the arched gateway to the east of the art gallery. Standing at the end of a long avenue flanked by lawns and the buildings of Robert Gordon's Institute of Technology is 'The Auld Hoose', the original building of the college, designed by William Adam, father of the better-known Adam Brothers, and completed in 1739. It was founded by Robert Gordon, another of Aberdeen's many merchants trading with the Baltic, as a 'hospital' or boarding school for the sons of poorer burgesses in Aberdeen. It is now a grant-aided day school (with a small boarding house for the sons of parents living abroad). As a member of the Headmasters' Conference it is also a 'public school' in the English, not the Scottish, sense.

One way to indicate its educational significance is to recall a story attributed (by Professor John Paton in his book *The Claim of Scotland*) to Ramsay MacDonald. One of the Premier's guests at Chequers represented to him that the Indian Civil Service

Aberdeen: the Castlegate and Union Street from the Salvation Army Citadel

should be restricted to young men educated at English public schools. Asked why, he said, "Because they are the only chaps who know how to handle the natives."

"Then perhaps," said the Prime Minister, "we might examine the evidence." He picked up the *Official Gazette* and read: "*United Provinces*: Governor—Sir Alexander MacPherson. Education: Robert Gordon's College and University of Aberdeen."

He then read out the data on a second governor and a third. In each case it was the same. All three had been educated at Gordon's College and Aberdeen University. What the interlocutor said is not recorded.

As we move west along Union Street from Union Bridge we pass Diamond Street and South Silver Street, leading to Golden Square, designed by Archibald Simpson. At the South Silver Street corner is the Music Hall with its stately pillars which he also designed. It was built in 1820 as a suite of assembly rooms and today in its largest hall Scottish National Orchestra concerts are held monthly throughout the winter.

Golden Square has lost its quiet secluded air since its central lawn was ploughed up and tarmacadamed to serve as a car park. Also a comparative novelty here is the massive granite statue of George, the fifth and last Duke of Gordon (1770–1836). It formerly stood in the Castlegate—an appropriate site for the first colonel of the territorial regiment of Aberdeen and the north-east of Scotland, The Gordon Highlanders.

Opposite the Music Hall are Crown Street and Dee Street and a little way along the latter, at the corner of Langstane Place is the Lang Stane, a granite monolith for which a niche has been provided in the wall of a store. It is probably a survivor of a Bronze Age stone circle. Some distance west on the same line of street (parallel to and south of Union Street), but now called Hardgate, is the Crab Stane, a squarish boulder also preserved in a special niche. Originally the boundary stone of a croft belonging to John Crab, a Flemish immigrant who became a hero of the War of Independence, it also marks the site of two notable battles— the Battle of the Crab Stane on 20th November 1571, between protagonists and antagonists of Mary Queen of Scots; and the Battle of the Justice Mills on 'Black Friday', 13th September 1644—the prelude to the deplorable sack of Aberdeen by the 'wild Irishes' and highlanders of the Marquess of Montrose.

Central Aberdeen: Union Street in foreground, St. Nicholas Church bottom right, Union Terrace top left, Rosemount Viaduct top centre Simpson's Old Infirmary top right.

The streets on both sides of this western half of Union Street were laid out on land belonging to the various craft guilds of the Seven Incorporated Trades of Aberdeen: Crown Street by the Hammermen, and Bon-Accord, Square, Terrace and Crescent farther west by Archibald Simpson for the Tailor craft. It is not surprising that this district is one of several conservation areas designated for preservation in view of their architectural merits. Union Street itself is another such area, while a third includes a large part of the Rubislaw ward to the west, and a fourth is Marine Terrace (in the Ferryhill ward) which was also designed by Archibald Simpson. Yet Simpson was not, it must be emphasized, the only architect of distinction at work in this creative period. Important also were the two Smiths: John, the first City Architect of Aberdeen, who designed the classical screen to St Nicholas Kirkyard which I have already mentioned; and his son and successor, William, who became the architect of Balmoral Castle.

As a fair generalization it could be said that both Simpson and the elder Smith excelled in classical styles, while their essays in the Gothic were comparatively mediocre. After the building of Balmoral Castle in 1853, however, the classical style was 'out' and neo-baronial was 'in'. It stayed 'in' in one form or another for the next sixty years, which is why as late as 1907 the general post office in Crown Street was designed like a medieval castle— a very grand and splendid one. And now when we come to the extreme western end of Union Street, at the intersection called Holburn Junction, we find the view closed by another castellated building, Christ's College (erected in 1850). It faces down the length of Union Street to the Salvation Army Citadel where we began this tour, one religious castle nodding to another. Queen Victoria's romanticism, however, cannot really be blamed for this vogue. It had actually begun in Aberdeen in the later Middle Ages, when, as we shall see when we move over to Old Aberdeen, St. Machar's Cathedral was given western towers with great machiolated warheads like a feudal fortress.

West of Holburn Junction Alford Place leads on to Albyn Place and Queen's Road through an area of stately terraces fronted by lawns and flower-beds and lined with great trees. This was the nineteenth-century design for gracious living, and no city in the world can boast so notable a succession of granite villadom. Fronting Albyn Place behind what is now a strip of public parkland is Rubislaw Terrace (1852), designed in a grand Abbotsford style by Mackenzie and Matthews from a sketch by James Giles; while in Albyn Place itself is the High School for Girls (1837) by Archibald Simpson. Renamed Harlaw Academy, it has been called the finest example of dressed granite in the city. More elaborate granite architecture is seen in Hamilton Place by John Bridgeford Pirie, who also designed the elaborate Gothic Queen's Cross Church, while exotic use of variegated stonework by Alexander Ellis is seen in St Mary's Episcopal Church, Carden Place (1862), nicknamed the 'tartan kirk'.

The traditional approach to Old Aberdeen, to which we may now turn, is by way of Broad Street, Gallowgate, Mounthooly, King's Crescent, Spital and College Bounds—a route known to generations of University students traversing the old high road from Aberdeen to the north, as 'the Spital Brae'. As, however, this route is now complicated by a traffic ban in the High Street of the Aulton, as Old Aberdeen is called, we may choose the simple and straightforward alternative of King Street, the new way to the north opened up in 1800.

After leaving the Castlegate, a little way down on the right is the rather inconspicuous Gothic frontage of St Andrews Episcopal Cathedral (Archibald Simpson, 1816). Its interior is the great feature. G. E. Street and Sir Robert Lorimer contributed to this, but its crowning glory is the Seabury Memorial restoration by Sir Ninian Comper. This was the gift of the bishops of the American Episcopal Church. Dedicated in 1948 it commemorates Samuel Seabury, first bishop of the United States, who was consecrated in Aberdeen in 1748. On the opposite side of King Street is the Civic Arts Centre, housed in the former North Parish Church (1830) modelled by John Smith on St Pancras Church, London. We pass from arts to sport farther down King Street, where, on the right, Merkland Road East leads to Pittodrie Park, the ground of Aberdeen Football Club. At St Machar Drive, flanked by the massive block of the new college of agriculture we turn left to enter Old Aberdeen.

St Machar Drive slices through the Aulton at its central point. The Old Aberdeen Town House stands with its back to it on its south side and faces the High Street, of which it is the terminal feature. Immediately opposite it on the north side of St Machar Drive begins the tree-shaded Chanonry leading to St Machar's

Cathedral, which stands on a high grassy platform overlooking
Seaton Park in the haughland or river meadow of the Don,
precisely at the point where, in a wide meander, it takes the shape
of a shepherd's crook. This was the site to which, according to
hallowed tradition, the saint was directed in the sixth century
and there he founded his church.

Early in the twelfth century King David I of Scotland, known
to history as "that sair sanct for the Crown" (costly saint for the
monarchy), transferred a bishop's see from Mortlach in Banffshire
to Old Aberdeen, then a village of "four ploughs" known as the
Kirkton of Seaton. Of the Norman cathedral then built nothing
now survives but a single carved stone preserved in the charter
room above the porch. It fell into ruin and a new cathedral was
commenced in 1357. It was never really completed, for by the
time of the Reformation 200 years later the new choir was not
yet finished. What we have today, therefore, is the nave, with
parts of the ruined transepts. It is aisled, and the two most easterly
pillars (fourteenth-century) are of sandstone, but the greater part
of the building is of granite. The building was crested with an
embattled parapet, and the two great western towers built around
1420 were strongly buttressed and boldly machiolated in the
military tradition, and crowned with battlemented parapets.
Between them the west front with its portal was given a great
window of seven lights. The whole composition, doubtless the
work of a local mason, is in its rude strength quite unlike that of

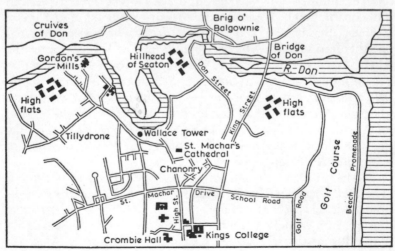

any other cathedral in the world. Internally its supreme feature is the heraldic ceiling dating from 1520 and consisting of forty-eight shields in three parallel rows. A great central tower built by Bishop Elphinstone (1431–1514) crashed in ruin in 1688.

William Elphinstone, statesman and Chancellor of Scotland was the founder of the University of Aberdeen. It was he who obtained the foundation bull by Pope Alexander IV dated 10th February 1494 in response to a petition by King James IV who had represented to the Pontiff that in the northern parts of his kingdom there were "men who are rude, ignorant of letters and almost barbarous". The opening words of the bull declare that "among the other blessings which mortal man is able to obtain in this fleeting life, it deserves to be reckoned not among the least that by earnest study he may win the pearl of knowledge, which shows the way to living well and happily . . . leads to a clear understanding of the secrets of the universe . . . and raises to eminence those born in the lowest estate". By the end of the same year King James had by charter created "the Cathedral city of Ald Aberdeen a true and free burgh of barony for ever". At this early date therefore all three elements in the Aulton were already in being: the church, the university and the burgh.

The ground plan of the burgh was very simple. It consists of the Chanonry, the ecclesiastical quarter originally lined by the manses and glebes of the cathedral clergy, and now by the stately homes of the university professors, which, leading north from the Old Aberdeen Town House to the gate of the cathedral, then turns at a right angle skirting the churchyard and debouches on Don Street to the east. Don Street itself leads back to the Town House, beyond which to the south extends the High Street, leading in turn to College Bounds which leads on to the Spital brae and the 'new town'. All this area is now part of 120 acres of land owned and developed by the university, who also own 110 more acres on the other side of the river Don. The surviving buildings from the past in this 'village community' are of all periods from the sixteenth to the nineteenth century.

They are of all scales from great rambling mansions to charming rows of single-storey tiled cottages, such as those in Grant's Place or Wrights and Coopers Place off the High Street, and they are all safe and have been, or are being, restored with money from a trust. Thus whatever happens the original Aulton will remain and in this context the idea of making the High Street a pedestrian precinct makes good sense. The good faith of the university is manifest in the care it is taking in this great scheme of preservation. But alongside this wonderful conservation area, on land formerly unoccupied by any buildings whatever—the ancient 'market lands' of the Aulton and the former college playing fields—the university, driven by the needs of very rapid expansion, has in the past two decades surrounded the ancient village with massive and towering departmental buildings and student halls of residence—and the corporation of Aberdeen, in the land beyond this outer ring of the 'university city', has reared successions of multi-storey flats. The result is that whereas only two decades ago one could stand on the northern end of Aberdeen's sea beach promenade and see the skyline of the Aulton broken only by two historic symbols—the towers of the cathedral and the Imperial Crown of King's College—both are now virtually lost in the welter of modernity.

That imperial crown tops the tower of King's College, which was built, along with the very beautiful college chapel, on the east side of College Bounds in the first years of the sixteenth century. From then till now it has remained a potent emotive symbol, revered by the native Aberdonian or student son of the university, generating, especially in the 'exile' waves of nostalgia. As A. W. Mair put it:

Crown of King's—and yonder the infinite thunder of ocean
  Breaks and beats on the shore as of old in the days that are sped;
Breaks as it beat of old: Ah me! but my heart in my breast will
  Beat never more as it beat in the golden days that are dead.

The crown, which an early description calls a "most curious and statelie work of hewin and corned stones, representing to the view of all beholders a brave pourtrait of the royal diademe" is only paralleled in Scotland by the crown of the High Kirk of St Giles in Edinburgh.

As an inscription on the west wall indicates the building which we now know as King's College Chapel, but which was then the Chapel of St Mary in the Nativity, was commenced on 2nd April 1500 and was finished in 1505. In flamboyant Gothic, it retains the arrangements and fittings of a medieval collegiate church in a better state of preservation than any other example in the British Isles. Its richly carved oaken rood screen and stalls have survived almost complete and are by far the finest example remaining of medieval Scottish ecclesiastical woodwork. No wonder that it is the dream and the privilege of a great number of graduates to be married in this holy of holies.

The tower and the chapel are the only parts of the original King's College that survive. To the south-east of the chapel is the Cromwell Tower, begun in 1658 to provide living accommodation for students. It is one more instance of Aberdeen's 'castle complex' that it took the form of "a huge and massive square tower, six storeys high, with a flat roof and an open parapet, for all the world like a Norman keep". But it was not finished until after the Restoration and thus came to include a billiard room as well as chambers for the scholars!

To the late nineteenth century King's College owes one more really fine building. This is the library, built on the site of the ancient kitchen and extending eastwards for over 200 feet. It is a long and lofty hall with double transepts, begun in 1870 and finished in 1885. The effect is very impressive and it can be fairly claimed that no library in Scotland is more magnificently housed. To sit in cloistered seclusion in one of the transepts copying a text is to feel privileged indeed. The same reverence can scarcely be felt for the university's twentieth-century creations, though some are at least spectacular, such as the futuristic-looking science library and the natural philosophy building with its curious mushroom-shaped vestibule. The zoology building in St Machar Drive is said to be an echo of Marischal College in contemporary idiom—though to the lay eye the resemblance is a little hard to detect. The visitor really requires no guide to these buildings; they thrust themselves upon his notice. Rather more retiring are the student halls of residence of which the best is surely the earliest— Crombie Hall to the west of College Bounds, built in 1960 as the first mixed hostel for students in Britain. The principle of having men and women students together in the same building with common lounges and dining halls has proved a great success.

The oldest inhabited domestic dwelling in the Aulton, or indeed in "both the towns of Aberdeen", is Chaplain's Court, No. 20 the Chanonry. It was part of a very much larger complex of buildings built at the south end of the bishop's garden by Bishop Gavin Dunbar in 1519. This contained accommodation for twenty vicars or chaplains who performed the common service of the cathedral. On the wall facing the Chanonry can be seen a shield surmounted by a mitre bearing Dunbar's arms—three cushions.

Old Aberdeen has always been kind and congenial to the elderly as well as inspiring to the young. In the Chanonry there are old folk still in the altogether charming group of cottages forming three sides of a square, set back from the street by trees and lawn and flower-beds. This is Mitchell's Hospital, built to "clothe and maintain five widows and five unmarried daughters of Merchant and Trade Burgesses of Old Aberdeen". Then there is Bede House, Nos 20 and 22 Don Street, built in 1676 and taken over at one period to house the 'bedesman' formerly housed in another 'hospital', founded by Bishop Gavin Dunbar (and supplied with a charter signed by King James V himself) in 1536. This characterful old building with a projecting tower and a corbelled stair turret is now let out to town council tenants, while closely adjoining it is Bede House Court, a model scheme of old peoples' houses built by the corporation. It should be added that, although they no longer live in a 'hospital' or even a 'bede house,' eight old men of Old Aberdeen still benefit by the bishop's benefaction. They are the official Bedesmen of the Aulton and receive a monthly pension and—in virtue of a very ancient privilege—3½ pounds weight of salmon from the heritors of the Cruives of Don and Nether Don fishings twice a year.

Another old house with fragrant memories is the Dower House, 49 Don Street. Built on the site of the cathedral treasurer's house its garden was found to contain numberless roots of the French or Aulton lily, the *fleur-de-lys*, which the treasurer had grown in fulfilment of his duty to keep the altars of the cathedral decked. Although Old Aberdeen ceased to be an independent municipality in 1891 the Aulton lily still blooms in its ancient coat of arms.

One more image to be harvested from the Aulton before we pass on: on the lawn beneath the Crown of King's lies the tomb of Bishop Elphinstone. No sarcophagus that I know of is so eloquent. Formerly in the chapel, it was re-sited here in accordance with a long-held plan, and the bronze figures of the Seven Virtues upon which the recumbent effigy of the Good Bishop was raised, were cast in Venice in 1914, and during the years of World War I, lay under the waters of the Grand Canal.

As we once more repass the cathedral, we may note that its battlemented towers are surmounted by twin spires of sandstone. Bishop Gavin Dunbar, who did so much to soften the asperities of his episcopal inheritance, had these built to replace the castle-like cap-houses with which they were originally crested.

Immediately to the west of the cathedral in a corner of Seaton Park rises the tall grassy mound of the Motte of Tillydrone, site of a twelfth-century timber fort commanding the ford of the Don at this point, while just beyond it is the recently restored and rebuilt Benholm's Lodging, more familiar to Aberdonians as the Wallace Tower, because of the effigy of a knight on an inset panel in one of its two round towers. This fine example of a Z-plan tower-house was originally built in 1616 in what is now the centre of 'new' Aberdeen, but was then just outside the built-up area, on the Netherkirkgate leading to St Nicholas Kirk. There it remained, though suffering partial concealment and some deterioration, until, in 1963, it was taken down, transported to Tillydrone and rebuilt practically stone by stone, its first tenant in its recreated state being most appropriately the late Dr W. Douglas Simpson, Scotland's leading expert on the medieval castle.

By Seaton Park one may walk through woods along the high right bank of the Don to the gorge of the river immediately above the Brig o' Balgownie, one of the most hauntingly beautiful Gothic survivals in Scotland, with great buttresses and a shapely pointed arch. It was built in the late thirteenth and early fourteenth centuries, and later so well endowed that money from the Brig Fund was more than adequate to build the new Bridge of Don, lower down the river, 400 years later. The old bridge is almost exactly as it was in Byron's day, when he terrified himself by thinking that Thomas the Rhymer's prophecy applied specifically to himself:

> Brig o' Balgownie,
> Wight is thy wa';
> Wi' a wife's ae son
> And a mare's ae foal
> Down shalt thou fa'.

As his mother's only son, mounted on a pony, he could not forget that the deep and dark pool on the west side of the bridge had been the death of many. The old houses on the south side of the bridge include an L-plan mansion mistakenly called the Chapter House. Its name should be the Dean's Lodging, for it was built by George Cruickshank, a Dean of Guild of Aberdeen, in 1653–5, and bears his coat of arms and those of his wife, Barbara Hervie of Elrick. This house and others nearby were restored by Aberdeen Corporation. The narrow cobbled rise of the carriageway over the bridge and the Cot-town of Balgownie on the other side, rebuilt by a private developer to make an attractive housing scheme, give this corner an old-world atmosphere.

The path from Seaton Park emerges on Don Street just above this Balgownie hamlet and without crossing the bridge one may descend stone steps on the other side of the street and follow a path high above the river bank to the new bridge and the start of Aberdeen's 2-mile-long sea-beach promenade. There is almost everything here that the solitary or the gregarious might ask of a seaside resort. Golf has been played on the Queen's Links since 1625. The sands of Aberdeen Bay—though natives persuade themselves that they have deteriorated—are still more than ample for the most fastidious connoisseur of foreshores; a large ballroom and restaurant, playing fields for children and adults, a sprinkling of shops and a fun fair—these diversify, without impinging too far on nature's own munificence.

Having traversed the entire width of the bay one arrives at another of Aberdeen's many conservation areas, Footdee. It is indeed at the 'foot' of the river Dee, in the angle between the Bay and the river mouth, at the base of the North Pier, but the name is a corruption of Futty, an ancient fishing hamlet. In 1809 harbour improvements necessitated the removal of this old village and a new one, on model lines for those days, was built here. It consisted of two squares of cottages each with a 'green' in the centre of the enclosed space which soon became built over with huts for the fishermen's nets and gear. Footdee still remains redolent of the atmosphere of an old-time fishing community though many of its inhabitants are workers in the nearby shipyards.

An account of Aberdeen's harbour itself must be left over to another chapter, appropriately the first of four on the Dee and its valley. It remains to take a rapid glance at the still expanding city far beyond the central core so far described. South of the Dee, opposite Footdee, is the peninsula of Girdleness with its lighthouse. There are splendid views over the city, Aberdeen Bay, the harbour and the rest of the town from the road which encircles this headland and leads to the Bay of Nigg beyond. A golf course intervenes between the lighthouse and the Torry and Balnagask housing areas and the industrial estate in the Vale of Tullos still farther inland. Farther south, beyond the Kirk of Nigg on its hilltop is the vast new housing and industrial estate of Altens, entirely an oil boom development with the H.Q. of Shell Exploration and Production nearby. On opposite sides of the Dee farther west are Ferryhill and Kincorth, the former also now a conservation area and containing the extensive Duthie Park with its winter gardens, cricket pitches and boating ponds. Beyond, in Ruthrieston, Kaimhill, Garthdee and Craigiebuckler one may trace in ever-widening circles the transition from the solid granite villas of the Victorian age to the genteel, granite-faced bungalows of the inter-war era, then the utilitarian brick and harl of today.

At a radius of approximately two miles from the city centre Aberdeen is girdled by an important by-pass or ring road extending in a wide semi-circle from the Bridge of Dee on the south to the former burgh of Woodside on the Don to the north. Named Anderson Drive after Sir Alexander Anderson, a great Victorian entrepreneur and Lord Provost of the city, this handsome motorway, centred for long stretches by flowerbeds, acts like the rim of a wheel from which all the main spokes converge, either directly or indirectly upon Union Street.

With some exceptions the area west of Anderson Drive is of post-war development. Here are Hazlehead (where the great wooded estate acquired in 1920 has served a double function, first in giving Aberdeen its noblest public park with its many acres of woodland, nature trail, golf courses, and early in the sixties, its handsomest housing estate, in which even the skyscraper flats fit into a sylvan setting), Summerhill, Mastrick and Northfield, vast municipal housing areas on what, before 1950, was simply "the country lying quiet and full of farms".

At Granitehill in Northfield, topped by the city's post office tower, that "extensive plain to the west of the city", which Union Street was designed 170 years ago to make accessible, reaches its greatest height, a mere 420 feet above sea level. But the multi-storey flats dotted around the area give views to take the breath away. To the east they look over the entire city and show the white-topped breakers rolling in upon Aberdeen Bay; to the north they overlook the hollow of the Don valley, with its paper and textile mills, its busy airport and the huge new suburbs of Dyce, Grandhome, and Bridge of Don; to the west they survey Brimmond Hill and the truncated cone and leonine hindquarters of Bennachie, that "grey king of common hills", while to the south beyond Hazlehead's white towers are the woods that slope to the Royal Dee.

Disregarding for a moment the oil servicing spectrum now so important, the greater number of the working population are employed either directly or indirectly by the fishing industry; granite, engineering, paper-making, shipbuild:ng and chemicals, are all significant, and textiles, while less so than in historic times, are still vital. But that is not all. Aberdeen is the main centre of commercial services in the north of Scotland. It is the market town of a region extending between 80 and 90 miles to the north-west. It is the funnel through which goods and services pass to the northern isles of Orkney and Shetland, and while the farmers of Aberdeenshire (one of the greatest arable and stock-rearing areas in Britain) and of Banff and Kincardine come to Aberdeen to buy and sell grain, livestock, feeding stuffs and implements, their wives and families are as much at home in Union Street and the other shopping thoroughfares—such as St Nicholas Street and George Street—as the city-dwellers themselves.

Out of natural resources that were meagre and unpromising Aberdeen has flourished—but only because it could look upon its hinterland and say in the words which Sir Alexander Gray used of Scotland as a whole:

> This is my country,
> The land that begat me,
> These windy spaces
> Are surely my own,
> And those that here toil
> In the sweat of their faces
> Are flesh of my flesh
> And bone of my bone.

To that hinterland, to the fancy-haunted valley of the Dee and its blue hills with their royal associations, to the Don renowned for 'horn and corn', to Kincardine, the land of 'Sunset Song', to the vales of the Ythan, the Ugie, the Deveron and the Bogie we must now turn, for they are an inseparable part of the story of Aberdeen, whose motto is "Bon-Accord" (good fellowship) and whose toast is the Toast of Bon-Accord: "Happy to meet, sorry to part, happy to meet again."

II

CASTLE COUNTRY: THE SHAPING OF A PROVINCE

Fair City of the Rivers Twain,
No child of idle dalliance thou;
The silvery borders of thy train
Come from the rugged mountains' brow.
William Forsyth.

FANTASTICALLY picturesque medieval castles, quaint planned villages of the eighteenth century, mysterious symbolic Pictish carving and sculpture, great stone circles of the Bronze Age abound in Aberdeen's hinterland. These, and a profuse heritage of ballad lore, are its special legacies from a past which will be briefly outlined in this chapter.

The countryside itself rests on a platform of metamorphic rock, widely interfused with granite, and occasionally crossed by sills of serpentine or strips of Old Red sandstone. It slopes down and fans out, north to the Moray Firth and east to the North Sea for 80 miles from a central core on the 4000-feet-high summit of the Cairngorm plateau. From this plateau emerge three main rivers—Dee, Don and Deveron—and it is only in their lower valleys, with their tributaries, and in the vales of two lesser rivers, the Ythan and the Ugie, that really kindly and fertile land is to be found.

The earliest inhabitants were Mesolithic pigmy flint folk who left their tiny tooth-like implements scattered about river terraces of the Dee near Banchory around 4000 B.C. After them came primitive strand-loopers haunting the shores. Next from 3000–2500 B.C. the first true farmers, Neolithic men of slight build with oval faces, sowed their barley and built long cairns found at Macduff in Banffshire, at Gourdon in Kincardine and at Cults on the western outskirts of Aberdeen.

Their numbers must have been few. But between 2000 and 1800 B.C. came a great wave of the Beaker Folk. They buried

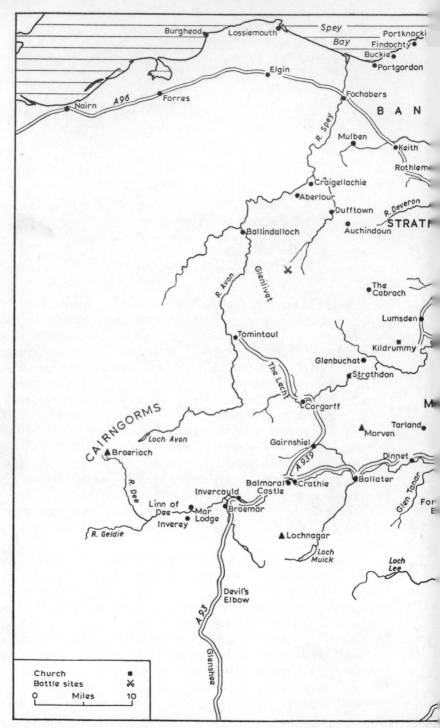

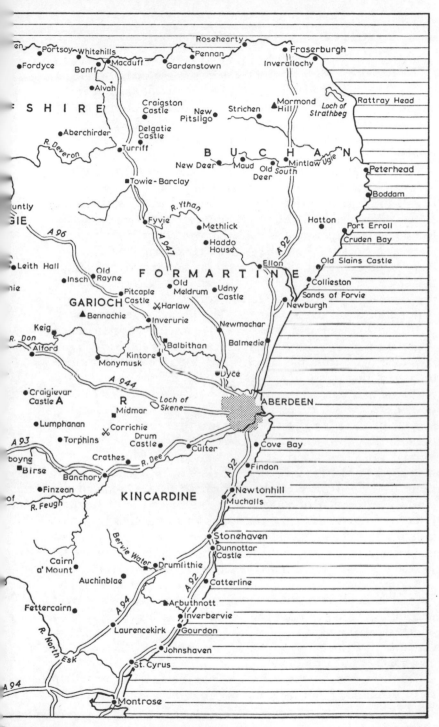

SCOTLAND

their dead singly in a crouched position in short stone cists and placed beside the body an urn, which from its shape is called a beaker. Landing all round the coast from their homeland at the mouth of the Rhine, which they had reached from Central Europe, these Beaker Folk, tall, and with round heads, square jaws and broad faces, are the true foundation stock of North-east Scotland.

Since the Beaker Folk colonized the area successive invasions have given it many waves of conquerors and ruling classes: Pictish and Celtic war lords, Scots from Dalriada, perhaps some Norse Vikings and certainly large numbers of Anglo-Normans. But underneath these upper crusts the man who remained tilling the soil, the man to whom the earth is "closer than the flesh of his body" is, as the Aberdeen University anatomists have established, the descendant of the Beaker Folk, and his physical type still predominates in North-east Scotland today.

Burial habits of course changed. The Bronze Age came. Soon on the skyline appeared those great recumbent stone circles of which over seventy are recorded between Dee and Spey. They take their name from the fact that, although the circle is formed by a great ring of upright standing stones, there is always in the south-western sector a large flat stone between two pillar-stones or 'flankers', which are usually the tallest in the circle. The most famous of these is at Daviot near Inverurie, and is a national monument. Others to see are at Old Keig near Alford, Sunhoney near Echt and Tomnaverie at Tarland. A few feet from the wall of the church at Midmar is one such circle, in which the recumbent stone is wedged between two enormous flankers—for all the world like the altar of some fearsome Druidic rite of sacrifice. I put my hand on the 'altar' and found that the sun had warmed it until it was like the chamber of an oven. But there is no proof that sacrificial rites were actually performed there. That the circles were linked with astronomical observations seems certain.

Another and more sinister kind of stone circle is on the low ground at Cullerlie, 9 miles west of Aberdeen. It consists of eight untrimmed boulders enclosing an area consecrated by fire in which there are eight small cairns. Here, it has been suggested, the child of a chieftain was buried, surrounded by the bodies of dependants slain at the funeral.

The Iron Age brought to the region great chains of hilltop forts. In the three north-eastern counties there are twenty-two,

Aberdeen Harbour: the three arms of water on the extreme left of the picture are the River Dee, the Albert Basin and the Victoria Dock

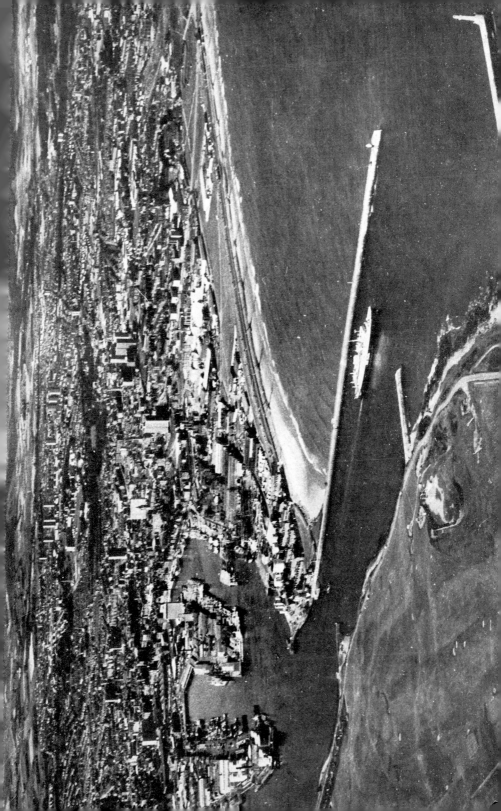

the most spectacular being on the Mither Tap on Bennachie (1689 feet), the Barmekin of Echt (900 feet), the Hill of Dunnideer and Tap o' Noth (1851 feet). Here, no doubt, the local inhabitants gathered to defy Septimus Severus or other Roman invaders.

The transition from paganism to Christianity has left us with a wonderful and mysterious legacy in this part of the world. There are over fifty sites where Pictish sculptured stones are to be found. They belong to three periods. In the first, between A.D. 600 and 800 these stones are rough boulders or only roughly dressed monoliths, on which are incised a wide variety of symbols taking the form of abstract patterns, animals, fishes or birds. The great majority of Aberdeenshire sculptured stones are of this class. In the second period (A.D. 800–1000) stones are carved in relief and contain, beside the old symbols the Christian Cross. Finally in the third period (A.D. 1000 or later) the pagan symbols—if indeed they are really pagan—have disappeared, and only the Cross, often marvellously enriched with Celtic interlacing remains. In some cases the incised stones also have inscriptions in Ogham— that curious 'code' alphabet of long successions of strokes and lines.

The most famous, and one of the most beautiful of these Pictish works of art is the Maiden Stone, which stands by the roadside at the 'back of Bennachie', a mile from the hamlet of Chapel of Garioch near Inverurie. It is a pillar of red granite 10 feet high. The front shows a man between two fish monsters (sometimes called 'Jonah and the two Whales'), an enriched cross and a panel with a disc and other decorative details. The other side depicts, in separate compartments, a centaur-like figure, a rectangle and Z-rod, an 'elephant' and a 'mirror and comb'. The experts tell us that the 'elephant, is not really an elephant, merely a beast with a long snout, curled feet and tail and lappets. Theories of the purpose and meaning of the symbols are legion. One may choose between the idea that the abstract patterns—crescents, discs, Z-rods and the like—are imitated from Celtic illuminated manuscripts, or the notion that they record the tattoo marks worn by the chieftains whom the stones are sometimes thought to commemorate.

The illuminated manuscript theory is not so far-fetched as it may seem, for from this region emanated the famous Book of Deer, a treasure comparable to the Book of Kells. Now in Cambridge University Library, where it was identified in 1857, it is an MS volume of eighty-six parchment folios containing the complete

Marischal College on graduation day

Gospel of St John and portions of the other three Gospels in Latin, transcribed about A.D. 700.

These beautifully illuminated Gospels were no doubt the work of Irish monks or Dalriadic Scots of the school of St Columba, but on the margins of the manuscript are added *notitia* in Gaelic of the eleventh or twelfth centuries. These jottings, of priceless historical value as a source of information about Celtic Scotland, were the work of the monks of Deer, 'the place of the oaks', a sylvan spot in the vale of the South Ugie 35 miles north of Aberdeen, where a monastery was founded by St Drostan, a Pict, shortly before Columba's day.

Drostan's foundation survived into the Columban period, and the *notitia* include an account of the monastery's founding strongly coloured by the Columban legends. Although we now believe that Drostan had in fact no contact with Columba, but 'colonized' this area of Buchan by crossing the Moray Firth from Caithness with his three disciples Colm, Medan and Fergus, the Book of Deer tells how Columba accompanied Drostan to Deer and saw him settled there before returning to Iona. As the two missionaries parted "their tears flowed" and Columba said, "Let this place be *Deara* [Gaelic 'tears'] from henceforth."

The jottings in the Book of Deer do however give us genuine insights into the fascinating but mysterious period when the burgh of Aberdeen was first founded. The Romans had known of it as Devana, a place marked in the fourth century map of Ptolemy as lying on the left bank of a river called 'Deva fluvius'—doubtless the Dee. But after that there is no mention until the Scottish king Alexander I (1107–24) lists "Aberdon" in a charter as one of his "principal towns". This charter was witnessed by Ruadri, the Celtic mormaer or Earl of Mar and Gartnait, Earl of Buchan. Then in 1125 the name occurs again, this time spelt Abberdeon, in the Book of Deer, in connection with a charter given by Gartnait to the monks. This document is witnessed by Ruadri, and also by another Celtic chieftain, Gillecoaim, the son of Muredach. The names of these two worthies survive today in two Aberdeen districts Ruthrieston (Ruadri's town) and Gilcolmston (Gillecoaim's town) in each of which there was a very ancient settlement, Gilcolmston having had a Bronze Age stone circle, and Ruthrieston a medieval motte. That word 'motte' takes us right out of the shadowy Celtic period and right into the clear light of history.

In 1057 Macbeth, who did not die in Dunsinane as Shakespeare's tragedy suggests, retreated across the Dee and was finally trapped and killed in the wood of Lumphanan in Aberdeenshire by Malcolm Canmore who then reigned in his stead, after disposing of Lady Macbeth's son Lulach the Fatuous. It was during the era of the dynasty which Malcolm founded through his marriage to Margaret the Saxon that the old Celtic civilization of Scotland —still very much alive when the monks of Deer were making their jottings in the book—was finally swept away and replaced by Norman feudalism.

The Book of Deer tells us that the secular power was wielded by "mormaer and toiseach". The kings who sprang from Malcolm and Margaret changed all that. They adopted William the Conqueror's recipe for a society based on the royal ownership of land, on feudal fief and vassalage, on written laws and charters and on trade conducted through channels regulated by special privileges granted by the sovereign. Essential props of this new order were the medieval castle, a Norman aristocracy imported from England by the Scottish kings, and the 'royal burghs', of which Aberdeen was one.

This great change did not come about overnight. If the Celtic mormaers were willing to toe the line they remained *in situ* as the king's men. If not, centuries of bloodshed might ensue, and this in fact happened in the turbulent province of Moray and the regions to the north of it. In the three north-east counties the Celtic mormaers of Mar and Buchan must have watched with some suspicion as King David I, the third son of Malcolm and Margaret, who reigned from 1124-53, started to 'plant' royal burghs on their doorstep like watchdogs, and ultimately such royal trading colonies were set up in Aberdeen, Kintore, Inverurie Banff and Cullen, the first three at least forming a wedge to keep Mar and Buchan apart and negative any combination between them inimical to the royal power.

That the Celtic overlords were not unwilling to learn from the new Anglo-Norman efficiency experts seems clear from the existence of Ruadri's motte at Ruthrieston, and it seems certain that at this period there were mottes at Nigg, Banchory Devenick, Ruthrieston and Tillydrone, forming in sum a ring of little fortresses around the outskirts of the infant burgh of Aberdeen.

Other interested parties were watching the birth of Aberdeen as a royal burgh. In the year of King David's death Eynsteinn,

King of Norway "spread his sails to the south and brought his ships to the town of Apardion, where he killed many people and wasted the city". It was no doubt a raid inspired by the thought that in this new emporium of trade there would be worthwhile loot. A saga touch is given to the affair in a poem by Einar Skulisson:

> I heard the overthrow of peoples;
> The clash of broken arms was loud;
> The King destroyed the peace
> Of the dwellers in Apardion.

But the Canmore kings continued their policy undaunted. In 1160 King David's grandson and successor Malcolm IV created his youngest brother David, afterwards Earl of Huntingdon, Lord of the Garioch, the province lying directly between Mar and Buchan. This potent prince, a hero of the Third Crusade and the direct ancestor of our present Royal Family, set up his 'castle', a motte and bailey stronghold, on the Bass of Inverurie, where the great grassy mound is a showplace today. Here it is easy to visualize exactly what these earthwork and timber castles—introduced into Britain by William the Conqueror and depicted in the Bayeux Tapestry—were really like.

The mound or motte, so steep and rounded that it was easy to defend, was crowned by a tall timber tower with a fighting platform supported on wooden brackets, all enclosed by a palisade of stout wooden staves, while on a lesser level close by was the bailey or courtyard, called today the Little Bass—both mounds being lapped by the waters of the Urie near its confluence with the Don. This timber fortress served as the Castle of Inverurie for three centuries and was the prototype of similar mottes scattered far and wide throughout the north-east: on the upper Don, the Doune of Invernochty and the Peel of Fichlie; between Don and Dee the Motte of Midmar; on Dee the mottes of Durris and Banchory Devenick; on the Feugh the Castle Hill of Strachan.

After Eynsteinn's raid Aberdeen had no more Viking trouble, but in 1162 King Malcolm entertained at his new royal burgh Sweyn Asliefson from Orkney, that buccaneering rogue who was "the Last of the Vikings", and they feasted together for a month.

Aberdeen's earliest surviving burgh charters, granted by King William the Lion, dated *circa* 1180 and 1200, can be seen in the Town House today, and the second lists the names of the first burgesses of whom we have any record. They were "William son of Norman, William, son of Hugh, and Gilbert, son of Joceline"—obviously Anglo-Normans to a man. This is what we would expect. The creation of a burgh was a deliberate act of policy. It was a 'new town', organized not merely for trade but for defence and, if not walled with stone, surrounded by an earthwork bank and ditch which could be easily defended and was pierced only by the 'ports' or defended gateways of the town. Aberdeen had six such ports: the Gallowgate Port to the north, the Upperkirkgate and Netherkirkgate ports to the west, the Shiprow Port to the south and Futty Port and Justice Port to the east.

Meanwhile the old Celtic mormaerdom of Buchan came to an end. Fergus, the last mormaer died without male issue, and in 1210 his daughter Marjory married—no doubt by the King's contrivance—William Comyn, descendant of Robert de Comines in France, who had come into Britain with William the Conqueror.

One of the first things this Norman aristocrat did was to found anew the Abbey of Deer—on a new site in the vale of the Ugie, and as a monastery of the Cistercian order. Shortly afterwards a blow was struck against the monopoly of the Celtic mormaer of Mar in the lands between the Don and the Dee. Around 1228 Thomas de Lundin, a Norman official who was the Door Ward of Scotland and whose family accordingly adopted the name Durward, put in a rival claim to inheritance of the Earldom of Mar, his mother being the daughter of a former earl.

Alexander II, who had by this time succeeded William the Lion, settled the dispute in such a way as to diminish the monolithic power of the Earl. He gave the Door Ward a large slice of the earldom, mainly in the Dee valley, and the Durward family now proceeded to duplicate in their new domain the strongholds which were the Celtic Earl's symbols of dominance, thus creating a sort of shadow earldom within the earldom.

In this period therefore the Anglo-Norman order had triumphed in Aberdeenshire. By the third decade of the thirteenth century Alexander II had at last subjugated the long-rebellious province of Moray to the north. To make his empire there more secure he built in Aberdeenshire, at Kildrummy on the upper Don a great stone courtyard castle intended to guard the route to Moray.

The contrast between this royal super-castle and the timber mottes that had hitherto be-sprinkled the north-east was striking.

But the evolution was logical. Wooden towers had been replaced by stone towers, timber palisades by stone curtain walls and the courtyard inside them had to be big enough to hold a little army. Such a castle was Kildrummy, the ruined shell of which remains today one of the wonders of the north.

Alexander decreed that it should have a plan based on the Chateau de Coucy in France which had been the home of his second wife Marie. Its great north wall is 250 feet long and it extends in the form of a semi-circle almost the same distance to the south. The massive curtain wall with its wall-walk is defended by six great circular or semi-circular towers. Along the inner face of the north wall were ranged the domestic buildings—the great hall, the solar or laird's private suite and the kitchen—while projecting from the east wall at an angle is the chapel with its three tall lancet windows of equal depth.

An accident of history gives Kildrummy features borrowed from both the French and the English schools of castle-building. Alexander gave it a great *donjon* or main keep in the French manner, the Snow Tower. But he died before the castle was finished, and when his successor Alexander III also died in 1286 Scotland was plunged into the long agony of its struggle for independence—and so it came to be that the castle was completed by Edward I of England, the 'Hammer of the Scots'. Edward gave it two great gatehouse towers, virtually identical with those of Harlech Castle in Wales, attributed to Edward's military engineer, Master James St George.

Ironically the castle had its baptism of fire defying Edward's power. In 1306, after launching the War of Independence, Robert the Bruce, Scotland's liberator king, sent his queen and her ladies to Kildrummy in the charge of his youngest brother Sir Nigel. In August and September the castle was besieged by Prince Edward of Caernarvon, the future Edward II. Nigel Bruce fought off every assault. Then treachery took a hand. Osbarn the smith, bribed by the English promise of as much gold as he could carry, fired the castle with the red-hot blade of a plough. The defenders were then compelled to surrender. Sir Nigel was beheaded at Berwick, and the English poured the gold they had promised—in molten form—down the blacksmith's throat. The west range of the castle's curtain wall was cast down and the fortress remained out of action until it was rebuilt after the battle of Bannockburn in 1314. Kildrummy withstood a second siege in 1335 when it was held by Dame Christian Bruce, sister of the king, on behalf of her husband Sir Andrew de Moray, then Regent of Scotland. On this occasion the 3,000 attackers raised the siege on the approach of the Regent, who then defeated them at the battle of Culblean—a turning point in the Second War of Independence.

In the thirteenth century Kildrummy had a 'poor relation'. This was the Castle of Coull near Aboyne. As I have mentioned, the Durward family, who had obtained a slice of the Earldom of Mar, duplicated the fortresses of the earldom to which they had laid claim, and Coull Castle was constructed by them as an imitation of Kildrummy. It was a courtyard castle with five circular towers. Throughout the first War of Independence it was held by the English or their puppets. In March 1307 King Edward sent urgent instructions that with other Scottish castles it was to be garrisoned by his supporters, in face of Bruce's intransigeance.

No account of its subsequent fate survives. But excavations have proved that it was set on fire and afterwards deliberately demolished. Vitrification and melted nails testify to the reality of the fire and what happened has been vividly pictured by Dr Douglas Simpson. He says: "I for one can never visit these grey ruins set amid the purple hills without picturing in my mind's eye a wild night when the farmers of Cromar rose in their scores to expel the hated Southron, when darkness was turned into lurid day by the flaming castle—when black against the fire the bodies of its garrison hung limply with twisted necks from makeshift gallows, while a savage peasantry, goaded to madness by long oppression, and now drunk besides with the heady wine of victory, danced their uncouth measures round the blazing ruin."

There was a third courtyard castle in the region at this time— the Castle of Aberdeen. Its fall was probably equally violent. On Christmas Eve 1307 Robert the Bruce, who had been lying ill at Inverurie, suddenly attacked and routed John Comyn, Earl of Buchan, at Barra near Oldmeldrum. The punitive Harrying of Buchan followed, and the fall of the English garrison in the Castle of Aberdeen seemed imminent.

In July 1308 Edward II ordered William le Betour, captain of his fleet, to sail immediately to succour the Castle of Aberdeen. He was probably too late. Tradition has it that, with the watchword "Bon-Accord" on their lips the Aberdonians rose, destroyed the castle and put the garrison to death. Robert the Bruce showed his gratitude to Aberdeen for this or other services in very tangible form. By charter in 1319 he gave to the burgesses in perpetual feu a large tract of land to the west of the town.

This was the Forest of Stocket, extending from 4 to 6 miles inland and girdling the outskirts of the city as far as the Mill of Brotherfield near Peterculter on the west and the eastern slopes of Brimmond Hill on the north. On part of this territory much of twentieth-century Aberdeen has been built, and if it had still belonged to the town the saving in capital expenditure would have been immense. But unfortunately, after holding it for over two hundred years, the magistrates of Aberdeen disposed of it piece by piece for ready cash.

Yet the inner meaning of this Freedom Lands story, as it has been called, goes deeper than any cash transaction. It gave the people of Aberdeen a stake in their own hinterland which was to have profound psychological consequences. The burgh had been 'planted' by the Canmore kings and manned by English, French and Flemings who were traders and craftsmen, not farmers. They were expected to act as a catalyst to stir up the sluggish economy of the region. By schoolroom definition a catalyst is a "substance which accelerates a reaction, itself remaining unchanged at the end of the reaction". Now, thanks to King Robert's gift, the citizens became more than a mere catalyst. They became landowners themselves. They identified themselves with their country cousins and shared with them an interest and a passion for improving their inheritance.

And how badly it stood in need of improvement! It has been pointed out that from the Cuttle Hill near the centre of the Freedom Lands "the hardy burger of 1319 would behold a dreary waste, broken here and there by little thickets of trees and stunted brushwood, a wilderness of marshy bog and stony crag, a rude primeval, undeveloped heath". On the same spot today one sees "a smiling and prosperous countryside, with orderly, well-cultivated fields producing luxurious crops, interspersed with beautiful plantations".

The labour involved in this transformation was almost beyond belief. At Kingswells within the Freedom Lands you can see immense ramparts of stones called 'Consumption Dykes'. These dykes or walls were so called because they 'consumed' the boulders that thickly littered every field, and had to be torn out by hand before the plough could get to work.

Unfortunately the Wars of Independence in Scotland did not usher in a golden age. Indeed men looked back to the age of Alexander III, before the trouble started, with poignant nostalgia:

> When Alexander our king was dead
> That Scotland led, in love and le,
> Away was sons of ale and bread,
> Of wine and wax, of gamyn and glee;
> Our gold was changed into lead!
> Christ, born into Virginitie,
> Succour Scotland and remeid,
> That stayed is in perplexity.

One consequence of the misery and anarchy of the times was the need for strong towers and fortified houses. This need was intensified by special circumstances in the three north-eastern counties, where there are over one hundred castles, either ruined or still occupied as stately homes, a great number of which are open to the public. This is indeed castle country and a great part of its history can be told in reference to the changes the north-eastern tower-house underwent from 1280 to 1660, when the last of the 'medieval' castles were still—anachronistically—being built.

Kildrummy was the last of the wide-spreading military courtyard castles in the area. These were replaced by grim keeps within which the kitchens and cellars, the great halls and the solars, instead of being arranged in a horizontal spread were upended to form a perpendicular sequence, "mere cells let into a solid mass of masonry". The first of these tower houses in the north-east was the Castle of Dunnideer on the top of a hill at Insch in the Garioch, built for Sir Jocelin de Balliol in 1260. It was followed around 1280 by the towers of Drum, Skene and Hallforest all within a radius of 10 to 12 miles from Aberdeen. Their immediate ancestry as modifications of the courtyard castle is apparent in their immensely thick walls and in the very primitive type of battlements, adaptations of crenellations on a curtain wall, while internally they consisted of five rooms one on top of the other within three great stone vaults, the upper two being sub-divided by timber floors. Drum, which remains in perfect preservation, will be described in Chapter III.

No great change in this style of castle-building occurred until near the end of the fourteenth century, when Sir William Keith, Great Marischal of Scotland, built himself the Keep of Dunnottar on its stupendous isolated rock south of Stonehaven. This was the first example in the area of an L-plan tower house. To the simple keep was added a wing at right angles, thus permitting one extra room on each floor of the building. As at Drum the projecting parapet of the battlements was supported on corbel blocks (which are just stone brackets replacing the wooden beams which carried the fighting platform on a timber motte), but at each of the four corners, and also above the main entrance, there were open rounds or turrets for guard duty—ancestors of the angle turrets which in succeeding centuries became great decorative as well as functional features of the Scottish castle. The Keep of Dunñottar was only the first of a whole range of buildings on this historic rock which will be further described in Chapter VII.

The fifteenth century opened with an act of fateful consequence at Kildrummy. The chief actor was Alexander Stewart, illegitimate son of the Wolf of Badenoch, himself a lawless royal princeling. He began his meteoric career as a sort of brigand chief and his first notable victim was Sir Malcolm Drummond, brother of Annabella, Queen of King Robert III, and husband of Isabel, Countess of Mar in her own right. Stewart's Highland henchmen seized Drummond while he was building a castle at Braemar and threw him into a dungeon where he soon died. Stewart then proceeded to the castle of Kildrummy where Isabel was in residence and compelled her to marry him.

In order to legalize his lawless deed he staged a dramatic charade at the gates of the castle. Tenantry and vassals were summoned to appear and with these as witnesses the usurper handed the keys of the castle to the Countess, in order, so he protested, that she might do with them as she pleased. The wronged woman then declared that she freely chose him as her husband and handed back to him the keys—along with the Earldom of Mar, the Lordship of the Garioch, the forest of Jedburgh and all her other possessions. From this moment Stewart, the self-made Earl of Mar, never looked back. Accepted as friend and protector of the city of Aberdeen, he organized and led the resistance to Donald, Lord of the Isles, which resulted in the Battle of Harlaw in 1411.

Aberdeen was scarcely interested in the dynastic dispute that led the Lord of the Isles to make war on the king and so to invade the 'laich country', but the townsfolk were aware that on his way south Donald had seized Dingwall and burned Inverness, and would reward his followers with the spoils of their own town if ever he occupied it. So they joined the barons of the north-east counties who had rallied under Stewart, and after a rendez-vous at Inverurie fought with them in the day-long battle which ensued at Harlaw, a mile or two to the north. After frightful carnage they remained in possession of the field and the Lord of the Isles retreated the way he had come.

The Provost of Aberdeen, Sir Robert Davidson and "Good Sir Alexander Irvine. The much renownit Laird of Drum" were among the slain, and, as Scott puts it, "the Coronach [lament] was cried from the Tay to the Buck of the Cabrach". Harlaw begat a hatred for the Highlander and his romantic trappings in low-land Aberdeenshire that was to last for centuries. Ballads mocked the drone of the pipes:

> As I cam in by Dunnideer,
> An' doun by Netherha,
> There was fifty thousand Heilandmen
> A-marching to Harlaw,
> *Wi' a dree dree dradie drumptie dree.*

A monument was erected on the "sair field" of Harlaw 500 years after the event—in 1911. As victor of Harlaw the upstart Earl of Mar cut a glorious figure at the court of France, and was appointed Lieutenant-Governor of the North, but the Countess died three years after her ordeal at Kildrummy, and when Stewart himself died in 1435 it was without leaving an heir. King James I then annexed the Earldom to the Crown.

This had disastrous results. Stewart had demonstrated that in this part of the world a strong man was needed. Tenants or stewards of the king could not provide the necessary strength, and a power vacuum ensued. Rival castles now grew thickly on the ground. Aberdeen turned first to the Irvines of Drum and then to the rising star of the Earls of Huntly for protection. Others signed 'bonds of Manrent' (treaties of mutual protection) with the Earls Marischal and the Earls of Erroll. Rivalry between the Forbeses on Donside and the Gordons in Strathbogie led to a bitter feud, and also to fruitful emulation in castle-building.

In 1440 the first Lord Forbes called in two master masons, John of Kemlock and William of Inverkip in Renfrewshire, to build him a new fortified dwelling of stone. What they built is called a 'palace house', the first of the type, and it happily survives today at Druminnor in the Old Red Sandstone gap which links Donside with Strathbogie. The name 'palace' is suggestive of special grandeur, but in its beginnings the Latin word *palatio* meant simply a hall-house, in which hall and solar, instead of being imprisoned in a perpendicular keep, adjoined each other on the same level, while the stair was accommodated in an angle tower of its own—in the case of Druminnor a massive round tower. In the next decade, and at Huntly only a few miles away, the first Earl of Huntly, head of the house of Gordon, built a new castle alongside his pre-existing L-plan tower house. It too was in the palace plan.

A few years later another type of castle appeared at Pitcaple in the Garioch, almost within sight of the battlefield of Harlaw. James II granted the lands of Pitcaple to David Leslie in 1457. The castle which he built was an early example of the Z-plan. In this, the central block of the building, whether tower-house or hall-house, was provided with two flanking towers, either round or square, at diagonally opposite corners. Thus each tower, with its gunloops, covered with fire the main block, which in its turn covered the towers. It is impossible to approach such a castle from any quarter without coming within range of the defenders' fire. Scotland has 170 of these Z-plan castles but Aberdeenshire has by far the greatest quota, and was the birth-place of the type.

At Pitcaple the flanking towers are both round and have that 'batter' or tapering profile which delights the eye, while in the delicate little angle turrets we see the beginning of a decorative theme soon to be carried to superlative lengths by the Aberdeen-shire castle builders. Mary Queen of Scots dined at Pitcaple in 1562 and danced under a thorn tree. Under this same tree her great-grandson Charles II likewise danced in 1650. That tree has gone, but nearby is a red maple planted by Queen Mary, consort of George V, in 1923.

The castle played its part in the Civil War. In 1645 Andrew Cant, firebrand preacher of the Covenant, was hi-jacked by the Royalists and held prisoner at Pitcaple for six weeks. Eventually he and his friends turned the tables on their jailers. They gained control of the castle, held it until relieved by allies, then set it on fire as they departed. Scorched stonework is still shown, but visitors are more impressed by the large well in the kitchen floor which supplied the castle with water.

In 1650 the great Royalist general, the Marquess of Montrose, arrived, a pitiful captive of his enemies, at Pitcaple, seated upon a pony to which his feet were tied with straw ropes. He was preceded by a public crier who proclaimed: "Here comes James Graham, a traitor to his country". Montrose was lodged in a room in the castle in which he was visited at midnight by the lady of Pitcaple, who, as it happened was his cousin. She offered him the chance of escape by a secret vent or garderobe flue within the thickness of the castle walls. But he declined saying: "Rather than go down to be smothered in that hole I'll take my chance at Edinburgh." They beheaded him there on 21st May.

On July of that same year Charles II, his erstwhile master, arrived here as the guest of the Leslie laird. After dancing under the thorn tree, he slept in a room still shown as the King's Room. Leslie followed his king to the battle of Worcester in the following year and gave his life in the Royalist cause.

Early in the nineteenth century there was tacked on to the old castle a modern wing designed by William Burn of Edinburgh. Tastefully done, it scarcely detracts from the beauty of the fifteenth-century pile.

In the sixteenth and seventeenth centuries Aberdeenshire developed a school of castle-building entirely its own, thanks to a race of master masons of whom the Bells in Mar and the Leipers in Buchan, together with another native genius whose name we do not know, are the prime exemplars. In Midmar's old churchyard a stone bears the legend:

HEIR LYIS GEORG BEL, MEASON, DECEISIT IN BALOGY
ANO 1575.

This George we believe to have been the designer of Midmar Castle, the first and among the very finest tower houses of the Aberdeenshire School. Although on the Z-plan like Pitcaple, one of its two flanking towers is square and the other round. On the main building are crow-stepped gables and large rectangular gabletted turrets resting on elaborate tiers of key-pattern corbelling. The square tower has circular corbelled turrets with conical roofs. The round tower is finished with an open battlemented parapet, while the staircase turret linking it to the main block rises high over all and is crowned by an ogee helmet from the peak of which a weather vane rises higher still. Ogee is an architect's term for features that are S-shaped in profile. Ogee roofs are popular in neo-classical buildings, but virtually unknown in medieval castles. Yet here was George Bell using it with that panache he displayed in all he did. At his hands Gothic turned into baroque and lost nothing in the process. Of the castles which he and his sons, John and David created, Stewart Cruden comments: "They are of great renown and compelling interest—so much so that critical analysis is stilled and description tends to dwell on their undoubted poetic quality".

The labours of the Bells extended over three-quarters of a century and, judging purely on their peculiarities of architectural style, one can attribute to them, besides Midmar, Crathes Castle (1553–1594), Castle Fraser (1567–1617), Old Cluny Castle (1604), Pitfichie Castle and Craigievar Castle (1626). In the same period the Leipers, Thomas the father and James, his son, were at work on such castles in Buchan as Arnage, Tolquhon, the House of Schivas and probably Fyvie and Craigston, while both Thomas and James were employed in Castle Fraser, where ultimately they had to play second fiddle to the genius of John Bell. The mysterious unknown mentioned earlier was the architect of Gight, Delgatie, Craig and Towie Barclay Castles, to be described in a later chapter.

One cannot escape the conclusion that north of Scotland lairds developed a special fondness for elaborate and beautiful tower houses which persisted long after they were strictly speaking necessary for defence. But we need not regret this. The thirty years of peace which followed the Union of the Crowns in 1603 permitted the younger Bells to go on happily assimilating to the medieval castle Renaissance and classical elements: ogee roofs, pillared balconies, magnificent timbered roofs and painted and pargetted ceilings. Then came the Civil War and after it while some handsome castles in the old manner were still built, the Bell genius had departed, leaving behind it works of art that give to the visitor to Deeside and its neighbouring valleys a unique aesthetic experience.

Complete and settled peace did not come to the north-east countryside until the eighteenth century.

After the last Jacobite Rebellion the Heritable Jurisdictions Act swept away the last of the special privileges enjoyed by Scottish barons. They turned from baronial rule, with 'power of pit and gallows' to commercial enterprise. They cleared away the huddles of wretched huts in which the peasants lived at the gates of their castles and covered the land with planned villages of stone, and devoted their energies to agricultural reform.

Sir Archibald Grant of Monymusk complained that his father had been saddled with an old castle "which had battlements and six different roofs of six different heights and directions, confusedly and inconveniently combined and all rotten", and in 1719 he was advised to pull it all down and build a "little but commodious house" in its place. Fortunately he did not do so, and we shall see what treasures were thus preserved.

For, after the Age of Reason came the Romantic Revival, and castles came into their own again. In the nineteenth century the very existence of the old castles inspired wealthy men to add their own beneficial contribution to the landscape of the north-east, converting treeless wilderness into flourishing woodland and land that remains fertile and lovely today.

In that century too, the age of the aristocratic 'improvers' gave way to the age of great tenant farmers and cattle breeders, perhaps the real makers of north-eastern prosperity. Certainly without them the region would be as backward as the Highlands, and as much in need of subsidized development. Instead, we have the situation that the three counties of Aberdeen, Banff and Kincardine covering an area of 3,000 square miles or one-tenth of the land surface of Scotland, account for almost a *quarter* of the arable acreage of the whole country.

This achievement is all the more wonderful when one remembers that even today moorland still covers half of the whole province, and in this half, despite all that forestry and hill farming can do, the economy is largely based on the sporting value of red deer and red grouse.

III

THE ROYAL DEE: THE LOWER REACHES

> Down rushes Dee,
> His cold clear tones
> Fresh from the mountains
> Ripple round stones.
>
> Claude Colleer Abbott.

On a fine spring day there can be few more exhilarating places in the world than the third tee of the Balnagask golf course in Aberdeen. The heavens are loud with a choir of skylarks. The turf is resilient and the view is superb. From the grassy plateau which roofs the long headland of Girdleness one looks down on the sea-gate of the city. Immediately to the north and almost at one's feet, bracketed off from the wide sweep of Aberdeen Bay by the lengthy, slender finger of the north pier is the Navigation Channel leading beyond the south breakwater to the wild emptiness of the North Sea. To the east the lighthouse, built in 1833 by Robert Stevenson, the father of Robert Louis, stands up like a piece of teacher's chalk, though there is no sign now of the light keepers' cows for which 8 acres of grazing land were originally provided.

To the north-west and the west are the three tongues of neatly squared-off water which form the present-day harbour of Aberdeen, and beyond them spreads the centre of the town with its steeples and skyscrapers. It is "bright snow-fed Dee", perpetually assisted by a busy dredger, which with its weight of water from the corries of the distant Cairngorms, scours out the Navigation Channel of Aberdeen and makes it fit to receive not merely the endless procession of dumpy diesel trawlers whose annual freight of £26,000,000 worth of fish maintains the output of the third fishing port of Britain, the freighters from the seven seas and above all the ceaselessly shuttling supply ships, safety boats, and pipe-laying barges that serve North Sea oil installations.

Of course what one sees today is a man-made landscape. Just

Brig o' Balgownie

Rubislaw Terrace, West End Aberdeen

as the land-hungry Aberdonians remade their wilderness of stony heath and marshy bog over many centuries into a prosperous and smiling countryside, so they also transformed their sea-gate. Looking down two hundred years ago from the same spot one would have seen a wide shallow basin of water which at low tide became a sandy delta. At an earlier period the narrow entrance channel was obstructed by shoals and sandbanks and by a large awkward chunk of rock called Knock Metellan. This in 1610 was removed by one David Anderson of Finzeauch, who earned the sobriquet of 'Davie-do-a'thing' by his feat of primitive but effective engineering. At low tide a necklace of empty casks was securely tethered to the rock, and when the tide rose it was quietly lifted from its bed and towed away—all for an inclusive fee of 300 merks.

Between 1869 and 1873 a new channel was excavated for the Dee enabling a large part of the harbour to be reclaimed. The land reclaimed from the estuary was laid out with streets and provided with sites for industrial use. The marvel is that from the thirteenth century, and despite all the defects of its sea-gate, Aberdeen was in the forefront of Scotland's trade with the continent of Europe.

Aberdeen's first commercial export was salmon. Then in the twelfth century an important trade developed with Flanders in wool, cloth, hides and skins. Trade with the Baltic followed in the fifteenth century and close links were developed with Danzig, while in the Netherlands, Campvere, the Scottish 'staple' or clearing house of continental trade loomed large. In 1685 Sir Patrick Drummond, Conservator of Scottish privileges on the continent reported that Aberdeen brought more money into Scotland than all its other towns.

Times have changed but there is still a cosmopolitan air about the city's commercial docks. On any day you will see cargoes of maize from Constanza on the Black Sea imported as farm feeding stuffs, much timber from Scandinavia and fertilizers from South America. There are regular freight services from West European ports from Dunkirk and Ghent to Helsinki and Abo, as well as from Canada and Portugal.

The façade of buildings along the north side of the Victoria and Upper Docks is a handsome one, including the charming eighteenth-century mansion that is now occupied by the Customs and Excise. The dominating Harbour Office with its tower dates from 1883. From this corner of the harbour there rises to the Castlegate in the centre of the town the only complete eighteenth-century street left in 'new' Aberdeen. Called Marischal Street, it dates from 1766 when the magistrates of Aberdeen reached an agreement with the last Earl Marischal to take over and demolish his town house called Marischal's Lodging on the south side of the Castlegate and lay out a new approach to the harbour on the ground which it occupied. The old house had rather gloomy associations, for it was there that in 1716 the disheartened chiefs of the Jacobite army in retreat after Sheriffmuir met to learn that the Old Pretender had returned to France, leaving them to their fate. Marischal Street has a uniform Georgian character which the Aberdeen Civic Society is anxious to conserve.

The commercial docks used to be cut off from the tidal harbour by dock gates and by St Clement's Bridge, east of which lay the ship-building yards of Footdee. The old dock gates and the bridge have been swept away to be replaced by the new open-plan port with its oil rig servicing facilities. But one vitally important shipyard, that of Hall, Russell and Company remains at Footdee, producing coasters and freighters, often of specialized design, tankers and car ferries for short sea crossings, while across the water, on the right bank of the Dee, another yard specializes in trawlers. At Footdee there was born the race of craft which revolutionized world transport by sea in the great days of sail—the Aberdeen Clippers.

In the 1850s the *Stornoway* and the *Chrysolite* pioneered British ascendancy in the race to China for tea. After 1852 Aberdeen shipbuilders built many fine clippers for the China run and also for cargo and passenger trade with Australia and South Africa. In the sixties classic models like the *Flying Spur, Yangtse, Black Prince* and *Jerusalem* were the envy of all sailing ship men; and the *Thermopylae*, racing the Clyde-built *Cutty Sark*, demonstrated that she was the fastest clipper in the world.

The inevitable change from sail to steam after the opening of the Suez Canal in 1869 did not destroy Aberdeen's shipbuilding prosperity. As late as 1890 Aberdeen yards turned out fifteen ships of 9,288 tons and employed over 2,500 men—but the passing of the clipper ships deprived us of a spectacle the lovely like of which we will not know again.

Meanwhile another maritime revolution transformed the economic life of the city. In 1882 a few local business men formed a syndicate and acquired a steam tug-boat called the *Toiler* "for the purpose of prosecuting trawl fishing". After six months the syndicate paid out a dividend of 100 per cent. Line fishing from scores of little havens all round the coasts of north-eastern Scotland reacted to the shock-wave of the new method. Fisher families from these tiny ports flooded into Aberdeen, and in particular to the new suburb of Torry on the Dee's south bank, where they were joined by businessmen from the English ports anxious to participate in the Aberdeen trawling boom.

By great good fortune, in which there was perhaps some foresight mingled, a long and useful tongue of water had been left between the enclosed docks and the river Dee when it was diverted into its present channel. This now became the Albert Basin, the home of Aberdeen's trawler fleet. A fish market was built around the upper end of it in 1889, and in twenty years the number of trawlers had risen (from the solitary *Toiler*) to 205, and about 25,000 people ashore and afloat were dependent on the new industry.

Aberdeen's fish trade has passed through many vicissitudes since, but a visit to the fish market, now on the threshold of a great scheme of modernization, is the one experience which no well-advised visitor to the town is allowed to miss. Despite the introduction of some catch-disposal by contract, the vast bulk of the daily fish landings is sold by auction and it is this which provides the colourful spectacle.

Vast numbers of haddocks and of cod are handled at Aberdeen Harbour in a year, and the classes and the functions of the men involved in the industry are almost as various as the fish, and this is one of the sources of controversy in discussions about the organization of the fish trade. There are the trawl-owners who provide the capital and the craft, the skippers and mates who officer the vessels, the trawlermen who man them, the fish-porters who land the catch, the fish salesmen who auction it, the fish merchants who buy it, process it and distribute it to the retailers and wholesalers and the transport agents who carry it to its ultimate destination, mostly on long-distance lorries.

Is all this complexity really necessary? More important is it desirable from an economic point of view? Mechanical handling might render the fish porters redundant. A contract system would make the fish salesmen obsolete. But then the excitement of the fish market spectacle would evaporate. To the bystander the thrill of seeing from two hundred to three hundred merchanting firms compete for the fish is worth a little concession to old-fashioned individualism. One thing will never be supplanted: the ardours and the endurances of the men who catch this harvest in icy, storm-tossed water. Even they, however, are being aided by the march of scientific advance.

Along the south bank of the Dee as one moves westward from the river's mouth are three significant institutions: the Unilever factory, which occupies premises first tenanted by the wartime Ministry of Food; the Torry Research Station of the Department of Scientific and Industrial Research; and the Marine Laboratory of the Department of Agriculture and Fisheries.

Each performs a distinct but inter-related function. The marine laboratory studies the fish in their own element and the means of locating them and catching them, as well as methods of fish farming. From the moment the fish is caught the research station takes over and studies how best they can be preserved, processed and prepared as food and kept in the pink of condition for human consumption. Unilever convert the know-how made available by the government scientists into viable commercial practice, utilizing and perfecting techniques of accelerated freeze-drying, and other methods.

The marine laboratory has its own fleet of research vessels. Its responsibility extends to advising the Government on the conservation of fish stocks in the northern half of the North Sea. It follows the migrations of the herring shoals and the plankton upon which they feed. It pries into the domestic life of the fish themselves. Indeed it was in the marine lab. at Torry that fascinated observers first watched the love-dance and the mating of the haddock—a performance that revealed that this fish does not procreate its young without the excitements of nuptial celebration.

It had been supposed that female haddocks spawned their eggs on their own, and that these were afterwards fertilized by the milt of the males in the vicinity, but in April 1967 at the aquarium in Torry astonished observers saw the complete courtship ritual and sexual embrace of the captive haddocks in a 700-gallon glass-fronted tank. They not only saw, they also heard, for technology now enables us to hear the noises made by fishes. Three of the Torry scientists, A. D. Hawkins, C. J. Chapman and D. J. Symonds later described the event in a paper.

The haddock were caught by hand line in Loch Ainort, Skye, in February 1967 and placed in the Torry aquarium. Beginning on 9th April a single female fish paired with one of a group of three males and spawned on repeated occasions. The male fish began their part in the drama by aggressive displays towards each other, accompanied by intense sound production. Then the dominant male and the mature female indulged in courtship displays. They danced in front and behind one another and extended their vertical fins. The male fish swaggered around with exaggerated swimming movements and actually changed colour. Two accessory pigment spots developed along each flank behind the well-known 'thumb-print' (traditionally said to be the mark of St Peter's thumb) which all haddocks carry. The male fish then slid round the female to a ventral position and eggs and milt were released simultaneously. The sounds made by the mating haddocks provided a dramatic running commentary. They were recorded on magnetic tape and as the courtship proceeded increased in frequency to give a humming noise. Sound production ceased during the embrace and after it the female retired to a secluded corner of the tank and the male returned to the floor and resumed sound production. The mating performance was repeated fourteen times in the next twenty days. An average number of 12,000 eggs was laid at each spawning—an estimated production of 168,000 eggs by this one fish.

Today the oil-servicing function is the dominant one at Aberdeen Harbour. Thanks to the oil-boom over £15 million of public and private investment has been committed to developments in the port since 1972. The conversion of the two former enclosed basins, Victoria Dock and the Upper Dock to full 24-hour tidal working at a cost of £3 million was a crucial factor. Over 20 oil rigs or platforms in the North Sea are being serviced from Aberdeen, and the port now has six major oil-exploration servicing bases. Support bases for their own exclusive use have been established by Amoco, Shell, Texaco, and Total. Amoco is on the Footdee side of the harbour at Pocra Quay. Texaco, Shell and Total are on the River Dee in the area of Old Torry, and there too, at Maitland's Quay West, is the Aberdeen Wood Group, who, with Seaforth Maritime's Seabase, at Waterloo Quay East, are providing 'non-stop shop' for services offered by Aberdeen companies.

The River Dee is a royal river from its mouth upwards. August after August the royal yacht *Britannia* sails up the navigation channel and berths at the Atlantic Wharf, one of the two deep-water berths on the north side of the Albert Basin, and the Queen and the members of her family disembark for the start of their annual holiday at Balmoral. Ever since Queen Victoria first came to Aberdeen—also by royal yacht—in 1848, a particularly intimate association has been built up between successive sovereigns and the city of Aberdeen. Seldom a year passes without the Queen, the Duke of Edinburgh or the Queen Mother fulfilling a number of engagements in the town and, as we shall see, the present Queen, then Princess Elizabeth, fulfilled her first public engagement 'out of convoy' when she opened an extension to the Aberdeen Sailors' Home in 1944 at the age of 18.

The built-up promontory of Point Law, with Albert Quay and its trawler jetties on one side and Mearns Quay on the other, separates the Albert Basin from the river, on the south bank of which is the Torry Dock.

It was not within the burgh boundaries of Aberdeen and it was not until the second half of the nineteenth century that Torry Farm and the Hill of Torry to the south of it began to be developed as a southward extension of the city. The lowest bridge over the river, Victoria Bridge, was built in 1880–81 to provide the main approach to the new suburb, beyond which to the west lies the Vale of Tullos, which, since the end of World War II has been intensively developed as an industrial area.

From a little below Victoria Bridge, where the river sweeps in a graceful curve from the south and south-west, Dee is lined by tree-fringed esplanades and this part of its course is the scene of boating regattas. These pass under the Wellington Bridge, a narrow suspension bridge which dates from 1830, and as far as the great curving viaduct which carries the railway from the south into the city. Above this the north bank is occupied by Duthie Park, presented to the city by Miss Elizabeth Crombie Duthie and opened by Princess Beatrice in 1883; while, on the south bank, the steep tree-girt bluff where Craiginches, the Aberdeen prison, conceals itself behind massive walls gives way to the more gently sloping sides of the Hill of Kincorth with its show-piece granite housing scheme.

At the west end of Duthie Park, Great Southern Road and the graceful modern King George VI Bridge form today the main motor approach to central Aberdeen from the south. The bridge was conceived simultaneously with the planning of Kincorth in the thirties of this century and was intended to divert the main flow of traffic from the sixteenth-century Bridge of Dee still farther to the west. It was not opened, however, until 1941, when Queen Elizabeth, now the Queen Mother, cut a tape and named the bridge after her husband, who was also present on that quiet wartime occasion. You must bear with me while I relate the incident which no one who was present then is likely to forget.

Aberdeen has been fortunate in its wartime civic heads. In World War I the Lord Provost was Sir James Taggart, a granite merchant who was blessed with an infectious sense of humour and a talent for funny stories in which his only serious rival was the first Marquess of Aberdeen and Temair. With these they lightened many a grim day for Aberdeen folk. In World War II the Lord Provost was Sir Thomas Mitchell, a baker by trade and a self-made man who had been born in very humble circumstances in the small rural burgh of Oldmeldrum and began his working life as a farm servant. A shrewd and energetic businessman, he had served long on the town council and was elected Provost, in competition with a distinguished lawyer, by a single vote.

He soon showed by his total lack of pomposity and affectation that he could win hearts. At the opening of the bridge he began his speech of welcome in great style, but, as he afterwards confessed, he had in his hand a small card with five words written on it "that I thought would put me on the rails again if I got lost". All was going well when he took a peep at the card, which instead of helping him threw him into confusion. He paused and turning to the King and Queen remarked in an audible whisper, "I'm afraid I'm making a hash of this!" They both laughed heartily and so did the crowd, whereupon he recovered himself and completed his speech without further mishap.

It was Sir Thomas who accompanied the present Queen three years later on her first solo engagement at the opening of the Sailor's Home. His long term as Lord Provost involved him in many royal occasions and private meetings with King George and his queen, for whom he was a special friend. The quality of this friendship became apparent when in 1959, shortly before his death at 90 years of age, she went to his bedside in an Aberdeen nursing-home. "Sir Thomas", she told the matron, "is a very old friend of mine. We have had many happy times together."

As Sir Thomas's posthumously published memoirs, recorded by Margaret Johnston in a book called *Ninety Wonderful Years,* revealed, the first of these "happy times" was in March 1940. On that occasion, when the Queen visited a naval hospital, he found himself at the station "all alone with no one to present me". The carriage door opened, the Queen alighted, and, said Sir Thomas, "she was the bonniest woman I have ever seen. . . . She came straight over to me with a smile on her face and shook my hand as if I had been a friend of long standing." He took her in the car provided along the sea front and showed her forty ships in line in what she confessed was the first wartime convoy she had seen. He showed her Bennachie, the favourite mountain of Aberdonians, and she said, "I wish we had been going up there!" To which Sir Thomas added, "and I said to myself, I wish we *had* been, and I'm not the only man who would have thought the same."

Sombre reference to a more remote historic past is implied by some of the street names in Kincorth immediately overlooking the sweep of the Dee between King George VI Bridge and the old bridge to the west. Here Covenanters Drive and Row and Faulds Gate, Crescent, Row and Wynd, commemorate the site on the hillside, long called Covenanters' Faulds, where the camp fires of the Army of the Covenant blazed on the night of 17th June 1639 before the Battle of the Bridge of Dee. That bridge, even then, was already a venerable structure. It had been built between 1520 and 1527 by Bishop Gavin Dunbar in fulfilment of the elaborate preparations made two decades before by Bishop Elphinstone.

The design was unique among Scottish bridges of that time. There were seven semi-circular ribbed arches; the roadway and arches were level and above each pier was a recess from the roadway for the added safety of foot passengers. The bridge also had, and still has today, an unprecedented array of coats of arms and commemorative inscriptions upon it: the arms of Scotland, of the Regent Albany, of Bishop Elphinstone and Bishop Dunbar. All these were fully tinctured in colour and the bridge had besides a chapel for wayfarers and a great protective port or gateway at the south end. The chapel and the port have gone, but the bridge itself remains one of the glories of Aberdeen and perhaps its finest single monument of the later Middle Ages. The battle which raged over it at the very moment when, all unknown to the combatants, the Pacification of Berwick was ending the First Bishops' War, has left no visible traces.

The Battle of the Bridge of Dee was an incident in the desolating period remembered simply as 'The Troubles', when Aberdeen became a cockpit of the Civil War. Owing to its long-established links with the Earls of Huntly, the burgh would have remained loyal to King Charles throughout the Great Rebellion, but the greater part of Scotland, incensed by the king's attempt to impose the usages of the Church of England upon the national Kirk, overwhelmingly supported the National Covenant.

On 17th June Montrose and his army from Tollohill (or the Hill of Kincorth) faced across the Dee a Royalist army under Viscount Aboyne encamped at Kaimhill (now, like Kincorth, a modern municipal housing estate). Between them lay the Bridge of Dee, where, during the two succeeding days, the battle raged. On the morning of the second day a cunning feint by the Covenanters—who sent 200 horse westward upriver as if to effect a crossing there—induced Lord Aboyne to withdraw his main forces in pursuit, leaving only some fifty musketeers under Lieutenant Crowner Johnston to hold the bridge. A chunk of masonry blown out of the bridge wounded Johnston on the thigh, and calling for a horse he advised his men to look to their own safety and make their way to the town.

The Covenanters took the bridge without more opposition and marched triumphantly into the town, where the citizens "for plain fear" fled "with their wives and children in their arms and carried on their backs—weeping and mourning most pitifully, straying their hair and not knowing where to go."

One of the victims of the battle, John Seton of Pitmedden, was the subject of a ballad which depicts his wife vainly pleading with him to remain at home:

> He looked over his left shoulder,
>   Cried "Soldier, follow me!"
> O, then she looked into his face,
>   An angry woman was she:
> "God send me back your steed again,
>   But never let me see thee!"

He was killed by a cannon ball and commemorated in his family's coat of arms in which one of the quarterings depicts a heart dripping blood.

West of the bridge on the south side of the river A943, the South Deeside road, after less than half a mile, crosses a tiny stream at Hilldowntree and leaving everything urban behind, runs into deep country. Here a side road strikes over the Mounth by the Blue Hill (467 feet) with a hill indicator pinpointing Cairngorm peaks far on the west. The view of the Deeside suburbia on the north side of the river takes the breath away. It reveals 7 miles of almost continuous riverside communities on the delta terraces, the villages of Cults, Bieldside, Murtle, Milltimber and Peterculter all served by the North Deeside road, A93, a glorious highway along which russet hedges gleam grandly, even in the low midwinter sunshine, while in spring, summer and autumn the trees cast a glorious tracery of light and shade. In this western 'lung' of Aberdeen, colonized by city-dwellers, the population has risen from 871 in 1801 to 9,000 at the present day.

This country road over the Mounth affording such a view follows the line of the ancient Causey Mounth pass across country referred to by Sir Walter Scott as the patrimony of Dugald Dalgetty in "A Legend of Montrose"—"five miles of desolate moorland"—but today the moorland has been chased into a corner, and along the riverside are country mansions in rich wooded policies, chief among them Banchory House. This was rebuilt by John Smith (Tudor Johnnie) of Aberdeen in 1840 as a replica of the extensions he made to Old Balmoral Castle. Curiously enough, Albert, the Prince Consort, stayed at Banchory House in 1859 and a granite obelisk at Catcraig nearby commemorates this visit.

Also in the grounds of Banchory House is the grassy mound of a twelfth-century motte. Here on the south side of the river we are in the parish of Banchory-Devenick or Lower Banchory, not to be confused with Banchory-Ternan 15 miles upstream. Devenick was a ninth-century saint who founded the church at Nether Banchory, while Ternan preceded him by four centuries. The church still lies close to the Dee on A943, and to serve it was built St Devenick's Bridge, known to all as the Shakkin' Briggie, erected in 1837 by Dr George Morrison of Elsick, the parish minister. This fairy-like suspension footbridge, long a favourite of walkers from Aberdeen, has been closed since Dee floods in 1958 wrecked its foundations. It joined the south bank to Cults, now a major residential growth-point with a pleasant square, an inn, a park and the popular Deeside Golf Club's riverside course.

West of Cults is Bieldside, long connected to Blairs in the south-bank parish of Maryculter, by a chain ferry. Blairs was an estate owned by the family of Menzies of Pitfodels, who in 1827 conveyed it to the bishops of the Roman Catholic Church so that its mansion house could be used as a seminary for priests. This was the origin of St Mary's College, the present buildings of which date from 1897, to which a large and handsome chapel, designed by Richard Curran of Warrington was added in 1901.

The treasures of Blairs include two famous portraits of Mary, Queen of Scots, several other historic portraits, illuminated manuscripts and over 150 early printed books. A miniature of Mary Stuart by Hilliard is known as 'the Jewel of Blairs'. The earliest manuscript in the library, a papal bull of privileges issued by Pope Alexander III to the monastery of Ratisbon has a peculiar interest to Aberdeen—for Ratisbon, once largely staffed by Scottish monks, is none other than Aberdeen's 'twin city' of Regensburg in Bavaria, with which many present-day civic links have been established. At the French Revolution archives of the Scots College in Paris were smuggled out to this country and now constitute the famous collection known as the Blairs Papers.

Until the twelfth century a single territory known as Culter (pronounced Kooter) extended along both banks of the Dee. Then around 1187 King William the Lion granted the Culter lands on the south side of the river to the Knights Templars who built a chapel there dedicated to their patroness, St Mary. As a chapel dedicated to St Peter stood on the north bank, the part of the Culter lands which it served became known as Peterculter, and Maryculter and Peterculter developed as separate parishes.

Maryculter's mansion house of Kingcausie fascinated Queen Victoria, who used to have the royal train halted so that she could view its Abbotsford-like façade. This had been embellished by the architect Bryce in 1853, but a part of the house dates from the sixteenth century and the present laird Mr James Irvine-Fortescue is the fifteenth in line of descent from Henry Irvine, who acquired the estate from the Knights of St John—successors of the Knights Templars—in 1535. Nearby are two famous natural features, the Corbie Linn, a charming waterfall, and the Thunder Hole, close to Maryculter House. Both are associated with the sad tale of a Saracen maid and the Crusader to whom she gave her heart but not her honour.

Close by the river the fragmentary ruins of St Mary's Chapel, built by the Templars in 1287, used by the Hospitallers who succeeded them for two centuries, and after that as the parish church, still survive. In 1787 the ancient structure was abandoned and the present parish church of Maryculter was built about a mile to the south. What was probably the old farmhouse of the Manse is now used as the Warden's House in a Boy Scout camping ground known as Templar's Park.

The Kirkton of Maryculter with its famous hostelry the 'Mill Inn' is linked to Milltimber on the north side of the Dee, 6½ miles west of Aberdeen, by Maryculter Bridge, built in 1895. Milltimber, to the west of the charming Den of Murtle, is now being developed as a dormitory suburb of Aberdeen with a private housing development of over 400 houses.

Overlooking the rapidly expanding village of Peterculter from the north-east is Culter House. This lovely house, the central block of which was built shortly after 1640 by Sir Alexander Cumin and bears his arms on a panel above the front door, is now occupied by over fifty boarders and members of the teaching staff of St Margaret's School for Girls. The last of the Cumins, another Alexander, voyaged to America with the object of visiting the Cherokee Indians. They crowned him their 'king' and along with six of the Cherokee chiefs he returned to Britain and laid his 'crown' at the feet of George II in Windsor Castle.

The shipyards and factories of Aberdeen apart, Peterculter is the only industrial community in Deeside. Over 600 of its folk are employed in the paper mills, founded in 1750 by an Englishman named Bartholomew Smith. Today the mills specialize in high-quality and coated paper for luxury publications. It is a remarkable fact that the visitor to Deeside, passing through Peterculter on the A93 highway, is scarcely aware that such an industrial complex exists, for it lies hidden from view far below the road and screened by trees in a loop of the Leuchar Burn near its confluence with the Dee. Some distance below this meeting of the waters the parish church of St Peter stands on a sunny slope closely overlooking the river just where it takes a magnificent curve around the meadowland of Templar's Park.

From the Bridge of Culter just west of the village one looks down upon a striking gorge, on a shelf of whose rocky wall stands the effigy of Rob Roy, in gaily painted highland dress. Here the Leuchar Burn has carved its way through solid rock on being elbowed off its original course by a bulky tail of boulder clay left by the Dee glacier as a legacy of the last Ice Age. Although the notorious Rob Roy Macgregor did in fact cross the Leuchar Burn after visiting a relative in Aberdeen, it was not at this point. But the effigy has a long history. It is the third on the site, the first being a ship's figurehead placed there, it is said, by carters from Aberdeen on delivering materials to the paper mill. When this decayed it was replaced by another wooden statue which stood for ninety years. In 1926 this was replaced by the present one as the result of a public subscription.

But now we leave suburbia completely behind and the river takes wider sweeps through a country of rising hills.

There is a great Roman marching camp at Normandykes above the Dee's left bank here, approached by the historic ford at Tilbouries, to the south of which stretches the ancient track of the Elsick Mounth pass which links up with the Causey Mounth north of Stonehaven. Normandykes is one of a chain of such camps, each of 120 acres in extent, traversing the three north-east counties: at Kair House in the Kincardine parish of Arbuth-nott, Raedykes (just north of Stonehaven), Normandykes on the Dee, Kintore on the Don, Glenmailen near the source of the Ythan (these last three being in Aberdeenshire), and Pass of Grange, near Keith (in Banffshire). All appear to have been built by the Emperor Septimus Severus in A.D. 208 or 209.

The North Deeside road leaves the river briefly, to follow the vale of the Leuchar Burn. Almost immediately we enter the parish of Drumoak (anciently Dalmaik) and soon reach the east lodge of Drum Castle estate (National Trust for Scotland).

This, one of the most fascinating show places in the Dee valley, is finely situated in the well-wooded plateau stretching west almost to the base of the Hill of Fare. The Tower of Drum (briefly mentioned in Chapter II), to which a Jacobean wing was added in 1619, was built as a watch-tower in the royal Forest of Drum, a hunting ground of the early Scottish kings. Over 70 feet high from the ground to the top of the battlements it is a quadrilateral with rounded corners to resist battering rams. There seems little doubt from internal evidence that its master-mason was none other than Richard Cementarius—'Richard the Mason' —the first recorded Provost or Alderman of Aberdeen. His mason's mark has been found on the fabric.

Internally the structure of this blunt and bulky keep consists of three great stone vaults placed one on top of the other. The basement, where the walls are 12 feet thick, was used as dungeon and storeroom and contained a well in one corner 3 feet in diameter and 18 feet deep. From it a straight stair within the thickness of the wall led to the great hall above, itself originally entered by an outside door in the wall approached by a ladder from the ground. The lofty vault of the great hall (now converted into a library and linked to the Jacobean house by a doorway cut through the wall) was subdivided to provide a solar separated from the hall by a wooden floor. Under the third or upper vault is the room now known as the large hall. It too had been subdivided by a timber floor into two chambers, the corbels supporting the floor being still visible, but today it forms a single most impressive hall with its great pointed vault 24 feet above the floor. This pointed vault provides the most important evidence linking the building with the Provost of Aberdeen. It is identical in form with the pointed Gothic arch of the Brig O' Balgownie. It has been conjectured that Richard the Mason, being an economical man, used the same wooden centring or scaffold for the construction of both jobs.

Although originally a spiral stair linked the Great Hall with all the upper rooms and emerged on to the battlements, the upper portion is now replaced by a timber stair from the large hall to the roof-walk. It is well worth while to climb this, not merely for the splendid view from the top, but also to examine the battlements themselves. They are unusually high, while the roof-walk behind them rises and falls in a series of steps between deeply set gutters with gargoyles to cast off the rain water. This must have made it awkward indeed for the defenders, so niches have been cut out in the battlements themselves to enable them to see over the top and shoot their arrows on the attackers—a gimmick which is unique in early castles.

An old traditional rhyme tells us:

> There be six great barons of the North:
> Fyvie, Findlater and Philorth,
> And if you would ken the other three:
> Pitsligo, Drum and Delgatie.

The barons of Drum were the Irvines, and it remained their home for 653 years, being handed over to the National Trust for Scotland by the widow of the last laird in May 1976.

During the early days of his struggle King Robert the Bruce

found shelter with William de Irwin or Irvine of Bonshaw in Annandale. He was struck by the manly bearing of the laird's son, also named William, and selected him as his armour-bearer and secretary. After Bannockburn he rewarded this faithful follower with the grant of the lands and forest of Drum and his charter, given at Berwick on 1st February 1323 is preserved in the charter room of Drum Castle. The last laird, H. Q. Forbes Irvine, was a descendant of William de Irwin. The third laird (mentioned in Chapter II) was the 'good Sir Alexander' who died in the Battle of Harlaw, and the fourth, also Sir Alexander, held the unique office of Captain and Governor of the town of Aberdeen in 1439. During the Civil War the castle was besieged by General Monro (in 1640) and plundered by Argyll and his wild Irish troops in 1644.

The eleventh laird whose first wife was Lady Mary Gordon, daughter of the second Marquess of Huntly, married a second time late in life. His choice was Margaret Coutts, a humble country girl of 16. The ballad "The Laird of Drum" rehearses the tale:

> The Laird o' Drum is a-hunting gane
>   All in the morning early;
> And he has spied a well-faured May,
>   Was shearing at her barley.

According to the ballad Margaret was a reluctant bride:

> For I'm ower low to be Lady o' Drum,
>   And your miss I'd scorn to be.

But having braved the ostracism of the laird's high-born friends and relations she had no doubt of her ultimate equality:

> Gin ye were dead, and I were dead,
>   And baith in grave had lain,
> Ere seven years were at an end
>   They'd not ken your dust frae mine.

As it happened she survived him, acted as his executor, and married another Irvine, the laird of Cults.

Drumoak which has never had a large population (it is now around 650) is one of the loveliest and is certainly the driest parish on Deeside. Perhaps this may have something to do with its popularity as a picnic spot. Here on a glebe field by the river every Saturday in June was for generations enlivened by bus loads and train loads of young people from Aberdeen Sunday Schools. In the extreme south-east corner, overlooking a beautiful sweep of the Dee, are the ruins of the ancient parish church.

The modern church high above the North Deeside Road was designed in a neo-Gothic mode by Archibald Simpson. Farther west and close to the river the neo-Classic façade of Park House is considered to be one of the best of Simpson's creations. Built for the laird of Park estate, William Moir, in 1822, and later the home of Sir Robert Williams, a pioneer of the African railways, it is now owned by Major H. F. B. Foster.

At the Mills of Drum in this parish an ancient ford links up with the Cryne's Corse Pass, the third of the Mounth passes, which leads to Laurencekirk in the Howe of the Mearns. Over this route in 1296 came Edward I of England in his role of 'Hammer of the Scots', accompanied by 30,000 men-at-arms and 5,000 mail-clad knights. They spent the night of 13th July at a "manour among the mountains", the motte and bailey Castle of Durris, now represented by the grassy mound of the Castle Hill on the south bank of the Dee a short distance above Park House.

Durris, which, like Dores in Inverness-shire, comes from the Gaelic word meaning a door, can show today a pleasant mixture of ancient and modern. On 1241-foot Cairn-mon-earn a television mast strikes the modern note, but there are still two traditional blacksmith's forges in the parish, while the oldest part of Durris House is an L-plan tower dating from 1620. The lairds of Durris were great tree-planters and the policies of the mansion contain a notable arboretum. The tiny Kirkton clusters on the right bank of the Burn of Sheeoch (the Fairy Burn). Some 3 miles upstream, where the Sheeoch is bridged by the Slug Road coming over the hills from Stonehaven, stands the farm of Blairydrine, scene of an interesting royal occasion in 1530.

As is well known, King James V of Scotland was particularly fond of travelling about his kingdom incognito. After a tiring journey over the Mounth he arrived at Blairydrine in search of refreshment. He was well received by the farmer, Monane Hogg, and on being told his name remarked that Hogg was a jolly good name for a farmer. Later he prevailed upon the Earl Marischal to make Monane the laird of his own land. As landed gentry the Hoggs were now entitled to their own coat of arms. The insignia granted them consisted of three hog's heads distilling

Pitcaple Castle

The Bass of Inverurie, motte of David of Huntingdon

blood surmounted by the crest of a right hand—King James's hand—and the motto *Dat Gloria Vires*, 'A Good Name Gives Strength'.

A little above the Bridge of Durris over the Dee, built in 1862, one sees standing out from the richly wooded slope on the north side of the river the gleaming coronet of Crathes Castle. We are now in the parish of Banchory-Ternan, the Upper Banchory, through and on the borders of which the Dee winds for 10 miles.

The form of the parish may look rather odd and anomalous on the map but from any reasonably elevated viewpoint the eye can take it all in at a glance. It is the little world that lies between the long isolated ridge of the Hill of Fare to the north, and the hills south of the Dee through which the Feugh, its largest tributary forces its way to the meeting of the waters at Banchory Lodge.

> There's Crathes with its stately towers,
> Inchmarlo with its leafy bowers,
> Raemoir, Tilquhillie, Hattonburn,
> Baldarroch and the Mill o' Hirn
>   Twixt Scolty and the Hill o' Fare.

Crathes first: since this sixteenth-century tower-house was handed over to the National Trust for Scotland by the late Sir James Burnett of Leys in 1951 it has become the most popular show place (next to Balmoral itself) in the Dee valley. When I first visited Crathes thirty-three years ago with the late Lady Burnett as my guide four lines by Yeats kept running in my head:

> How but in custom and in ceremony
> Are innocence and beauty born?
> Ceremony's a name for the rich horn
> And custom for the spreading laurel tree.

There over the mantelpiece in the great hall was the rich horn—of fluted ivory with four bands of gilt and three crystals—which will remain for all time the heirloom and emblem of the Burnett family. This horn, the Horn of Leys, is believed to have been the original horn of tenure in virtue of which Robert the Bruce granted the lands of Leys to Alexander Burnard in 1323.

Now, it will be remembered that in February of that year King Robert granted to William de Irwin the royal domain of Drum, along with which the hereditary office of King's Forester

Crathes Castle

normally pertained. But a difficulty arose when it was found that this office had already been given to Alexander de Burnard. To overcome this, and by way of compensation for loss of office, the King gave Burnard by charter dated 28th March the lands which formed the kernel of the barony of Leys. Both lairds claimed the official arms of the King's Forester, a silver shield emblazoned with three holly leaves. This poser was solved by the introduction of heraldic 'differences'. Both families—who have been good neighbours for over 600 years—still display the holly leaves, but the Burnetts have in addition the Forester's Badge, a black hunting horn.

The Burnards were a Saxon family settled in England before the Norman Conquest. They came to Scotland in the train of King David I to assist him in his schemes of feudalization and settled in the Scottish Borders—like so many other territorial families who later migrated to the north. Their first home on Deeside was a castle on the crannog or artificial island which Iron Age lake-dwellers had built, probably about A.D. 100, on the Loch of Leys, half way between Banchory and the Hill of Fare. It was not until 1553 that the building of Crathes Castle, 3 miles to the east, began. The work was started by Alexander Burnett, the ninth laird, and completed by his great-grandson in 1594.

Crathes is one of the master-works of the Aberdeenshire castle-building school associated with the Bells of Midmar. Probably due to a break in the building programme its design is a little unusual. It is an L-plan tower-house, and, as Stewart Cruden has pointed out in *The Scottish Castle*, it contains a re-entrant stair tower of unusual size, extending from the re-entrant angle to the gable-end of the principal wing, which is thus two wings wide. "By this extension", says Cruden, "the stair tower is absorbed into the main block. As this is correspondingly enlarged, the lesser wing is small in relation to it and projects with diminished effect. The plan of the whole is a square with a small oblong area subtracted from it. This produces a lumpish elevation and unsatisfactory oblique views."

There is undoubtedly something in this expert opinion. But to balance it the views of Dr Douglas Simpson demand quotation. "Externally", he says, "this tower-house forms one of the most spectacular architectural conceptions in Scotland. Its regal coronet of round and square turrets, dormer windows with

quaint finials and gargoyles of fantastic or grotesque design vie
with the riotous exuberance of its ornate corbelling in forming a
composition vibrant with elan and joy in life."

Joy in life! That is undoubtedly the keynote and never did Dr
Simpson's enthusiasm take wing more eloquently than in his
tribute to the Crathes interiors. Of them he wrote in *The Earldom
of Mar*:

A great house which has been in continuous occupation for centuries is always an inspiring sight. . . . If it should chance that the
house be still occupied by the descendants of those who built it, if
it should retain the very furniture with which they surrounded
themselves when the harl was still damp upon its walls, and if the
tinctured pomp of heraldry and the glowing imagery of medieval
fancy with which they clad their walls should still survive to greet
our eyes as we pass from room to room—then surely we have to
deal with a pearl of great price among the nation's jewels.

Each visitor to Crathes will find his own favourite features.
The tower room has barbaric splendour. It is a lofty vaulted
room in which the native stonework has been laid bare, while
hanging from the ceilings are the original pendants bearing the
Burnett arms, one of them dated 1554. Three rooms contain
remarkable ceiling decorations uncovered after long concealment
in 1877. The Chamber of the Nine Nobles depicts three pagan
heroes: Hector of Troy, Alexander the Great and Julius Caesar:
three Old Testament heroes: Joshua, David and Judas Macca-
baeus; and three Christian champions: King Arthur, Charle-
magne and Godfrey of Bouillon. Painted in 1602 each hero is
eulogized in a black-letter rhyme and the series ends with the
query

> Gude redar tell me or you pass
> Whilk of these myn maist valiant was?

The Chamber of the Nine Muses also finds room for the Cardinal
Virtues while the paintings in the Green Lady's Room are more
miscellaneous. The Green Lady has not been haunting this apartment of late, but workmen in Victorian times found the skeletons
of a woman and a child behind the fireplace. At the top of the
house the long gallery has an oak-panelled ceiling unique in
Scotland. Perhaps the most famous scion of the Burnett family

was Gilbert, Bishop of Salisbury, historian and adviser of William of Orange.

Instead of the "green laurels" mentioned by Yeats Crathes has its yew hedges planted in 1702 and a garden of eight sections as renowned as the building itself. A third attraction is the nature trail in the surrounding woodlands opened by the National Trust in 1970. At Mill of Crathes there are two of Deeside's Pictish sculptured stones each bearing crosses.

Almost opposite Crathes on a side road on the south bank of the Dee is Tilquhillie Castle (1576) a Z-plan tower house with a massive central keep and square towers at diagonally opposite corners. It is the ancestral home of the Douglas family and here in 1868 was born Norman Douglas, the author of *South Wind*. It is a far cry from Tilquhillie to the Isle of Capri, where this urbane literary man died in 1952, but he remained strongly attached to his Deeside birthplace.

There is a link between the Douglases of Tilquhillie and the third of Banchory-Ternan's castles, ruined Cluny-Crichton Castle near the foot of the Hill of Fare. It was on marrying a daughter of Sir Robert Douglas, a seventeenth-century laird of Tilquhillie, that George Crichton of Cluny began building it. Never actually completed it remains a striking landmark. A mile to the east of it off B977 is Raemoir Hotel. Behind the modern hostelry is the old hall-house of Raemoir (1680) which bears the arms of Margaret Skene and her husband, James Hogg of Blairy-drine, a descendant of the farmer who entertained James V.

Some 3 miles farther along B977, which skirts the south-eastern flank of the Hill of Fare, is a monument erected by the Deeside Field Club in 1952—a stone with a plaque—to commemorate the Battle of Corrichie in 1562. This battle, in which the power of the Earls of Huntly was levelled in the dust, was a traumatic experience for the people of the north-east. The intransigence of Sir John Gordon, son of the fourth Earl, was the immediate cause of the battle but behind that lay the intense conflict between the pro-Catholic Earl and Lord James Stuart, the Protestant half-brother of Mary Queen of Scots.

Huntly had been anxious to lead a Catholic coup on behalf of Queen Mary, herself a Catholic, and oust the Protestant faction through which she was ruling the country. But in this he was repeatedly rebuffed, and during the Queen's progress in the north the defiance of Sir John and the apparent inability of the

Earl to bring him to submission gave a handle to his Protestant enemies to convict him of treason. On 28th October 1562, while the Queen remained in Aberdeen, her forces under Lord James Stuart, now newly-made Earl of Moray, manoeuvred and clashed with the Earl of Huntly's supporters on the eastern shoulder of the Hill of Fare, then covered by forest. Repeated charges by the Gordons failed, and they were driven in rout into the vale of Corrichie. At the height of the battle the Earl fell dead from his horse. His body was taken to Aberdeen and ultimately to Edinburgh for sentence of forfeiture, while Sir John Gordon and five other leading Gordons were publicly decapitated by the 'Maiden' in the Castlegate of Aberdeen. Such a spectacle of utter downfall and humiliation of the ruling family in the province— John Douglas, the builder of Tilquhillie Castle, was only one of the many local lairds who fought on Huntly's side—no doubt had a profound effect. Ballad threnodies for Corrichie were sung:

> Mourn ye Highlands and mourn ye Lowlands,
>   I trow ye hae meikle need,
> For the bonny burn o' Corrichie
>   Has run this day wi' bluid.

The common man, aware that whatever befell his lot would be little the better, speaks from the heart in the final stanza:

> I wis our Quine had better friends,
>   I wis our countrie better peace;
> I wis our lords would na discord;
>   I wis our weirs at hame may cease.

In the midst of this beautiful and historic countryside is the small modern burgh of Banchory with a population of around 2,500. Apart from Aberdeen it is the largest 'populated place' in the whole valley. A sawmill, a lavender factory (much visited as a showplace by tourists) and a slaughterhouse, are its only industries, but its attraction as a residential area is great. Inquiries from intending settlers come from all over Scotland, particularly from those who want to find or build a house in good time for their retirement.

Modern Banchory dates from 1805, when the first feus of what was then called Arbeadie village were taken up. By 1841 there were fifty-two houses occupied by seventy-two families forming a population of 350, and by the end of the century this

had swelled to 1,400. Most of modern Banchory is still concentrated along the long line of the High Street, the built-up part
of the North Deeside Road, but pleasant terraces rising to a
considerable height look down upon it from the north, while on
the south Dee Street leads past the recreation ground and the
fine riverside golf course to Banchory Bridge over the Dee,
which dates from 1799, although it had to be partially rebuilt in
1829 and is now being again reconstructed.

Banchory's most historic site is the kirkyard at the east of the
town. Here St Ternan had his fifth century monastery and here
stood the medieval church, slight traces of which remain. Near
here in 1488 Sir Alexander Burnett established a burgh of barony
called the Kirkton of Leys. There is a Pictish wheeled cross at
Banchory Manse and the shaft of the Kirkton's market cross is in
the Burnett Park. A watch-tower in the kirkyard has a bell made
by Peter Ostens of Rotterdam in 1644. The only relic of St
Ternan himself is his 'ronnecht' or Celtic handbell at Inverey
House. The 'new' Banchory at Arbeadie became a police burgh
in 1885.

A memorial tablet in the High Street commemorates Scott
Skinner the 'Strathspey King' (1834–1927), a master of fiddle
music whose best known composition was probably "The
Miller o' Hirn". The mill can still be seen a few miles north-east
of the town. Half a mile south of the burgh, where the Feugh on
its way to join the Dee foams its way through a gorge of reddish
quartz-porphyry, is the Brig o' Feugh overlooking spectacular
falls where salmon leap a succession of sills. It dates from 1790, as
does the old Toll House at its west end. To lessen traffic dangers
a pedestrian footbridge has been built for the salmon-watchers
just above the old brig. It is a blot on a natural beauty spot and
can only be justified as a temporary expedient. Banchory Lodge
Hotel on Dee's north bank opposite its confluence with the
Feugh caters for the salmon anglers and the burgh has several
other fine hotels.

On the estate of Blackhall south of the Dee and at the foot of
the Hill of Scolty with its conspicuous summit tower commemorating General Burnett of Banchory, the Grouse Ecology Unit
has established itself in the old stables. The history of this venture
goes back to 1956 when a Grouse Inquiry was financed by the
Scottish Landowners' Federation. At that time there was an
alarming drop in the demand for grouse moors and their average

rental was running at the rate of £1 per brace. Now the situation has improved and moors let at £5 per brace. But what started as an emergency rescue operation continues with wider aims. In 1960 the Nature Conservancy took over responsibility for the work which is now incorporated in the Conservancy's Mountains and Moorlands Habitat Team. There is a scientific and technical staff of fifteen investigating grouse, deer and the associated botanical and forestry problems.

The red grouse is the only species of wild bird peculiar to the British Isles, so research on it is unique and cannot be duplicated anywhere else on earth. The scientists under Dr Adam Watson and Dr David Jenkins have shown that improved moor management can bring back the good old days of big grouse yields. Grouse are very selective feeders and respond to specially fertilized heather in a spectacular way, nesting earlier and rearing up to four times as many young.

IV

THE ROYAL DEE: THE MIDDLE REACHES

When I see some dark hill point its crest to the sky
   I think of the rocks that o'ershadow Culblean;
When I see the soft blue of a love-speaking eye,
   I think of those eyes that endeared the rude scene.
George Gordon, Lord Byron.

DOWN the valley of the Feugh and its tributary the Dye comes the fourth and historically the most important of the eight Mounth passes, the Cairn a'Mounth, which is traversed by a modern motor road. Nightly in winter one hears on the broadcast road reports whether the Fettercairn–Banchory road (B974) is still blocked or "passable but difficult". By this route Macbeth retreated northwards in 1057 and Edward I marched southwards in 1296. The road crosses the watershed between the Howe of the Mearns at 1,475 feet, yielding a magnificent view over the greater part of the Mearns.

It crosses the Water of Dye by two bridges: the old Brig o' Dye built by Sir Alexander Fraser of Durris in 1681, and the Brig o' Bogindreep. Another bridge, over the Feugh, brings it to Strachan (pronounced Straan), the kirktown of this upland parish dominated by four hills: Mount Battock (2555 feet), Clochnaben (1900 feet), Kerloch (1747 feet) and Mount Shade (1662 feet). Its three streams, Feugh, Aven and Dye come together in the Haugh of Strachan where also is the Castlehill of Strachan, site of a medieval motte.

Although the permanent population is only 470, this gives no idea of its use by tourists who choose it as a beguiling alternative route to the upper reaches of the Dee valley. The Brig o' Dye, 9 miles from Banchory, is only 3 more from the summit of Clochnaben. The name means 'the stone on the mountain' and refers to an eccentric boulder 95 feet high which makes the summit conspicuous. Joseph Knowles' poem attributes it to a quarrel between the Devil and his wife:

"Have at you now, you beldame" roared the Fiend,
    And hurled the rock through the resounding skies;
Dreadful it fell, and crushed his breathless friend,
    And there entombed Her Hellish Highness lies.

The parish of Strachan has produced a number of famous men.
Thomas Reid, founder of the Scottish or Common Sense School
of philosophy and author of *An Inquiry into the Human Mind* was
born here. He was a son of Lewis Reid, parish minister of
Strachan, and his wife Margaret Gregory, the sixteenth child
of David Gregory of Kinnairdie, a family famous for mathe-
matical genius. She herself had no fewer than twenty-nine children
by the parish minister!

The Feugh is 20 miles long, rising on the Hill of Cammie on
the Aberdeenshire-Angus border, and a choice of roads enables
one to follow its course far up into the Forest of Birse, or to
return to the Dee valley by alternative routes, both highly
picturesque and both approximating to ancient branches of the
Cairn a'Mounth crossing north of Strachan. The first of these,
branching off on the right from B976 at the Feughside Inn traverses
the Shooting Greens of Strachan and, at a point near Muckle Ord
on the Aberdeenshire-Kincardine county boundary, affords a
magnificent view looking west up the Dee valley. The second is
the upper portion of B976 itself which turns north opposite the
Mill of Clinter to cross over the Corsedarder pass. This road skirts
the estate and community of Finzean, a name which means 'the
Fair Place' and has been made most famous perhaps by the landscape paintings and snow scenes of Joseph Farquharson, R.A., one
of its lairds.

Finzean (pronounced Fing-an), which, like all the upper valley
of the Feugh, lies within the Aberdeenshire parish of Birse, is a
delightful self-contained community. The parish, which is large
and scattered (it is 10 miles long and 10 broad and has a land area
of 31,591 acres), really consists of three portions: upper Feughside
including Finzean and the Forest of Birse above it, Mid Strath
or Glencat in the centre and the Deeside portion along the right
bank of the Dee. The parish church is in the Deeside portion so
that in historic times all the dwellers on the Feugh had a long
trek over the hills to reach their kirk. They had to endure this
until the nineteenth century when the Farquharsons, who have
been lairds on Feughside for 390 years, secured the creation of the

quoad sacra parish of Finzean. Now this parish within a parish has a church, school and social centre of its own, and one is surprised at the number of houses strung out along the valley road on either side of the red-roofed Finzean Public Hall, built in 1928 by Joseph Farquharson, the artist laird, for the benefit of his tenants.

The Corsedarder pass takes its name from the Corsedarder Stone, a great granite monolith which was broken in two parts by workmen while making the present road over the hill to Glencat and Deeside, and afterwards clamped together with an iron clasp and re-erected on its original position on the west side of the road by the orders of Archibald Farquharson of Finzean. It is traditionally claimed to mark the site of a conflict at the dawn of Scottish history. King Dardanus was said to have reigned over the Picts for the space of four years. According to the chroniclers he was a great tyrant and fell into all sorts of vices, so that the nobles and commons rebelled against him, and in A.D. 81 so the story goes, he was taken and beheaded by his own subjects—and buried at the very spot where the Corsedarder Stone now stands.

Nearby, at the summit of the pass, at a height of 745 feet, stands overlooking the valley of the Dee on one side and the valley of the Feugh on the other, the war memorial in honour of the men of Birse and Finzean who fell in the two world wars. From this point the road descends, and crossing the Burn of Cattie passes the hamlet of Marywell and the school of Ballogie, and links up with the South Deeside road (A973) midway between Potarch Bridge and Aboyne.

Before proceeding along this road let us look back to the upper vale of the Feugh. From the point where the Corsedarder road leaves it, the beautiful Forest of Birse road continues westward for another 5 miles, the stream foaming over boulders through a landscape that becomes increasingly rougher and barer. At Ballochan one passes the tiny Forest of Birse Church, converted out of an abandoned school in 1890, and then—surprise! surprise! —one reaches right at the end of the road the turreted and splendid Castle of Birse, in this century magnificently restored and added to by the late Annie, Viscountess Cowdray. It has a fascinating history.

All this land originally belonged to the Bishops of Aberdeen, to whom it was granted in 1242 by King Alexander II. They divided the arable part of it into twenty-four 'touns' or holdings, leased to as many tenants, and then, towards the end of the medieval period, they sold the Forest of Birse to the Gordons of Cluny, by whom the castle was built about the end of the sixteenth century.

Commanding the Fungle, a track over the hills from Aboyne which crosses the upper Feugh and links up with the Fir Mounth pass from Dinnet to Glen Esk, Birse Castle was originally a plain keep in plan with the addition of a round tower at one angle only. Its most famous laird was Sir Thomas Gordon:

> High on the bonnie hills o' Birse,
>   Stan's good Sir Thomas's tower,
> And far and wide the oak tree spread
>   That shades his lady's bower.

By 1791 there was a community of 147 with 120 acres of land under the plough here, but illicit distilling was their main source of livelihood. When the castle itself was abandoned Highland caterans took up their abode in the ruins and made raids on cattle lower down the Feugh. Now the restored castle is let to shooting tenants.

In 1851 the population of Birse parish stood at 1,533. Today it has fallen to 714. The school at Birse on the Dee side of the hills has been closed; the school at Finzean still flourishes while the school at Ballogie, in the Mid Strath, recently won a hard-fought battle against closure.

Ballogie House, on a tree-girt site overlooking the Burn of Cattie was built in 1856 by James Dyce Nicol. The grouse moors here are famous and year after year chalk up bumper bags on 'The Twelfth'. The Corsedarder pass road reaches the Dee near the House of Balnacraig. James Innes, who built the house in 1735, was the target of Cumberland's militia after Culloden, having been 'out' with Bonnie Prince Charlie. While he hid from the redcoats in the summer house, his wife Catherine Gordon saved the house from ruin.

The soldiers arrived footsore and weary and hungry too—for Catherine had gathered in all the food in the neighbourhood and set her servants baking for dear life. She regaled the men with a feast under the trees in the grounds and invited their officers to come in and dine in the parlour of Balnacraig. They bore an order to arrest the laird and burn the house as that of a rebel. But they were hungry, and they went in and ate boiled chicken and gooseberry tarts and cream. They toasted the Lady of Balnacraig and declared that, rebel though her husband was, the house would be spared. The redcoats for their part left the premises in a state of high inebriation, watched by the 'hunted' laird who was lurking nearby.

Birse Church lies on a quiet country by-road off A973. Dedicated to St Michael, it contains the Crusader's Stone, a sculptured grave-slab depicting two cross-hilted swords.

At the extreme north-west corner of the parish is Birsemore Loch, a beauty spot beloved by Queen Mary, consort of George V. At the invitation of her friend Lady Cowdray she was in the habit of taking a picnic tea there at a little cottage reserved for her use.

At the other end of Birse, its north-eastern tip on the Dee, is Potarch, once famed for fairs and now for picnics, close to the handsome bridge built there in 1812 across a gorge of porphyry. Its site is 50 yards below the narrows where Cyard Young, a freebooter, leapt across the river when fleeing from justice in 1800. His leap however, did not save him from being hanged at Aberdeen in the following year, after being convicted of manslaughter.

While the graceful Bridge of Potarch was being built and two of its three arches were complete a flotilla of logs came down the river and crashed into the unfinished masonry, ruining the work of months. As a result an Act of Parliament was framed prohibiting the floating of timber under bridges in the course of erection. The Muckle Spate of 1829 tore away part of the rock under the foundations of the bridge. It was repaired, and remains today one of the glories of Deeside.

By this beautiful bridge one may return to the North Deeside road a few miles west of Banchory. Between that burgh and Potarch, despite the heavily wooded country, one may catch a glimpse here and there of the filter beds of the Aberdeen Waterworks—for Aberdeen, which owes to the Royal Dee so much else, is also indebted to it for its water supply, by a scheme completed and opened by Queen Victoria in 1866. The intake is at Cairnton, between Invercanny and Potarch.

A mile west of Potarch, where the river above the Potarch gorge is running in a quiet open reach, A93 runs through the long main street of Kincardine O'Neil, the oldest village on Deeside. Its total population is only 166 and it never seems to have recovered from the setback it received when by-passed by the Deeside Railway in 1857, though now that the railway is dead it has a brighter future. It has old-world charm and one ancient monument of great interest, the now roofless medieval church of St Mary, which took its origin in the hospice and chapel established there by Alan Durward in the thirteenth century.

In Chapter II I told how Thomas de Lundin, the Door Ward of Scotland, secured a slice of the Earldom of Mar. This included the Lordship of O'Neil. To link it with the Cairn a'Mounth pass, Thomas built the first bridge over the Dee. This timber structure has long vanished, but in 1231 Thomas's son, Alan Durward, established a hospice and chapel for the benefit of travellers using the bridge. The chapel became the parish church, and served until 1733, when its heather-thatched roof caught fire. It was re-roofed and slated, but in 1859 the fabric was considered unsafe and the present parish church was built on the other side of the road and opened in 1862. Now the venerable old kirk is cared for by the Department of the Environment.

Two miles north-east of Kincardine O'Neil is Torphins (population 561), on the Beltie Burn, one of the communities given life by the wide detour away from the river taken by the Deeside Railway, which was finally closed in 1966. In the Barony of Learney Torphins has always lived and breathed and had its being. In 1857 it consisted of a few thatched cottages near an old wayside inn. But the Baron of Learney, Colonel Thomas Innes, welcomed the arrival of the railway and from 1859 when the line was opened development was rapid.

At Torphins the Deeside Railway passes through a cutting 50 feet deep and quarter of a mile long and known as Satan's Den. In less than 2 miles from the village both rail and road (A980) cross the Beltie Burn and enter the parish of Lumphanan.

This is Aberdeenshire's Macbeth country. It lies amid gentle hills bounded by greater heights with noble outlines on the west. The parish has a total population of 717 and its largest centre of settlement is a modern village of 247 folk. It has a few shops, an inn called the 'Macbeth Arms', a fine modern school built in 1965, and dominating the whole scene from a conspicuous knoll backed by wooded slopes, is the Stothart Memorial Church (1870) with a tall tower topped by a soaring steeple. All this is really the consequence of the coming of the Deeside Railway.

For in Lumphanan the ancient and the modern subsist side by

side. Little more than half a mile to the south-west on the road leading back to the Dee valley at Dess is the original Kirkton of Lumphanan, a hamlet that remained unaffected when the railway arrived in 1859. In the centre of it is St Finan's Church, simple, comely, built in 1762, with a pleasing decorative belfry—but otherwise no trace of the Gothic grandeur of its sister church across the way.

Lumphanan means 'the Cell of St Finan', one of four disciples of St Kentigern who proselytized here in the seventh century. Most famous of the antiquities in the parish are the Peel of Lumphanan, Macbeth's Cairn and Macbeth's Stone, said to be the actual spot where that king was slain.

As his kingdom toppled about his ears he no doubt sought some strength where he could hold out to the last. The Peel of Lumphanan may have been that place, for the Department of the Environment, who look after it today, say there may quite well have been a 'castle' of a kind there in 1057. Standing close to the road to Dess as it passes under the railway, it is described as "a first-rate example of a shell keep—an enclosed castle on a mound, protected by a wall round the summit and earthworks and ditches round the base."

Macbeth's Cairn, now almost hidden by a surrounding protective clump of trees, is on a sloping field on the farm of Perkhill about a mile north of the village (on A980). But it was *not* erected over the burial place of Macbeth. It is clearly a prehistoric cairn far older in origin than the year 1057—and it has now been established that Macbeth, like so many of the early Scottish kings, was buried on the holy isle of Iona.

Now that we are on A980 let us carry on up it to the northern tip of the parish at the Crossroads of Lumphanan. Here there is an inn and a small cluster of houses at the point where A980 crosses A974, the Aberdeen-Tarland road. We are here just beyond the highest point of the watershed between the Dee and Don valleys, but it will be well worthwhile to continue for 2 miles more along A980, which now follows the Donward-flowing Leochel Burn, till we come to the avenue leading west to Craigievar Castle, the crowning glory of the Aberdeenshire school of castle-building. The most superlative tribute to Craigievar was paid by Mr Stewart Cruden, who, as we saw earlier, was a severe critic of the design of Crathes.

"As a testimony of taste," he wrote, "Craigievar ranks with

any representative building in Britain. As a work of art it claims a Scottish place in the front rank of European architecture. . . . There is a sort of sublimity about the front elevation . . . a serene assurance not communicated by any other tower-house however pleasing. No infelicity of mass or exaggeration of detail suggest room for improvement. Quite perfect, lightly poised upon the ground, it is the apotheosis of its type". These are strong words but I agree with every one of them. Craigievar is the nearest thing to a fairy-tale castle that I know. Although we have no documentary proof of the fact, it was so obviously designed by I. Bell, the architect of Crathes, Cluny and Castle Fraser, that it can be assumed to be his 'ninth symphony' in stone.

Set in most attractive country, in grounds meticulously cared for by the National Trust for Scotland who acquired it from the late Lord Sempill, Craigievar was completed in the year 1626 and has remained virtually unaltered ever since.

Craigievar is an *L*-plan tower house with a square tower in the re-entrant angle. On the ground floor it is a model of stark sobriety. On the first floor the corbelled stair turrets (there are two of them) spring out of the face of the building. Three more storeys intervene and then the angle turrets sprout (there are six of them) linked by a richly decorative corbel table encircling the building two storeys below its actual roof level. The majority have simple conical roofs, but crowning the whole edifice, alongside an open platform with a pillared Renaissance balustrade, are two turrets with gracefully segmented ogee helmets. Nor is this all. Each of the four elevations of the building has a different profile, the biggest contrast of all being between the south and the north faces.

I. Bell was obviously having fun. And it is this architectural gaiety which is the keynote of Craigievar. For all this it is still a pretty safe place to be in if pursued by a batch of evil men. The walls are stout and strong and there are two spiral staircases right to the top of the house—but only one way in, the arched doorway in the tower, protected first by a stout wooden door, and then by an iron yett. Scottish yetts (the word simply means gate) are unique. English craftsmen never adopted the cunning system of interweaved iron bars which gave these protective grilles great strength.

The mingling of medieval and Renaissance features so conspicuous outside the castle is also prominent within. The central portion of the great hall at Craigievar is covered by a lofty medieval groined vault, but this vault is clad in Renaissance plaster with strapwork and decorative pendants, as well as medallion portraits of Biblical and classical worthies. At the lower end of the hall are the screens with minstrel's gallery above—a tradition that goes back to the Dark Ages when Saxon heroes feasted in their banqueting halls. But—and this is the delicious paradox——the woodwork of the screens is carved with classical arcading and crowned with a Renaissance balustrade.

The great fireplace is basically Gothic, but above the lintel is a heavy Renaissance stucco cornice, and on either side of the sculptured achievement of the Royal Arms of the United Kingdom (said to be the finest thing of the kind in Scotland) are two caryatids, male and female.

In stressing the virtuosity of Craigievar as an architectural *jeu d'esprit* one should not overlook the charm of its intimacy as a family home. This was first borne in upon me over thirty years ago when I was shown round the house by Lady Sempill, wife of the eighteenth Baron. High up near the roof of the house are the arcaded box beds where the domestic staff slept, and here I saw an array of wooden 'patterns' for stockings, each labelled with the names of the members of the family for whom the stockings were to be made by some eident knitter in the dear dead days beyond recall. Craigievar is in fact a miniature epitome of the social history of Scotland over three centuries. So late as 1842 the floors of the main rooms were strewn every morning with fresh rushes gathered in the meadows below the castle. Until the middle of the eighteenth century the baronies of Scotland had their barony courts for dispensing local justice. These were frequently held in the great hall at Craigievar, and the court books, which survive, are full of human interest. One rude character, for example, for calling the minister a liar, was ordered to be put in the stocks during the baron baillie's pleasure. All together it was wise to follow the advice on the arms of Red Sir John, dated 1668: "Doe Not Vaiken Sleiping Dogs".

As we return southwards to rejoin the North Deeside road at Dess (where the former station building has been converted into a pottery by a local craftsman, Stewart Johnston) there is one more point of special interest on the A980 road. About a mile north of the station to the west of the road lies the site of the

Craigievar Castle

Loch of Auchlossan. Where, less than a decade ago, the dark outline of the hill of Mortlich was mirrored in a great expanse of still water, one can drive across the centre of the loch amid fields of waving grain. There is nothing new, however, about this alternation between watery waste and productive farmland. It has been going on at intervals ever since J. W. Barclay first drained the Loch in 1860. Great quantities of straw from the Loch of Auchlossan fed the big population of horses on Deeside in the days of Queen Victoria's 'tourist' boom which brought many a fine carriage to the area.

There is a waterfall at Slog of Dess, a short distance south of the station, and by this point the road has crossed the parish boundary and we are now in the parish of Aboyne and Glentanar. The village of Aboyne (30 miles west of Aberdeen) is properly speaking Charleston of Aboyne, so named after Charles, first Earl of Aboyne, who in 1670 obtained a charter authorizing him to erect a burgh or barony in close proximity to his domain, Aboyne Castle, the main lodge gates of which stand at one corner of the village.

For well over a century, thanks to the royal presence at Balmoral, Deeside has been the darling valley of rich men who have lavished improvements on it which otherwise it would never have enjoyed. This is nowhere more obvious than at Aboyne, where the whole village bears the stamp of Sir William Cunliffe Brooks, millionaire banker and laird of Glentanar, who, we are told, "had an absolute passion for building and road-making" and who became very closely linked to Aboyne when his daughter married the eleventh Marquess of Huntly. He built most of modern Aboyne, and he also brought a spate of changes to Aboyne Castle itself, where the whole story of Aboyne begins—unless, that is, one cares to dip back into prehistoric times. In that case one can carry the tale back to the Neolithic era.

Two miles north-west of the village there is an extraordinary collection of cairns—903 of them have been counted—which has been named the Balnagowan Necropolis. Most of them belong to the Bronze Age, but at least one is a long cairn of the New Stone Age. In this area too is St Mochrieha's Cross, an incised equal-armed cross. Mochrieha, it is believed, was the same St Machar who gives his name to the Cathedral of Old Aberdeen, and since the 1929 union of the churches the parish church of Aboyne—although originally dedicated to St Adamnan, the

'The Twelfth': grouse drive on a Deeside moor near Dinnet

biographer of Columba—has been called St Machar's. The next most ancient antiquity is the Formaston Stone, a Pictish sculptured stone of Class II. It is a fine cross slab with symbols, including the 'mirror', and Ogham characters, now preserved in the gardens of Aboyne Castle. It came originally from Formaston, one of the three old hamlets in the area which preceded the creation of Charleston of Aboyne. Formaston was the ancient kirktown around the old kirkyard a mile east of the village. The second hamlet, called Bonty, stood at the ford of the Dee below the present Bridge of Aboyne (rebuilt in 1871), its site being marked by the Boat Inn. Dalwhing, the third hamlet, lay on the south bank of the Dee.

The great mystery about the early history of Aboyne is the precise location of its earliest castle, although there is no doubt at all that a castle existed and was of major importance from a very early period. The oldest part of the present structure, a seventeenth-century tower, has been recently restored, and the Victorian additions demolished. Originally the noble House of Gordon made their advent at Aboyne when a Keith heiress brought the lands of Aboyne, Glentanar, Glenmuick and Cluny into the family. Until the seventeenth century Aboyne was held by the Earls of Huntly and often bestowed on their second sons. It was Charles, fourth son of the second Marquess, who by his exertions in the Royalist cause helped to sway the Cromwellian General Monck in favour of the Restoration and was rewarded by being created Earl of Aboyne in 1670.

In popular imagination the first Earl is the hero—or villain—of the ballad "The Earl of Aboyne" which begins:

> The Earl of Aboyne is to England gane
> And a' his merry men wi' him.
> Sair was the heart his fair lady had
> Because she wasna wi' him.

Then follows a tale of rumour and panic, of the return of the Earl, and a further misunderstanding, and of the broken-hearted death of "bonny Peggy Irvine". Originally separate, the parishes of Aboyne and Glentanar were united about this time.

The glen of the Tanar, a right-bank tributary of the Dee 12 miles long is one of the most spectacularly beautiful vales on Deeside, famous for its still-surviving indigenous Scottish pinewoods, part of the ancient Caledonian Forest, but it was at this time a desperately poor and primitive area, for, apart from floating the logs down the Dee in time of spate, there was no easy way of moving the timber.

In 1732 the Countess of Aboyne introduced the first sawmill to deal with the problem. Work was doubtless interrupted by the 1745 Rebellion, when Lord Lewis Gordon raised an Aboyne Battalion for Bonnie Prince Charlie. But in 1797 a ship entirely of oak from Aboyne was built in Aberdeen and named *The Countess of Aboyne*.

In 1836 George, fifth Earl of Aboyne succeeded to the Marquessate of Huntly on the death of the fifth and last Duke of Gordon, thus becoming Cock o' the North, as the head of the house of Gordon is called. The twelfth Marquess, Douglas Charles Lindsey Gordon, is the present chief, besides being premier Marquess of Scotland. This is reflected in the pageantry at Aboyne Games, when he makes ceremonial entry with attendant chieftains. The Games, originally on the day preceding the Braemar Gathering, are now held on an August Saturday.

The first Aboyne Games of the present series were held in 1867. The Green of Charleston, a grassy triangle about half a mile long, around which the village is built, thus became the arena of doughty deeds by outstanding Highland athletes, including the most famous of them all, Donald Dinnie from Birse.

Donald Dinnie (1837–1916) started competing in the games at their inception, became a professional at the age of 30, took part in 11,000 contests, winning 150 championships and earning about £26,000 in prize money. Although all his records in the main events have been subsequently broken no one could equal his all-round achievement.

In 1952 the organizers of Aboyne Games made history by introducing the 'Aboyne dress' for women dancers, really a revival of the graceful women's costume of the eighteenth century—designed to replace the kilt and tunic bespattered by medals that was being worn at Highland games. They have also attempted to restore women's dances to replace the male dances like the Highland Fling as a girls' competitive dance.

It was in 1869 that Cunliffe Brooks first came to Glentanar as tenant of the estate which he subsequently owned. He kept a regular staff of 250 workmen and before he died had rebuilt Glen Tanar House and nearly every farm and cottage on the estate. In 1870 he began building the beautiful Chapel of St Lesmo. It is still one of the marvels of Glentanar. The pews are lined with deerskin and the altar is a great stone found in the bed of the Tanar. Sir William was followed in Glentanar soon after his death by the first Baron Glentanar, then Mr George Coats, who bought the estate in 1905. His son, Lord Glentanar, devoted himself to forestry and hill farming.

Despite the pressure of national need in the war years, when 3,200,000 cubic feet of timber was felled in Glentanar, the remains of the indigenous pinewoods were spared, and their natural regeneration which had been virtually halted for a century, was after 1940 specially encouraged and has made a significant advance. Glentanar has 5,000 acres of woodland and 30 per cent of the stocked and partially stocked area is indigenous forest. This priceless relic of the old Wood of Caledon is now effectively seeding itself. Besides this there is a planting programme of at least 100 acres a year.

Both the roads west of Aboyne are lovely, but the South Deeside road is perhaps the more spectacular. Soon after crossing Aboyne Bridge one has a glimpse over an island in the river of the handsome house of Rhu-na-Haven, designed by Sir Robert Lorimer in 1911. In springtime this delectable mansion is environed by acres of daffodil-starred lawns. The road now passes under the wooded shoulder of Craigendinnie to Bridge of Ess over the rock-strewn gorge of the Tanar, with its tower, one of the many landmarks created by Cunliffe Brooks.

Two miles farther on by a wide meander of the Dee is the old ruined kirk and the kirkyard of Glentanar. Here a grey granite cross marks the grave of James Robertson of Ballaterach and his wife and daughter Mary—the heroine of Byron's poem "When I Roved a Young Highlander". How wonderful is the power of words! Lord Byron's apostrophe to Mary Robertson half convinces us that he is recalling a grand passion, but this girl was only 14 at the time, and she was decidedly the plainest of the two Robertson sisters, while Byron himself was only a little lame boy of 8, recovering from an unromantic bout of scarlet fever. Indeed so improbable does the whole thing seem that some have preferred to think the Mary concerned was his cousin Mary Duff (mentioned in Chapter I). But, as we know from his subsequent career the poet was, in the words of one Scottish critic, "unco wastefu' o' Marys".

When I roved a young Highlander o'er the dark heath,
    And climbed thy steep summit, O Morven of snow,
To gaze on the torrent that thundered beneath
    Or the mist of the tempest that gathered below,
Untutored by science, a stranger to fear,
    And rude as the rocks where my infancy grew,
No feeling save one, to my bosom was dear;
    Need I say, my sweet Mary, 'twas centred in you?

The question was rhetorical, and *Hours of Idleness*, in which the poem appeared, represents the romantic posturing of the young blood. But the few weeks which Byron spent at Ballaterach farm in 1796 provided him with furniture of the mind upon which he continued to draw for the rest of his stormy life. The savagery of the Deeside mountain tops he somehow equated with the wild streaks in his own ancestry and the devil-daring extremes of his own temperament. He succeeded in making them symbols of personal freedom. He reflected in a passage of some genuine psychological insight on the power of first impressions:

He who first met the Highlands swelling blue
Will love each peak that shows a kindred hue,
Hail in each crag a friend's familiar face,
And clasp the mountain in his mind's embrace.

That dynamic "clasping" of the mountain is the only thing about this that would be recognized by his early Deeside acquaintances as characteristic of the spoilt, unruly child who roved the dark heath around Ballaterach. To the carpenter at Deecastle (about 3 miles west of Glentanar Kirk) he was a holy terror. This worthy declared that Master Byron was "neither tae haud nor tae bind [neither to hold nor to bind]" and that he would not keep his hands off any of the tools in the workshop and "spoiled them completely before he would let them go". To escape this mischievous meddling the craftsman was in the habit of shutting up his shop and making himself scarce whenever Byron was seen approaching. But there must have been rapture in it for Byron. He tells us:

Long have I roamed through lands which are not mine,
Adored the Alp and loved the Apennine,
Revered Parnassus, and beheld the steep,
Jove's Ida and Olympus crown the deep;

But 'twas not all long ages' lore, not all
Their nature held me in their thrilling thrall;
The infant rapture still survived the boy,
And Lochnagar with Ida looked o'er Troy. . . .

Ah, Lochnagar! you say, when do we meet up with that storied peak? We are really anticipating things, for the mountain is not visible from this low-lying stretch of the South Deeside road. But there is one famous viewpoint from which it can be seen amid the splendid company of its attendant heights. To reach it we must retrace our way to Aboyne village and take the road (B9094) which leads due north. This goes by way of Balnagowan to the crossroads of Coull, the small parish which contains the ruined courtyard castle whose story was told in Chapter II. At the crossroads near the church we bear right and ascend the slope which will bring us to A974 at the Slack of Tillylodge.

Here, a short distance west of the road junction, is the view indicator set up by the Deeside Field Club to mark its jubilee in 1970 at a point known as the Queen's View. The whole of the foreground is occupied by the green fertile basin of Cromar, while beyond it the stalwart solidity of Morven's great bulk stands up along the west. But let us turn our eyes to the east first of all and then follow summit by summit in a wide three-quarters circle the story that the indicator has to tell. Due east is Corse Hill (1,383 feet), then a shade to the south Craiglich (1,583 feet) with its monument, then Leadlich (1,278 feet), and Mortlich (1,248 feet) which now stands between us and Aboyne. These are all nearby hills, but now our view leaps across the Dee, invisible in its hollow, and overlooking all the glen of the Tanar reaches to the crest of the Mounth barrier at Braid Cairn (2,907 feet) and Mount Keen (3,077 feet) quite unmistakable because of its sharp cone. Still moving west the indicator now picks out two slightly closer hills, Cairn Leughan (2,205 feet) and across the deep defile of Glen Muick the graceful Coyles of Muick. It is only beyond them, towering over all—and given rather good visibility—that one sees the long serrated ridge of Lochnagar, rising to its majestic summit of 3,786 feet at Cac Carn Beag. This is the limit of the view to the south-west, because the whole western horizon is blocked by the much nearer and almost continuous ridge of Culblean Hill (1,983 feet) and Morven (2,862 feet). One more height the indicator pinpoints, much nearer but at the extreme north-western limit of its range, and this is Pressendye (2,032 feet), part of the hill-barrier which cuts off the Howe of Cromar from the Don valley to the north.

One of the numerous interpretations of the name Cromar is 'the sheepfold of the god' and a divine sheepfold it certainly is. Let us press on down the "rose-red road winding down the southern slopes of the heathery hills" to the village of Tarland, its centre.

We shall not be escorted on our way as Ishbel, first Marchioness of Aberdeen and Temair was in 1878, when a convoy of tenants on horse-back accompanied her and her husband into the delectable vale of the Tarland Burn, but we may pause, as she often did, at the earth-house of Culsh on the left-hand side of the road. It is a long, low, narrow and curved tunnel, dry-built of undressed surface stones, roofed over with massive lintels and approached by a flight of steps into the ground, in which it is completely insulated except at the entrance.

A little farther on, on the other side of the road, one passes the farm of East-town with its tall silo tower designed to hold 700 tons of silage, its crop store for 200 tons of moist grain and its vast hangar-like cattle court, 315 feet long with a span of 64 feet (big enough to tuck away a fleet of aircraft) which in fact accommodates in ease and comfort 300 weaned calves. This is one of the phenomena of the MacRobert 'empire' in Cromar. Tarland is a parish of 6,300 acres but the MacRobert Trust, centred at Douneside, now owns a territory of 9,476 acres extending into adjoining parishes and, beside the Douneside farms at its core, there are eighteen rented farms.

All this was really the creation of Sir Alexander MacRobert, born at Ann Street, Aberdeen, in 1854, in humble circumstances. While still a young man he went to India as manager of the Cawnpore Woollen Mills, and this was the beginning of a business career which brought him great wealth. In 1888 he bought a small house, Burnside as it was then called, on the lands of Ranna, as a home for his parents. By 1906, both parents having died, he enlarged the little house at Burnside for his own use, and that was the beginning of the Douneside which was in time to transform the pattern and economy of the whole Tarland countryside. Sir Alexander was twice married. By his second wife Rachel Workman he had three sons, Alasdair, Roderic and Iain. Each in turn succeeded to the baronetcy Sir Alexander left behind when he died in 1922. Alasdair was killed in a flying accident in 1938 and Roderic and Iain lost their lives in the Second World War while serving with the RAF. In their memory Lady MacRobert presented to the Government a Stirling bomber, 'MacRobert's Reply' and four Hurricane fighters—three named after her sons and the fourth 'MacRobert's Salute to Russia'.

The estate of Cromar had been acquired from the Marquess of Aberdeen in 1918, and Lady MacRobert and her co-trustees purchased the Melgum estate in 1929. Upon these lands they developed great farming enterprises. Besides the three Douneside pedigree herds of Aberdeen-Angus, British Friesian and Highland cattle and a commercial herd of cross-bred cattle, there are some 1,000 Blackface and 700 Greyface sheep along with 1,726 acres of woodland and 1,800 acres of hill land.

The charitable work of the MacRobert Trust is perhaps more important than its actual farming operations. The handsome House of Cromar, originally built for the first Marquess of Aberdeen, became Alastrean House (a name intended to denote 'Hearth of Honour for Winged Heroes of the Stars') and still serves as a house of rest and recreation for RAF officers, while a group of farms called 'Alamein' were used as training centres for young men entering the farming industry. Grants for many purposes are made by the trust. The restoration of Old Aberdeen in conjunction with Aberdeen University (mentioned in Chapter I) and the endowment of a MacRobert Art Centre at Stirling University costing £250,000 are among the trust's activities, while in Tarland itself a MacRobert Memorial Hall was established

Tarland village (population 396) with its parish (population 638) is one of the oldest communities on Deeside. On the fold of land overlooking the village from the south a notice points the way to the Bronze Age stone circle of Tomnaverie. That takes us back 4,500 years. Then at some time in the sixth century Tarland was visited by St Moluag of Lismore, whose name the parish kirk bears.

The Civil War was unkind. In 1644 the whole area, like much of Deeside was ravaged by a punitive force of Argyll's Highlanders. The old kirk, built in 1762, still stands in ruins in the kirkyard at the east of the village square. In 1870 a new and imposing church was built in a commanding position overlooking the golf course east of the village and serves as a landmark for miles around.

Beyond Tarland to the west is the parish of Logie-Coldstone

where gentle cultivated hills sweep down to the wooded skirts of Morven.

> There's a land of wonders in the lee of Morven,
>   Along the road by bonnie Bellastraid,
> From Davan's brink to hill-bright Tillypronie
>   Through Blelack's woods in loveliness arrayed.
> The Cross of Migvie and its vanished castle,
>   And Newkirk dreaming by its sombre steeple:
> These I remember as a child remembers
>   A land of wonders—and of happy people.

The village of Newkirk (population 74) on A97, the road from Deeside to Strathdon, got its name when the two parishes of Logie-in-Mar and Coldstone were united in 1618 and a new and "centrical" kirk was built to serve both districts. The present church dates from 1780 though the sombre steeple was added later. The population of the joint parish today is 532.

Let's traverse the parish from north to south. Tillypronie House, on the high ground overlooking the vale under Morven is the Scottish home of the Hon. Gavin Astor. A former laird Sir John F. Clark brought to its garden the Tomachar Stone, a Pictish sculptured stone of Class I. Its symbols are the two-legged rectangle intersected by the Z-rod with the crescent and V-rod below. Tomachar, 'the hillock of the stone', from which it came lies nearer Newkirk. At Migvie, a little to the south is the Migvie Stone, one of the finest Pictish cross-slabs in the north-east. Besides the huge Celtic cross with its delicate interlacing it bears four other symbols: a double disc and Z-rod, crescent and V-rod, a pair of shears and a knight on horseback. Migvie is also the site of a thirteenth-century courtyard castle, the capital messuage of the Lordship of Cromar. Nothing but the rude foundations of this remain, but there is a charming little church dating from 1770.

South of Newkirk the road runs through the lovely woods of Blelack with glimpses of Morven and Culblean through the trees on the west and avenues leading to Blelack House on the east. From the middle of the seventeenth century to the end of the eighteenth Blelack was held by the 'red' Gordons to whom a traditional jingle prophesied doom in the words:

> Dool, dool to Blelack,
>   And dool to Blelack's heir
> For driving us frae the Seely Howe
>   To the cauld Hill O' Fare.

This was a curse uttered by a race of fairies or 'little people' when they were expelled by the Gordons from the sheltered nook in which they had settled at Blelack and had perforce to take up more draughty quarters on the Hill of Fare. A modern fairy-tale called "The Ashwood Train" by R. E. Jackson (Mrs Thomas Innes of Learney) imagines their return to the Blelack of today.

In the '45 Rebellion Charles Gordon of Blelack and his neighbour Gordon of Pronie (the Tillypronie of today) went off to join Bonnie Prince Charlie in Edinburgh. After they had done so the minister of Logie-Coldstone was engaged in prayer one Sunday morning at Newkirk and had just besought the Deity to "scatter the army of the Rebels and bring their counsels to nought" when he was interrupted by the Lady of Blelack, seated in the congregation, who with an oath cried out, "How dare ye say that an' my Charlie wi' them!"

Just south of Blelack is Balnastraid, now an experimental farm of the North of Scotland College of Agriculture. Three hundred years ago over twelve people lived and worked on the same land. The name Baile na Sraide, in Gaelic, means 'town of the street', in other words a farm-toun with a row of croft cottages.

In 1695 the tenant was John Cattanach. Fifty years later his successor another John Cattanach became notorious. He lorded it over a numerous community at the big house known as the 'Ha' of Bellastraid' (as the name is still sometimes spelt and pronounced) and fought with Gordon of Blelack in the '45. After Culloden he quietly returned to Bellastraid and for a time defied all attempts to take him into custody. A messenger-at-arms named Cuthbert was dispatched by the authorities in Aberdeen to capture him alive or dead. Before bearding the lion in his den Cuthbert spent the night at a nearby inn. As he emerged on the following morning he met Cattanach face to face.

"A sharp morning, sir!" said Cattanach, "and what may ye be after today?"

"And who are you?" said Cuthbert haughtily, "that you claim the right to know?"

"I am Cattanach of Balnastraid, and I believe I have a right to know," came the retort.

Cuthbert thereupon pulled out a horse pistol, aimed at Cattanach and pulled the trigger. But maybe it had been tampered with overnight, for all that happened was a little flash in the pan.

"Ha, ha, my man," said Cattanach, "is that what you're after. We'll let you see better-gaun graith here!"

He then produced his musket and shot the messenger-at-arms through the heart, leaving him dead on the threshold. There he lay till the authorities in Aberdeen were told what had happened. Or not quite—because Cattanach was a firm believer in the local superstition that if a murderer could by any chance contrive to see daylight beneath the body of his victim he would escape the punishment due to his crime. He therefore hastened to the nearby farm of the Davan and enlisted the aid of a crony there called MacCombie, whom he persuaded to lift the corpse of Cuthbert. Having seen daylight under it, he then returned to Balnastraid well content.

The day after that a posse of dragoons came out from Aberdeen, but when they got to Balnastraid the bird had flown. Cattanach lurked about the country for months, moving from one hiding place to another, and eventually succeeded in smuggling himself overseas to foreign parts.

Just south of Balnastraid there is a crossroads. Here A97 turns west and, skirting the northern and western side of Loch Davan and the western side of Loch Kinord, joins the North Deeside road at Cambus o' May, while B9119, passing the hamlet of Ordie, runs straight as a die across the Muir of Dinnet on the eastern side of the two lochs to the village of Dinnet and to Dinnet Bridge over the Dee on the south of it.

Let's take the Dinnet road first. The Muir of Dinnet is one of the great topographical features of Deeside. It marks the final pause, the holding of the breath so to speak of the Deeside landscape between hilly uplands and Highlands proper. Near the Mill of Dinnet on the North Deeside road at the point where the Burn of Dinnet passes under it the Deeside Field Club have erected a stone which announces to the traveller "YOU ARE NOW IN THE HIGHLANDS". But Dr Douglas Simpson considered this a little premature. He saw the true gateway to the Highlands as the Pass of Ballater at least 5 miles farther west.

Dinnet (population 73) is a modern village owing its origin to the Deeside Railway. A new *quoad sacra* parish was set up here in 1886. Its first minister was John Grant Michie, author of *Deeside Tales* and books on Loch Kinord and Logie-Coldstone.

West of Dinnet the South Deeside road skirts an ancient

oakwood on its way to Deecastle and Cambus O' May, while the North Deeside road runs through the Muir of Dinnet, since 1977 a national nature reserve of 3,805 acres, sustaining a population of 12 human beings and up to 7,000 wild ducks and geese. Dinnet House, north of the river, is the manor of Kinord, one of the largest territorial 'empires' of Deeside, extending westward from the outskirts of Aboyne to the left bank of the River Gairn above Ballater. The Muir is a great brown undulating heath, glorious with the purple of the bell heather during July and August, though now it is reverting to woodland of birchen scrub, which was its ancient state. Suddenly, however, this wild desolate expanse gives way to softer country disclosing at the foot of Culblean two gleaming sheets of water, the twin lochs, Kinord and Davan.

Loch Davan, which lies farthest to the north, is formed by a hollow in the sheet of boulder clay deposited by the grinding weight of a vanished glacier. Loch Kinord has an even stranger origin. It lies on the site of a great lobe of 'dead ice' which at one time obstructed the flow of melting waters from the icefield in the Ballater basin farther west. It was this ancient overflow channel rudely carved out in the declivity between Culblean and its southern spur Cnoc Dubh (1,067 feet), which formed the spectacular gorge of the Burn o' the Vat with its great rocky cave on the hillside (easily approached by a footpath from Vat Cottage on the A97 road and one of Deeside's most popular picnic spots). The Vat cavern, narrowly open to the sky above but ringed with solid rock, is often called Rob Roy's Cave, though its real tutelary spirit is not Rob but Gilderoy, the most notorious of the seventeenth-century freebooters who infested the area.

The landless Macgregors were the cat's paws of violence in the Highlands. As Michie tells in his *Deeside Tales* a band of them were invited to Deeside "to try their hands on some desperadoes who had broken loose there". They soon settled that hash, but refused to go back to the wilds of Rannoch whence they had come. Instead they settled in the Dens of Culblean behind the Vat and took to cattle lifting with such success that the whole country around felt the cure to be worse than the disease.

Loch Kinord, the eastern shores of which are the site of a Boy Scout camping ground, is adorned with two islands, at least one of which, and probably both, are man-made. Crannog Island, formed by successive layers of stone and earth, held together by intersecting mortised timbers and tethered by a girdle of piles, resembles many European lake dwellings. Its companion Castle Island remained inhabited long after the lake-dwellers had departed—as a medieval fortress.

Loch Davan also had its fortalice known as the 'Ha' of Ruthven' and both castles played their part in the brief but decisive campaign which proved the turning point of the Second War of Independence in the year 1335. On the high land between the two lochs the Deeside Field Club erected in 1956 the Culblean Battle Memorial Stone to mark the site of this decisive clash.

As mentioned in Chapter II, this campaign opened with a siege of Kildrummy Castle—held by Dame Christian Bruce, on behalf of her husband Sir Andrew de Moray, who was acting as Regent of Scotland during the exile in France of King David II. She was attacked there by David de Strathbogie, Earl of Atholl, a pro-English quisling, and an army of 3,000 men. While this siege was going on the Earl learned that Sir Andrew was approaching in his rear with a formidable force. He then raised the siege and turned south to face his greater adversary, who had by this time arrived at the Ha' of Ruthven.

The two armies met in the grey of the morning of St Andrews Day, 30th November 1335, on the slopes of Culblean Hill. The Earl was surprised and slain and his routed followers hid themselves in the wood of oak and birches which then covered the far slopes of the hill. One of the Earl's men, Sir Robert Menzies, took possession of the Castle of Kinord, where he was safe for the time being on the island fortress, but he afterwards capitulated and pledged his fidelity to the Scottish cause.

During the Civil War the Castle of Kinord again saw action. In 1646 it was restored and garrisoned by the Marquess of Huntly in the cause of King Charles. It was then besieged and surrendered to the Covenanting General Leslie's troops. Two years later, by Act of Parliament, it was ordered to be slighted. The demolition was carried out with such thoroughness that not a trace of it remains. Yet Loch Kinord today is still a lively place in summer. Scouts navigate it with their canoes and the battles of old are fought over again in play.

At Cambus o' May a short distance west of the point where the North Deeside road and A97 converge, the river, richly wooded on both banks, is spanned by a fairy-like suspension footbridge erected in 1905. Here we are 38 miles from Aberdeen and, with the wide open expanse of moorland left behind, we are entering an enclosed valley, the floor of which is seldom more than 400 yards wide for the next 20 miles.

So narrow in fact is the shelf of land above the defile of the river that when the Deeside Railway reached Cambus o' May it was necessary to slice off a corner of the gable of the old River Inn to fit in the railroad track between it and the road. The railway is now silent and the inn is now a cottage, but that odd slice remains to catch the eye.

Although the valley is now narrow it is never dull. Two geological factors have dowered it with picturesqueness. Millennia ago the river meandered widely in a comparatively flat plateau. The land was then uplifted into mountain masses, and the river incised a deep channel, but the old meanders remained, giving a perpetual kaleidoscope of changing views so that every bend produces a new perspective. Then came the Ice Ages. Glaciers converged with tremendous pressure on the upper valley and the force of glacial erosion came into play, giving even the smaller hills that rugged contour which makes for landscape spectacle. There is a fine example of this as the road sweeps round the big curve of the river west of Cambus. You see in the west a cup-shaped gap from which the river flows, with a hill like a smaller cup turned upside down in the middle. That inverted cup is Craigendarroch, the Crag of the Oaks. To the south of it, on what was a patch of barren moorland below the confluence of the Dee with its two tributaries the Muick and the Gairn, lies the burgh of Ballater. To the north, in the narrow precipitous gap between Craigendarroch and Creagan Riach, is the Pass of Ballater, the true gateway to the Highlands.

While there is still about a mile and a half to go before we reach this pass, there face each other across the river the two historic antecedents of Ballater: the old ruined Kirk of Tullich and the Inn of Pannanich with its famous wells.

Tullich lies low in the haughland on the north side of the river and all that there is to see there now is the ruined kirk with its picturesque circular wall; several Pictish sculptured stones of Class I, the best bearing the double disc and Z-rod, the elephant and the mirror symbols; and, not far away, another Pictish earth-house like the one at Culsh. But it is indeed a famous place.

> For blythe and merry we'll be a'
> As lang as we hae breath to draw,
> And dance till we be like to fa'
> The Reel o' Tullochgorum.

Tullich, Tulloch, Tullochgorum . . . the controversy about the
origin of this famous reel will doubtless go on till the end of time.
John Skinner, himself a Deeside man, really meant Tullich, I
think, but was beguiled by the demands of rhyme into confusing
the issue. For me it seems crystal clear that these lines do refer to
the Kirkyard of Tullich, where even today one can so easily
imagine how it must have been on that wintry Sunday morning
when the congregation, goaded by a terrific nip in the air, danced
with ever more and more abandon, as they waited for the storm-
stayed minister to come and let them into the shelter of the kirk.

But Tullich's story does not begin with the reel. Although the
kirk dates from about A.D. 1400 it was built on the site of St
Nathalan's Chapel. About this obscure Deeside saint there is a
delightful story. Having committed a "great sin" he locked
himself in an iron girdle and cast the key into the Key Pool of the
Dee near Tullich. Then he went to Rome seeking absolution.
The key turned up in a fish's belly and the saint knew that he had
won divine pardon.

Over a century ago Dr Joseph Robertson, the historian, in a
spoof guide to Deeside which he wrote for James Brown, a
Ballater coachman, made playful fun of this legend. It was he
said "a Popish trick" for "what trout, pike, eel, salmon, grilse
or other fish should swallow a key (which as it could not eat iron
it would have no incentive to do) in the Dee at Ballater, and then
swim down the Dee, round the Girdleness, away along the coast,
through the Channel—across the tumultuous Bay of Biscay—
along the shores of Spain and Portugal, then turn through the
Straits of Gibraltar and up through the Mediterranean till it
came to Italy?"

"Doubtless," continued the good doctor, "if this fish did swim
all this long weary way with the key in its belly, it must have been
sick and tired of it, and as glad to the full to get rid of it, as was
Saint Nathalan to find it. That heavy iron girdle must, it is certain,
have occasioned him a world of trouble and been an inconvenience
to him not to be described."

St Nathalan died at Tullich on 8th January 678. The kirk was partly reconstructed after the Reformation. It has a fine doorway of yellow freestone in the Early English style at the west end of the north wall. Once a thriving village, Tullich is claimed to have been a royal burgh in the Middle Ages, although its credentials as such are said to have been lost by Sir Walter Scott when he was entrusted with them by William Farquharson, the founder of Ballater.

Across the river at this point the South Deeside road runs high on the lower slopes of Pannanich Hill. A little to the east of Tullich there was here in the old days a hamlet known as Cobble-town of Dalmuchie. Around 1760 an old woman of this neigh-bourhood miraculously cured herself of scrofula by bathing in a bog to which she had been 'guided' by dreams. The fame of her cure was exploited by Colonel Francis Farquharson of Monaltrie (William Farquharson's uncle) on his return to the land of his fathers after the twenty years' exile that had followed his capture at Culloden and narrow escape from execution as a rebel. At the Cobbletown he built the inn, Pannanich Lodge, and created a spa which was soon the rage of fashionable society. As Pannanich Lodge is still there today, along with its upper and lower wells (which played so essential a part in the foundation of Ballater), some small account must be given of its romantic Jacobite progenitor.

Nicknamed the Baron Ban (fair-haired) because of his fair curly locks, Francis Farquharson (1710–90) son of the laird of Monaltrie and factor to his uncle John Farquharson of Invercauld, commanded the Aboyne Battalion of 300 men in Bonnie Prince Charlie's army.

It is difficult for us to understand today the extent to which the aristocracy of Deeside and indeed of the Highlands as a whole were divided by the Jacobite rebellions. Here it was not a case of whole clans or families opting for one side or the other. Fathers and sons, brothers and cousins, even husbands and wives were severed by their conflicting notions of loyalty or self-interest. While his uncle and other relatives stayed cannily at home Francis made the perilous choice, influenced it is said by his employer's daughter, his own cousin, Lady McIntosh, known to the Jacobites as Colonel Ann, whose husband, the McIntosh of McIntosh, remained loyal to King George.

Most of the Aboyne Battalion were slaughtered at Culloden. Francis was captured, shipped from Inverness to London, sen-

The Dee at Pannanich

The Burgh of Ballater with Craigendarroch, 'The Hill of the Oaks', behind

tenced to death by hanging and was on his way to the gibbet on Kensington Common on 28th November 1746 when a reprieve came out of the blue. It is said that a wealthy lady, Margaret Eyre of Hessop, fell in love with him at first sight and appealed successfully for his life, though the fact that his father was a Justice of the Peace and firm friend of the Government may have helped. It was pleaded on his behalf that before the '45 he had "promoted industry among the poor, built roads and bridges and started charity schools".

In 1766 he returned to Deeside. The foundation of spas was almost a patent profession by ex-Jacobites. The Baron Ban had the waters which had cured the old wife analysed, enclosed them in elegant fountains, and the great Pannanich boom began. By the early 1780's the pardoned rebel was being hailed in stylish verses:

> Our children's children shall revere thy plan
> And praise Monaltrie as the friend of Man.

The inn at Pannanich has a magnificent view. It is a hotel-in-two-halves, between which the coaches rumbled in Georgian days with their health-hunting cargo. And the wells themselves are still patronized. Some years ago Miss Mary Gray the licensee of the inn invited me to 'take the waters'. I found them clear and pleasant-tasted and, though they are rich in iron, they can be drunk with zest, despite the disillusioning conclusions of modern science that the cures they effected were miracles of faith.

However, the phenomenon of Pannanich gave the final spur to other acts of faith that were necessary before Ballater could come into being. The three united parishes of Glenmuick, Tullich and Glengairn had long needed a focal point. In 1798 the foundation stone of a "centrical kirk on the moor" was laid. After the church was opened in 1800 William Farquharson, the Baron Ban's nephew set about laying out the new village on the black moor that surrounded it.

On our way there by the North Deeside road we may glimpse Monaltrie House which the Baron Ban rebuilt in 1782—to replace the ruins of the ancestral home which had been burned to the ground by King George's redcoats in 1746. Monaltrie, which is approached by the Pass of Ballater road, is now the centre of a small but attractive animal park. Meanwhile the North Deeside road sweeps on to Ballater and enters it immediately to the

The Queen presents colours to the 3rd Battalion, the Gordon Highlanders on the lawn in front of Balmoral Castle

Balmoral Castle: the ballroom, tower and part of the north front

north of the present bridge over the Dee, the story of which is told by a plaque on the west parapet: "A bridge of stone was built about 100 yards east of this site in 1783 and was swept away by flood in 1799. A second bridge of stone was built by Telford 60 feet east of this site in 1809 and was swept away by flood in 1829. It was replaced by a wooden bridge in 1834 which lasted till 6th November 1885, when this bridge, built by County Road Trustees, was opened by H.M. Queen Victoria who named it the Royal Bridge. Long may it stand. . . ."

Ballater's population in 1971 was 982, while in the whole of the joint parish of which it is the centre, a parish between 10 to 16 miles long and 6 to 12 miles broad and embracing 87,335 acres, there were only 508 more people. This shows a decline of about 100 per cent since 1921. Before a single house in Ballater was built there were 2,117 folk in its now depopulated hinterland.

These figures are not quoted to point a lugubrious moral. Rural depopulation is universal throughout Britain. But they do show how for 150 years Ballater has acted as a magnet, not only to the tourist from afar but to the indigenous population of the area. They also mirror the social history of Upper Deeside, in which three main phases can be detected. From the Dark Ages to the Union of the Crowns this region was a hunting forest or playground for kings and barons. Between the seventeenth and the nineteenth centuries it was overspread by the small nucleated settlements of subsistence agriculture, encouraged at first as nurseries of fighting men, then gradually swept away by the pressure of economic rationalization and replaced by a new kind of hunting forest or natural playground—at first for the noble, the wealthy and the royal, but eventually for the common man. The process continues. Ballater, with about forty boarding houses and hotels, is adjusting itself to the change from long-residence resort to the short-term, stay-a-night-or-two car-tourist era. It has one advantage over other resorts which find themselves in the same boat—across the Muick, beyond the Gairn on its western doorstep, lie the royal holiday estates that are centred in Balmoral.

A planned community from the start (where a worthy called Sandy Dunn followed William Farquharson with a plough as he was measuring and laying out the streets and was "sometimes like to lose him amid the broom"), Ballater is on the checkerboard plan. Its main thoroughfare, Bridge Street, lined with shops, many of which display the insignia to which royal warrant-holders are entitled, runs north from the bridge to the Station Square and is intersected half way along by The Square, a wide and long village green, on which the only building is the stately Glenmuick Church.

A high green hill, Craig Coillich—the Hill of the Old Women —1,250 feet, rises abruptly from the verge of the South Deeside road on the south side of the bridge. Craigendarroch, the cup-shaped Crag of the Oaks already mentioned, rises precipitously a little north of the North Deeside road at the other end of Bridge Street to an exactly similar height. Ballater has the freedom of both, though Craigendarroch, having the best views and being girdled half way up by a convenient path, is the favourite. Yet it is to Craig Coillich with its summit cairn that the hill race which is the highlight of Ballater Highland Games in August is run, and since the games are held in the Monaltrie Park, itself almost under the shadow of Craigendarroch, the competitors can be followed as they sprint through the town and up the rocky tree-cumbered slopes.

Although there are a few old streets near the river dating from its earliest days, Ballater is mainly a Victorian creation. Long straight residential streets run westward to the golf course on the wide flood-plain where the Dee describes a great semi-circle from the mouth of the Gairn to the mouth of the Muick. This delectable course in its amphitheatre of hills is bordered on the south by a large well-serviced caravan site just above the bridge, while on the north runs the riverside path, sacred to pedestrians only, known as the Old Line, which accompanies the Dee in its boulder-strewn rocky gorge to Invergairn. Ballater owes this pleasant amenity to Queen Victoria, who insisted that the Deeside Railway should abandon any plan to carry its track west of Ballater. The portion which had already been engineered thus became available as a lovers' walk.

To those who know it best Ballater (Gaelic: *baile challater*, 'town of the wooded stream') means not merely memories of innumerable royal arrivals and departures at the Station Square, not merely the lights and bustle of the Victoria Barracks when the Royal Guard is in occupation, not merely the excitements of unrehearsed royal shopping expeditions, but the scent of pine needles, the sound of rushing waters, and that hush of gloaming when the Coyles of Muick are haloed in a sunset glow.

V

BALMORAL: THE SAGA OF A ROYAL DOMAIN

> Away ye gay landscapes, ye gardens of roses;
>   In you let the minions of luxury rove;
> Restore me the rocks where the snowflake reposes,
>   For still they are sacred to freedom and love.
> Yet Caledonia, beloved are thy mountains,
>   Round their white summits though elements war,
> Though cataracts foam, 'stead of smooth-flowing fountains,
>   I sigh for the valley of dark Lochnagar.
>
> Lord Byron.

BALLATER is 42 miles from Aberdeen. Braemar is rather more than 58. Between them lie 16 miles of superlatively beautiful country, every mile of which is permeated by royal associations. It would be possible to describe it step by step, but the best way is surely to begin at the mid-point, Balmoral Castle itself, for it will be found that everything will fall naturally into place around the home which Queen Victoria created as a refuge from protocol, red tape and the endless cares that beset the crowned head.

Lord Byron's poem on Lochnagar was set to music as a splendid dramatic song, and as a song of patriotism and euphoric abandon it is best remembered. He saw an unbridgeable gap between rugged romantic grandeur and the "tame and domestic" beauties of soft English countryside. Victoria saw this contrast too, but she showed that it was possible to have the best of both worlds. Under the window of her sitting room on the west front of Balmoral Castle, so designed as to give a superb view of the Cairngorms, there is a charming rose-garden. But Byron's dark Lochnagar remains the indispensable back-drop.

The Castle lies 50 miles west of Aberdeen on a flat green shelf of meadowland on the Dee's south bank, so close to the river that the sound of its waters is heard through every open window in the house. Directly south of it and separated from it only by a lawn and garden of a few hundred yards rises the hill of Craig

Gowan (1,430 feet), and from this point successive wooded ridges and hills rise in height as they recede southwards through the Forest of Balmoral to the long ridge of Lochnagar with its eleven summits of over 3,000 feet.

The shape of the Balmoral countryside can be easily defined taking the Lochnagar ridge as its keel. Between Ballater and Braemar on the south bank of the river there are five tributary glens, two large and three small: Glen Muick with its loch 8½ miles above the Bridge of Muick at Ballater; Glen Girnock, a little farther west; Glen Gelder, immediately to the west of Balmoral; the glen of the Garbh Allt with its falls in the Forest of Ballochbuie; and Glen Clunie, the water of which is 12 miles long and accompanies the famous Cairnwell Pass north of the Devil's Elbow on its way from Perth to Braemar.

In the beginning, however, it was only Balmoral and its forest, which lured Victoria and Albert. The Queen's long love affair with Scotland was chronicled by herself with simplicity and frankness in *Leaves from the Journal of Our Life in the Highlands* (1868) and *More Leaves* (1883). Two books of extracts from these journals have recently been published, so there is little excuse left for the wilful denigrators of Victoria who would attribute to her a bogus sentimentality and a false cult of Highland romanticism, sometimes cynically dubbed Balmorality. As a sovereign Victoria had her faults so savagely delineated by Lytton Strachey and others, but it is a fact that Deeside brought out the best in her character. She was the first British sovereign to acclimatize herself to Scotland for 250 years. She was 23, two years married and expecting her third child, Princess Alice, great-grandmother of the present Duke of Edinburgh, when she and the Prince Consort first entered Scottish waters in the yacht *Royal George* on 31st August 1842.

It is easy to smile at her gushing enthusiasm: "We then came in sight of the Scotch coast, which is very beautiful, so dark, rocky, bold and wild. . . ." Or at Taymouth on 7th September: "The *coup-d'oeil* was indescribable. . . . It seemed as if a great chieftain in olden feudal times was receiving his sovereign. It was princely and romantic." The spell had begun to work. There was no doubt to begin with a tincture of romantic illusion, but there were no illusions when she wrote twenty-seven years later: "The departure from Scotland, that loved and blessed land . . . was very painful and the *sehnsucht* for it very great. It is not all the pure air, the quiet and beautiful country which renders it so delightful—it is the atmosphere of loving affection and hearty attachment of the people around Balmoral which *warms* the heart and does one good".

The story of how, following a very wet summer at Ardverikie in the Perthshire highlands in 1847, Victoria and Albert were persuaded by Sir James Clark, the queen's doctor, to try the drier climate of Deeside is well known. The royal family arrived at Aberdeen on board the royal yacht early on the morning of Thursday 7th September 1848—twelve hours before its scheduled time! This was due to a mistake on the part of an official who, under the misapprehension that the maximum speed of the vessel was 10 knots, had ordered full speed ahead, with the result that it had left its North Sea escort far behind and gave the Aberdeen authorities a panic awakening. They were soon on hand, however, to present their loyal addresses, received by the Queen in a black and white straw bonnet and tartan shawl. Prince Albert then took the children for a tour of the city, and the drive to Balmoral began at 8.30 a.m. the next day.

This journey up the Dee valley was a non-stop fête. The first triumphal arch was a massive structure at Aberdeen Harbour. There was another at Cuparston "where an immense crowd received her Majesty with loud cheering". There were others at Cults, Murtle, Culter, Drum, Park and Crathes (where the slogan was "Mearns hails its Queen"). The first of the two arches at Banchory was of "gigantic dimensions, composed entirely of heather, and surmounted by a figure of the British Crown, six feet high by five and a half wide, formed of dahlias and other flowers". Private citizens also made their arches. About 100 yards west of Banchory the farmer of Kineskie had devised one entirely of oats, barley and wheat, so neatly arranged that the ears only were visible. The Blackhall arch was entirely of stags' heads, Inchmarlo's was festooned with flowers, Potarch had a huge Gothic affair. At Aboyne the Queen walked on a carpet of Gordon tartan to lunch with the Countess. At Ballater cannon boomed from the top of Craigendarroch. Finally at Crathie, a mile and a half from Balmoral the last arch proclaimed "Welcome to your Highland home, Victoria and Albert".

The Queen wrote in her journal: "We arrived at Balmoral at a quarter to three. It is a pretty little castle in the old Scottish style. There is a picturesque tower and garden in front, with a high wooded hill; at the back there is wood down to the Dee, and the hills rise all around. . . ." They took a meal at once, rushed out of doors and climbed Craig Gowan. The view "reminded us very much of Thuringerwald. It was so calm, and so solitary. . . . All seemed to breathe freedom and peace, and to make one forget the world and its sad turmoils."

Victoria's reference to a "picturesque tower" in this entry raises an interesting point. Both Ivor Brown in his book on Balmoral and the current Balmoral Estate Office guide to the castle policies, following the Reverend Dr John Stirton's history of Crathie, assume that the "pretty little castle" of 1848, was the second on the site, having been built in its entirety by John Smith ('Tudor Johnnie') of Aberdeen for Sir Robert Gordon in 1835, after the total demolition of the previous castle dating from 1550. I feel sure this is an error.

Both W. Wyld's painting of Old Balmoral and a photograph of it taken in 1855 by George Washington Wilson before its final demolition, show this "picturesque tower" to have been the original fortified tower-house of the link plan, with a round tower abutting on one angle of a large square keep of the sixteenth century. What John Smith did was to build a large addition to the old tower, an addition more or less in the Abbotsford manner which included another square tower and a turret.

Balmoral, originally part of the Earldom of Mar, first appears in written record as "Bouchmorale" in 1452. It recurs again in the Exchequer Rolls of Scotland for 1539 when Alexander and John Gordon are mentioned as "tenants of Balmurrell". An heiress Anne carried it into the Farquharson family on marrying Charles Farquharson, second son of William Farquharson of Inverey. Its long Jacobite associations begin when Charles Farquharson fought under 'Bonnie Dundee' in the battle of Killiecrankie, in which he was severely wounded. His nephew, known to history as 'Balmoral the Brave' fought on the Jacobite side in both the '15 and '45 Rebellions. He won his sobriquet at the battle of Falkirk on 17th January 1746. As he marched at the head of his men a bullet hit him in the shoulder and his henchmen cried "Four men to carry our wounded chief to the rear!"

"Never!" cried Balmoral. "Four men to carry your chief at the head of his children into the thickest of the fight!"

The estate was forfeited after the Rebellion and bought by the Earl of Fife, whose trustees leased the old castle and estate to

Sir Robert Gordon, a retired diplomat who was the brother of the Prime Minister Earl of Aberdeen.

Besides adding the modern extension to the old castle Sir Robert at the same time established the Balmoral deer forest. In the summer of 1847, while Victoria and Albert were suffering, along with Sir James Clark, the ceaseless torrents that pursued them in the West Highlands, Sir James's son, convalescing from an illness, was enjoying fine weather as Sir Robert's guest at Balmoral. There had been some discussion about this when the news came that Sir Robert had died suddenly at his breakfast table at Balmoral. Prince Albert then entered into negotiations with the Fife Trustees and took up the unexpired lease of the property.

The acquisition of a permanent royal home in the Highlands was not a matter to be embarked on lightly. In Chapter I, I mentioned how James Giles, the Aberdeen artist, helped to make up the Queen's mind. He drew sketches which were specially commissioned by Victoria and Albert to give them a clear idea of Balmoral and its neighbourhood. One of these showed a Sunday morning service in the parish kirk of Crathie, whose minister was the Reverend Archibald Anderson. It depicted the minister's collie dog Towser curled up on the pulpit steps while his master preached. The Queen and the Prince went to the kirk. But Towser had been left at home that day. On Monday morning her Majesty sent an equerry to the manse to inquire if anything had happened to the dog. If, as she hoped, he was alive and well, she would like to see him in his old place on the pulpit steps. And so Towser was restored to his position of privilege. He always behaved decorously in church—but if the sermon was a few minutes longer than usual he got up and stretched himself, yawning audibly.

A week after her first arrival at Balmoral, Victoria climbed Lochnagar by way of Ballochbuie Forest, going pony-back from the Old Bridge of Invercauld—the picturesque old military bridge that had been built by General Wade's successors in 1752. As they climbed the view grew finer and finer—"no road, but not bad ground, moss, heather and stones". Albert went off to shoot ptarmigan, and returned with a brace. And then, when they had nearly reached the top, the mist drifted over in thick clouds. After four hours Victoria dismounted and scrambled up the last steep stony place on foot. All ready for her there was a seat in a little nook and a picnic lunch. "But, alas!" she records "nothing whatever to be seen; and it was cold, wet and cheerless.... Coming down the wind blew a hurricane the mist being like rain, and everything quite dark with it. Bowman [Mr. Farquharson's keeper] and Macdonald, who preceded us, looked like ghosts. ... When we had gone on about an hour and a quarter or an hour and a half, the fog disappeared like magic, and all was sunshine below. Most provoking!—and yet one felt happy to see sunshine and daylight again. . . ."

Thus Victoria with prosaic simplicity. What would Byron have said in the same circumstances?

> Shades of the dead! have I not heard your voices
> Rise on the night-rolling breath of the gale?
> Surely the soul of the hero rejoices
> And rides on the wind o'er his own Highland vale.
> Round Lochnagar while the stormy mist gathers,
> Winter presides in his cold icy car;
> Clouds there encircle the forms of my fathers;
> They dwell in the tempests of dark Lochnagar.

Lochnagar, which the Queen was to have other opportunities of climbing and seeing at its best, means the 'loch of the goats' and takes its name from the small loch at the foot of the great eastern corrie with its mighty crescent of cliffs. Towering over the loch is the Black Spout which rises 1,200 feet, largely in sheer precipice, from the 2,575 feet level of the water. In 1924 the Cairngorm Club erected an indicator on the summit which shows all the prominent landmarks within view, from the Caithness hills in the north, Ben Nevis in the west and in the south Ben Lomond, the Pentlands and the last Cheviot in England 108 miles away. Usual modes of approach for the many who climb it are from Ballater via Glen Muick and from Braemar by Loch Callater. The mountain is of coarse red granite, which weathers into gigantic blocks of stone like masonry. In the early summer masses of creeping azalea tinge with pink great areas of the upper slopes.

The Queen's first Balmoral holiday lasted only three weeks, but in November 1848 negotiations began for the purchase or lease of the estates of Abergeldie and Birkhall and of Balmoral itself. Birkhall, the long narrow estate stretching along the left bank of the River Muick from the Bridge of Muick at Ballater to the lower slopes of Lochnagar, was bought in the name of the

Prince of Wales, the future Edward VII, then only 7. Abergeldie, occupying the whole area between Birkhall and Balmoral, was rented from its fifteenth laird, Michael Francis Gordon, and remained on lease to the royal family for a century. The royal domain, 12 miles long, on the south bank of the Dee, was not completed until thirty years later with the purchase in 1878 of Ballochbuie Forest, the largest indigenous pinewood in Scotland, which lies immediately to the west of the Balmoral estate. In addition large grouse moors in Glengairn, north of the Dee, are rented.

The deal with the Earl of Fife's trustees for the purchase of Balmoral proved to be rather complicated, and so it was not until June 1852 that Prince Albert purchased the land outright for £31,500. It was thus his personal estate and did not come under the elaborate administration of other royal residences. This meant a very great deal to the royal couple. They celebrated the event by the building of the Purchase Cairn on Craig Gowan on 11th October.

Although the Prince Consort, then 33, had only nine more years to live, he supervised in that time the complete transformation of the estate and the building of the present Balmoral Castle. In fact it could be said that the changes that have taken place since his death in 1861 are all comparatively minor. Even before the Purchase Cairn was built he had been in long and earnest consultation with William Smith, City Architect of Aberdeen, the son and successor of 'Tudor Johnnie'. It had become clear that Old Balmoral would have to be replaced by a larger structure capable of accommodating the royal household for the lengthy autumn stay which soon became the rule. The new castle was designed to house 130 people and was disposed around its central feature, a clock tower 25 feet square rising to 80 feet, and topped by a round turret with flagstaff bringing the total height to 100 feet.

The building has two main blocks: the royal and guest apartments with a stately south front, and the 'offices', both linked to the tower by small two-storey wings. The style is the nineteenth-century 'Scotch Baronial', garnished with round towers and small angle turrets—but a very restrained and simple example of the genre. Each of the two blocks has a central courtyard and the main entrance is a battlemented *porte-cochère* or carriage porch bearing the arms of Prince Albert in marble.

The south face of the tower bears a stone carving of the Royal Arms of Scotland while on the window gables between the tower and the entrance porch are six of the crests of Saxe-Coburg in gilt. The west front, overlooking the rose garden, has two bay windows. Beneath the smaller are the royal crests of Scotland and England, together with the crest of the Prince of Wales. Under the larger are a series of bas-reliefs by J. E. Thomas. These depict St George with his dragon, St Andrew, the patron saint of Scotland with his X-shaped cross, and, in a larger panel in the centre, St Hubert, the patron saint of all hunters.

Apart from Thomas's contribution, Balmoral was virtually a local creation. The finely dressed ashlar of which it is built is of light grey granite quarried at Invergelder on the Balmoral estate, while the roofing slates are from Foudland in central Aberdeenshire. The largest single room in the house is the ball-room (68 feet long by 25 feet) on a lower level than the rest of the building on the shelving river terrace to the north. Its exterior façade carries another bas relief by J. E. Thomas showing King Malcolm Canmore presiding over the eleventh-century 'Braemar Gathering', which he is said to have instituted. King Malcolm is also commemorated by an imposing life-size bronze statue by Theed in the flagged hall or vestibule of the castle entered from the *porte-cochère*. Prince Albert, it is clear, liked to think that the way of life he initiated at Balmoral had a precedent in venerable antiquity. Stags' heads and a boar's head from an animal shot by the Prince in Germany were ranged round the vestibule, which opens on to the main corridor of the house leading past the dining room to the drawing room suite with billiard room, drawing room and library.

In the early days lavish use was made of tartan for decoration, the Royal, Hunting and Dress Stuart tartans being used for hangings, upholstery and floor coverings, while wallpapers had a thistle theme with the Queen's monogram. Subsequent royal chatelaines have preferred pastel shades. Heating in Victoria's day was a sore point. She preferred very moderate heating, and disgruntled courtiers and ladies-in-waiting, for whom a spell at Balmoral was something like banishment, coined the unkind description of the castle as 'the house of a thousand draughts'. But all that is changed now.

The new Balmoral had been purposely built 100 yards north-west of the old castle so that it could continue to be used during the course of construction. Work began in 1853 and Victoria and Albert, with an old shoe thrown after them for luck, took up quarters in the new building in 1855. "This dear Paradise", as the Queen later called it, was finally complete in 1856 and the old castle was demolished, a memorial stone, still visible in the garden today being left to mark the spot. But Albert's work was not yet finished. He had begun improving the estate in 1849. Cottages were rebuilt. A great series of plantations was made and his last project, uncompleted at his death, was the model dairy, which functioned continuously for more than a century and only ceased to be used in 1965, when the Balmoral Ayrshire dairy herd was sold. This has been replaced by two beef herds, a fold of pedigree Highland cattle started by the present Queen in 1955, and a herd of Luing cattle formed in 1966.

The human impact of Victoria and Albert on their tenantry was immediate. As early as 1849 Charles Greville was writing: "He shoots every morning, returns to luncheon, and then they walk and drive. She is running in and out of the house all day long, and often goes out alone, walks into the cottages, sits down and chats with the old women." They literally ran about all over the place. They knew everyone, and adults and children alike had cause to realize it. In the days before properly fenced fields a certain Maggie was herding the cows on a Balmoral croft when she was joined by a girl friend, Mary, and Mary's little 5-year-old brother Kenneth. As the two girls wanted to gossip, Kenneth was told off to watch the cows. When the cows got into the corn in the next field Kenneth failed to raise the alarm, and when Victoria and Albert reached the scene the little boy was being furiously scolded by the girls.

"Maggie!" cried the Queen. Timidly Maggie approached the presence. "You should remember", said her Majesty gently, "that Kenneth is a little boy and does not know about keeping cows off the corn. It would be a better idea to put up a string so that they cannot get at it."

"Yes, Ma'am," said Maggie meekly. But the Prince Consort laughed heartily and pointed out that string would hardly be adequate for the purpose, and the royal couple departed chuckling over the joke.

Even more typical is the story of the royal concern for a family where the breadwinner was dying of a wasting disease. Prince Albert called daily with suggestions for dainties that might induce him to take a bite. Princess Alice, on the eve of her wedding brought a china tea service and, laying it on the table, said, "I hope you will take a cup of tea from these for my sake."

"But," said his widow afterwards, "he wasna even able to do that".

In the interim Prince Albert himself died suddenly of typhoid. Next May the Queen "with her broken heart" came to Balmoral. Her first call was at the widow's cottage. "And", said the widow, "we both cried. The Queen cried and I cried. I controlled myself as soon as I could and asked her pardon for crying. And 'Oh', she said, she was so thankful to cry with someone who knew exactly how she felt. And afterwards she said: 'You saw your husband's death coming, but I—I did not see mine. It was so sudden.' "

Before his death the Prince Consort had made important changes in the layout of Balmoral's approaches. Formerly there had been a South Deeside road extending the whole way from the Bridge of Muick at Ballater through the Balmoral estate to the Old Bridge of Invercauld near Braemar. To secure greater privacy he built an iron bridge at Balmoral, opposite the present Gate Lodge to the castle, in 1859, by which the South Deeside road, now terminating at this point, was carried to the north side of the river, joining up with the north road at Crathie Post Office. At the other end of the private domain thus created he built a new bridge at Invercauld a short distance west of the Old Bridge, which now became a private bridge within the royal domain. It remains, however, so close to the public road that its antique beauty can be fully enjoyed, and with its background of the glorious Ballochbuie pines it makes the most popular and widely publicized of Deeside beauty spots. Ballochbuie—'the bonniest plaid in Scotland'—takes its name from the Gaelic *bealach buidhe*, 'the yellow pass', and its 'bonniest plaid' sobriquet comes from a tradition that when it was sold by a MacGregor of Ballochbuie to a Farquharson of Invercauld the bargain was sealed by a tartan plaid.

Balmoral's privacy has also been secured by careful tree-planting. Trees thickly line the North Deeside road immediately opposite the castle, while the north and west fronts of the building are also screened by trees so that only the upper part of the clock tower with its flag-staff is visible at the nearest points to public roads. But there are two famous viewpoints at a greater distance. One is on A939, the hilly road from Crathie to Bridge of Bush,

Gairnshiel and Strathdon. Here, high above Crathie, the entire castle can be seen centring a vast panorama with Lochnagar in the background. The other view is from a sector of the North Deeside road near Inver where, looking back along the river, the west front of the castle displays itself.

The rule of privacy however is not rigidly maintained when the royal family are not in residence. Throughout the months of May, June and July the grounds of the castle are open to the public every week day for a small charge in aid of selected charities. Crathie Church, with all its treasures, is also open to visitors throughout the summer months. One sunny day just before the castle gardens closed for the season I paid them a visit. The two car parks were full. An unending stream of sightseers passed through the turnstile at Gate Lodge. Flock after flock of silent pilgrims trooped into the nave of Crathie Kirk and listened attentively while Mrs Douglas Fairweather briefly described the features of the sanctuary. Across the way on its adjoining height Crathie Post Office somehow managed to accommodate a non-stop queue for picture-postcards and ice-cream blocks. From the hillock on which the post office perches one had a perfect view of the whole animated scene. What struck me was that I had never seen so large a concourse of people behaving with such exemplary rectitude. They were not being herded or marshalled. The police were scarcely in evidence, but nobody jostled his neighbour, fooled around or tried to jump his turn. Although there must have been many hundreds of people there the hush of the countryside still enfolded them.

From Gate Lodge with its wrought-iron gates made by a local blacksmith in 1925 a carriageway of just under half a mile leads through fine old trees to the south front of the castle. It is not difficult in front of the *porte-cochère* to picture to oneself the many state occasions celebrated here from the arrival of the Czar of all the Russias to the less formal greetings that awaited the savants of the British Association or the Australian cricket team led by Don Bradman. Here Gladstone and Disraeli, and Prime Ministers and Ministers-in-Attendance down all the vicissitudes of British history since, have come to take up their quarters. And the grounds themselves are a history book of national and domestic events within the Royal Family, for at almost every turn there are memorials. Outstanding are the massive statues to Queen Victoria and to Prince Albert in the golf course east of the entrance drive, and the cairns on the hillsides and hilltops, of which the most prominent is the Prince Albert Cairn on Craig Low-rigan. Beyond the spacious lawn to the south are two features of special interest—Garden Cottage, where Queen Victoria loved to deal with her correspondence in pleasing seclusion; and the gardens devised by Queen Mary between 1923 and 1925, which have been extended in recent years to incorporate a large kitchen garden.

While at Balmoral it is inevitable that some reference must be made to John Brown, Queen Victoria's personal attendant, the butt of so much malicious gossip and angry resentment down the years. He too has his memorial in the grounds—a statue in the woods to the south of the old dairy. Brown was the son of a farmer who had also been a school teacher and who, when young John was 5, moved to Bush farm at Crathie. John had been singled out for advancement in the royal service by the Prince Consort, and in the years of her widowhood the Queen turned to this blunt, unflappable Highlander as her shield from a world from which she shrank. Beginning as a lad in the stables in the old Balmoral Castle in 1842, he became ghillie to Prince Albert in 1849, was promoted to leading the Queen's pony in 1852, and in 1865 was "upper servant and permanent personal attendant to the Queen".

Victoria was convinced that on more than one occasion his presence of mind in emergency had saved her life. There was the unlucky jaunt to Loch Muick in 1863 when the royal carriage overturned and John Brown jumped from the toppling vehicle and rescued the ladies when it crashed, and there was the incident in the grounds of Buckingham Palace in February 1871, when a half-mad Irishman called Arthur O'Connor put a pistol to the Queen's head in order to compel her to sign a document. Brown snatched the pistol and held down the man—thus vindicating his much envied role as the gallant watchdog. Then in 1882 he captured another assailant, the insane Roderick Maclean, at Windsor Station. When he died in 1883 the Queen contemplated writing his life story. Dissuaded from this by the Dean of Windsor, she commissioned the Poet Laureate to write the inscription for the Boehm memorial statue and he produced a verse beginning "Friend more than servant, Loyal truthful, brave. . . ."

Brown has been painted as an arrogant, alcoholic major-domo.

His bluntness was certainly unquestioned. But it is well to remember that his long service to the Queen must have involved him in personal sacrifice. He might well have preferred to marry and retire from his arduous duties. Instead he wore himself out in his Queen's service. For that, perhaps, his rough tongue and his moments of overbearing officiousness may be forgiven.

For Brown the Queen had built the cottage in the grounds called Baile na Coile, which is now the home of the resident factor. Karim Cottage, on the road leading to the stables to the east of the castle, was built for Victoria's Indian secretary, the Munshi Abdul Karim—another retainer who achieved intense unpopularity—during the last years of her reign.

Queen Victoria loved Balmoral so much that she came to spend a third of every year there—a month in May and three months in the autumn. She hated to leave the place before snow was on the ground in November. She began as a young woman by climbing Craig Gowan at least once a day. In her later years she went for a brisk carriage drive twice a day—morning and afternoon, with changes of horses awaiting her at the Invercauld Arms Inn at Ballater. For shorter outings in the grounds she used her rubber-wheeled garden chair.

The pursuit of seclusion was always a passion and to gratify it there arose the four mountain shiels which could also serve as hunting lodges or bothies. The nearest of these was Queen's Cottage in Glen Gelder, about 3 miles due south of the castle. Sometimes called Ruigh nan Bhan Righ, 'The Queen's Shiel', and looking directly over the Gelder where it brawls over a bed of boulders, this little house has remained popular as a royal picnic rendezvous right down to the present day—ever since Victoria entertained the exiled Empress Eugenie of France there to an afternoon tea "with some excellent brown trout cooked in oatmeal".

There are two shiels in Glenmuick, the oldest and the nearest of them Alltnaguibhsaich (Gaelic: 'burn of the firwood'), now a very substantial mansion where the late Princess Marina and her family spent many Deeside seasons. It lies beyond the picturesque Linn of Muick, a waterfall almost 40 feet high, and about a mile short of the lower end of Loch Muick itself, at the end of the road on the Balmoral side of the glen. Victoria and Albert knew it as 'The Hut' and used it frequently from 1849 onwards.

After the Prince Consort's death Victoria felt reluctant to

The summit of Lochnagar

return to Alltnaguibhsaich Lodge and built a new shiel higher up the Glen at Glass-allt on the pine-covered delta formed by that burn as it dashes down the hillside to join Loch Muick. She called it her 'Widow's House' and spent a first night there on 1st October, 1868.

The fourth royal shiel stands near the Falls of Garrawalt in the heart of Ballochbuie Forest, in a country which looks as if it had been the plaything of giants, so bestrewn is it by huge boulders. It is called the Danzig Shiel, from the old sawmill, operated by a Danziger, which once stood on the site. Lord Kitchener was entertained here to afternoon tea by Queen Mary.

Two more shiels, more recent than Queen Victoria's day, lie on the north side of the Dee in the countryside where most of the Balmoral grouse-shooting takes place. One is at Gairnshiel and became a favourite picnic haunt of the young family of King George VI—Her Majesty the Queen and Princess Margaret. Converted to its new use it was affectionately dubbed Teapot Cottage. Gairnshiel Lodge itself is also used as a hunting lodge while the old church of the glen, quite close to Teapot Cottage, is still in use. While staying at Ballater I have found it one of the pleasantest ways of spending Sunday afternoon to join the mini-bus starting from the Station Square, which conveys worshippers from the burgh to the tiny church in the glen, where they are joined by the families in the glen itself.

On the way one crosses the lovely old hump-backed Gairnshiel Bridge, sometimes erroneously called a Wade bridge but actually built a little after his day in 1751. The modern road A939 crosses it, following the route of the old military highway from Deeside to Strathdon.

More remote still is the royal shiel at Auchtavan, a favourite retreat of Queen Elizabeth the Queen Mother. Auchtavan is the last house in lonely Glen Feardar, the mountain stream which joins the Dee on its north bank a little below the inn at Inver, west of Crathie. It stands at an altitude of 1,500 feet above sea level and yields a fine view of Lochnagar.

It was not to be expected that Queen Victoria's successors would devote so much time to Balmoral as she did. But their loyalty to this delectable personal possession (for each succeeding Sovereign receives it as a private bequest) has been by any count remarkable. King Edward VII, it is true, never stayed longer than a month there and sometimes less, but King George V had a

Braemar village and the games arena on Gathering Day

greater affection for it and made a point of staying at Balmoral for eight weeks in the autumn. So did King George VI, and the present Queen and her family are usually in residence for two months. They glory in it as a base for the open-air life. Miss Mabel Anderson has summed it up in the words: "The whole family goes out in weather that most people would think mad." And she tells of royal days spent shooting on the hills followed by evenings fishing on the river.

This may be the place to explain the sporting aspect of the royal domain. It would be wrong to think that Royal Deeside's fame as a hunting, fishing and shooting playground dates from Queen Victoria's arrival on the scene in 1848. A few statistics may help to clear up misconceptions. Balmoral lies within the parish of Crathie and Braemar, by far the largest in Aberdeenshire. It extends to 286 square miles and includes several lochs. If the water area is deducted it has 182,219 acres of which 165,647 acres consist of well-stocked deer forests with a gross annual value of over £2,066. The rest of the land is made up of woodlands (11,500 acres), grouse moors, and arable land (2,400 acres).

This enormous wilderness, with a tiny fringe of farming country in the river valley, has been a hunting paradise from the earliest times. It is only the nature of the hunting that has changed. In the eleventh century Malcolm Canmore built a castle at Braemar as a hunting seat. He and his successors regarded the deer forests as royal hunting grounds specially and eternally reserved for their own enjoyment. The position had not very much altered by the early seventeenth century when the Earl of Mar, as the King's representative, enjoyed the prerogative of organizing deer hunts on a huge and spectacular scale. There are many references to such hunts, but the most vivid and detailed comes down to us in the book called *The Penniless Pilgrimage* by John Taylor, the Water Poet, dated 1618. He told how five hundred to six hundred men were dispatched "early in the morning" to scour an area "seven, eight or ten miles in circumference" to bring down herds of deer in enormous numbers to an appointed rendezvous where the "lords and gentlemen" awaited them. At one hunt he attended "in the space of two hours four score fat deer were slain".

Such massacres, which involved the use of deerhounds, appear to have continued into the eighteenth century, but after the Jacobite Rebellions attempts were made to introduce hill sheep which did not meet with much success. In 1778 Glen Lui in the upper valley was cleared of sheep and reverted to deer forest. It is claimed that the present era of Highland sport really dates from 1800, when Sir John Maxwell took a ten-year lease of Abergeldie. In 1826 the Forest of Mar was advertised as "the finest shooting district in Scotland" and Mar Lodge was let at £1,800 per annum.

In the early part of the century the great game drive, the *battue en masse* did continue. At Breadalbane in 1842, as Queen Victoria records in her journal, the Earl himself with 300 Highlanders went out beating for the royal guests. The organized hunt must have been a spectacular occasion, but the bag as the Queen records it was a modest affair of "nineteen roedeer, several hares and pheasants and three brace of grouse".

But very soon the real sportsman preferred the individual ardours of the deer-stalk to the mass slaughter of game. This demanded a far higher degree of skill and for the Prince Consort at Balmoral normally involved a walk with a gun or rifle and a couple of ghillies.

The Prince Consort's successors as lairds of Balmoral have all been good shots. Edward VII learned shooting as a boy and before he was 18 boasted of killing two stags to his father's one. George V had superb skill with a rifle and in grouse drives his inerrable aim was famous. Eric Linklater, who watched him in a day's shooting at Geallaig Hill, to the north of Balmoral, has testified that "every bird that fell to the King's gun was dead in the air before it dropped. When a large covey came, and another closely followed, there were two, three, four dead birds in the air before the first had fallen. ... It was the very summit of marksmanship".

Edward VIII was not so deeply interested in Balmoral, but George VI had inherited his father's passion for a day on the moors and in his later years, when leg trouble was a certain handicap, he took advantage of cross-country motoring to get to the less accessible grouse-butts. The Duke of Edinburgh continues the tradition of high skill on the moors.

Beginning with the 12th, grouse shooting and deer stalking continue throughout August and September. October brings partridge shooting and wild duck and hare hunts and November pheasant shooting.

While the period of royal residence at Balmoral brings a great influx of temporary staff to the castle and its domain the all-the-year-round population is surprisingly small. Census figures bring this out clearly. In June 1961 the population of the Balmoral Castle estate was 86. At Easter Balmoral, the small village on the verge of the castle grounds there were 27 more folk, at Crathie hamlet 39, at Inver 17 and on the Abergeldie Castle estate 18. The Communion roll of the parish church amounts to 238 and the children at Crathie School number 33.

Since the dawn of Christianity in the district there have been five Crathie Churches. A standing stone on the slope above the North Deeside road 3 miles east of Crathie hamlet marks the spot where a ninth-century saint, Manire, established the first one. He is believed to have died and been buried there in A.D. 824. Almost opposite Balmoral Castle a deep pool on the river Dee bears the name Pollmanire, the 'pool of Manire'.

The ruins of the next church, dating from the Middle Ages, stand in the old kirkyard of Crathie, close to the present manse of the parish, on the flat haughland north of the river about 2 miles farther west. At the end of the eighteenth century this fell into disrepair and a third church was built high up on the slope above the North Deeside road—on the same site where the present church now towers over the valley. Opened in 1804 this plain and unadorned building, whose only feature was a belfry in the south gable, was the one already mentioned where Queen Victoria worshipped from 1848 to 1893. She became extremely devoted to it, but the only drawback was that in the open gallery she was under every eye. Gapers at royal worshippers are no new thing.

> It's Crathie Kirk—the door's nae steeked,
> Gang in and when ye weel have keeked
> For the Queen's pew—gin ye shall look
> Ye'll see her cushion and her Book.

While the present church was being built between April 1893 and June 1895 a temporary wooden church served the congregation, who had worshipped for two Sundays in the iron ballroom at Balmoral Castle until this was ready. Designed by A. Marshall Mackenzie, the architect of Marischal College, the Crathie Church of today, with its massive square tower, is of light grey granite from Inver and is cruciform in plan with a semi-circular apse.

Worshippers enter by the open porch in the west gable while there is a private entrance known as the Queen's Porch giving access to the south transept, reserved for the Sovereign and the members of the Royal Family. The north transept is occupied by the heritors of the church, the lairds of Invercauld and Abergeldie. Many gifts by members of the Royal family enrich the interior. The hexagonal pulpit incorporates fifteen varieties of Scottish granite and a collection of pebbles gathered by Princess Louise on the isle of Iona. The communion table, of variegated Iona marble backed by a richly carved oak screen, forms a memorial to Edward VII. The font of Rubislaw granite was the gift of the Duke and Duchess of Connaught. The stained glass is also fine. The great rose window in the west gable commemorates the Reverend John McInnes, minister of Crathie from 1715–48. He was one of the many who pleaded for the life of the Baron Ban (mentioned in the last chapter), and his errand of mercy on that occasion in 1746 involved a horseback journey to London.

The quality of the choir and the music at Crathie Church have long been famous. This stems in fact from a very old local tradition, for the parish in the eighteenth century was a nest of superlative fiddlers and pipers. Family tradition in the parish is also very strong. The Session Clerk of the Church is the village postmaster, Mr Albert Thomson, whose family have been the postmasters of Crathie for 128 years. On Sundays during the royal stay at Balmoral hundreds and sometimes thousands of sightseers line the short route from the castle to the kirk. This phenomenon has come to be accepted as inevitable and car parks are provided for the touring coaches and cars that bring the spectators.

Some of the limelight directed at the Royal Family inevitably falls on the Queen's neighbours. It surprises some folk to learn that almost within sight of Balmoral there is a thriving distillery. On the Abergeldie estate, within a mile of the castle, is the Royal Lochnagar Distillery, which dates from 1825, when it was built by John Robertson of Crathie, an old smuggler, who decided that it would be a good idea to go 'legitimate'. The distillery was acquired by John Begg in 1845, and three days after their arrival at Balmoral in 1848 Queen Victoria and Prince Albert paid it a visit. Permission was given for the use of the prefix 'Royal' to the whisky made at Lochnagar and the product was supplied to the castle. It is I am told a wonderful whisky with a subtle flavour of sherry from the cask in which it has been matured. At one time it was the most expensive whisky in Scotland. The firm of John

Begg became a subsidiary of the Distillers Company Limited in 1916.

On a lovely site at the foot of the slope on which the distillery stands, on the south bank of the river 2 miles below Balmoral and 6½ miles west of Ballater, within a few yards of the Dee, is Abergeldie Castle. A beautiful grove of birches—that tree which is more characteristic of the Dee valley than any other—inspired the old air "The Birks of Abergeldie" of which Burns made use for his more famous "Birks of Aberfeldy"—but having seen them both I should say that as trees the Abergeldie birches are superior!

The castle dates from around 1550. Built on the 'link' plan, an intermediate stage between the medieval keep and the L-plan Renaissance tower house, it consists of a rectangular main building four storeys high and double the width of the single keep, with crow-stepped gables and a round stair tower in the south-west angle, to which at a much later date a clock and a cupola were added. There is also an elaborately corbelled turret on the north-east angle of the building.

The same family of Gordons have owned Abergeldie since 1481. The laird who built the castle, Alexander, the fourth of his line, became known to history as 'Black Alister'. Although he took part in the movement to expel the French from Scotland in 1560, he followed the Earl of Huntly to Corrichie in 1562 and was imprisoned at St. Andrews for his part in that fray. On being pardoned by Mary Queen of Scots he became one of her loyalest supporters, but nothing he could do could save that ill-fated queen. For the remainder of his life 'Black Alister' was deeply involved in the desperate feud between the Gordons and the Forbeses. In 1592 his stout castle resisted the invasion of Deeside by the Mackintoshes and other clans from the west known as the Great Spulzie, but the invaders passed on down the valley and killed his kinsman Henry Gordon of Knock and the lairds of Braickley and Toldhu. They conspicuously exempted from this fate the Forbes laird of Strathgirnock, lying between Abergeldie and Glenmuick.

This laird, Arthur Forbes, known as 'Black Airter', now became the sinister opposing figure whose conflict with 'Black Alister' was to have frightful consequences, particularly for the Gordons of Knock, whose ruined keep still stands on the hill to the west of Ballater golf course. In 'Black Airter's' absence his house at

Strathgirnock was burned by avenging Gordons, but peace was temporarily patched up and he returned. The next source of bloodshed was an ill-fated love affair. Francis Gordon of Knock fell in love with 'Black Airter's' daughter and made the mistake of visiting his prospective father-in-law to ask for a 'thigging' or betrothal gift. Forbes took this as an insult and struck him a blow with his sword—still as he thought sheathed in its scabbard—but the scabbard flew off, and off came the young man's head.

'Black Airter' now went into hiding, and the young man's father, the laird of Knock, took possession of Strathgirnock and dispossessed 'Airter's' tenants. 'Airter' then returned and, with a group of followers, surprised the seven sons of Gordon of Knock cutting peats on his former lands. He slew them all, and sticking their spades into the ground impaled each of their heads on the implements. A servant from Knock arrived on the scene bearing a meal for the peat-cutters, and, taking in the frightful scene of carnage at a glance, hastened back to the castle. He blurted out the news to the laird as he stood at the head of his staircase, upon which the old man, overcome by the shock, fell over the bannisters to his own death.

The seventh Gordon laird, another Alexander, was a prominent Royalist in the Civil War, and when Deeside fell to the tender mercies of the Covenanters the castle was ordered to be razed to the ground. But fortunately the sentence was never carried out. It was again in the battlefront in the campaign of John Graham of Claverhouse ('Bonnie Dundee') following the 'Glorious Revolution', when it became a pawn in the struggles between the Jacobites and the Government forces under General Mackay. Claverhouse himself used it as a temporary base while raising the Highland clans, but in due course it was taken and garrisoned by General Mackay's forces in 1689. A small garrison of seventy men were left in charge, but no sooner had the main body of the Government army turned their backs on it than the Jacobites under the 'Black Colonel', John Farquharson of Inverey, swept down valley and cut it off from supplies. This time General Mackay meant to stand no nonsense. After relieving his be-leaguered garrison in August 1690 and beating off the 'Black Colonel' in a sharp engagement in which he himself strangely escaped while under the very horses' feet, the whole country for miles around was effectively scorched. Reporting to the Government on his activities Mackay said the castle would have been lost within three days had it not been "timely succoured". He added that "to terrify others from the like attempts I burned twelve miles of a very fertile Highland country and at least twelve or fourteen hundred houses. I left order to permit none to rebuild but by delivering up their arms and swearing allegiance to their Majesties William and Mary."

After the castle was rented to Queen Victoria it became the home of her mother the Duchess of Kent, who lived there for many years. Another royal resident for a time was the Empress Eugenie, widow of Napoleon III. But eventually it became the Deeside home of the Prince of Wales, the future King Edward VII and his children, and in more recent times has served to accommodate various guests of the Royal Family while at Balmoral. It makes a fine setting for social or ceremonial occasions and garden parties, fetes and official receptions have been held on its lawns. Now, however, the present laird of Abergeldie, Mr John Howard Seaton Gordon, has resumed personal occupancy of the castle.

The pretty suspension footbridge which links the castle with the north bank of the Dee was built in 1885. Before that, on the same site, there was a rope and cradle bridge which was one of the sights of Deeside. A sort of primitive cableway, it consisted of a rope suspended from posts on either side of the river from which the cradle or basket containing the passenger hung. On getting into the cradle the passenger was carried half way across without any effort on his part, after which he levered himself up on to the far bank by pulling on the rope with his hands.

There were of course several accidents. An exciseman named Bruce, anxious to get to the other side in pursuit of whisky smugglers, lost his life by the breaking of the rope when the river was in flood. Two other victims were Peter Frankie, the game-keeper at Altnaguibhsaich and his bride Barbara Brown, drowned on their wedding day—it was thought through the malice of a disappointed suitor of Barbara, who was a very popular and beautiful girl.

Near Abergeldie, on the north side of the Dee, are slopes which in recent years became available as a nursery run for novice skiers and drew large numbers of winter sports enthusiasts, though the increasing developments at Cairnwell at the Devil's Elbow have tended to concentrate ski-ing activity there. Below Abergeldie the changing panorama of wood and hill is at its loveliest. On the North Deeside road, commanding a magnificent sweep of the river is the old coaching inn of Coilacreich, still a popular rendezvous, while on the South Deeside road is the little community of Girnock with a population of twenty-four, the remnants of a much greater scattering of crofting folk. The tenacity with which the old community clung to its identity is exemplified in the story of the miller of Girnock whose two young children attended the local school. When it was threatened with closure he engaged a workman with twelve of a family— and the closure was postponed.

Below Girnock, where the strath of the Girnock is guarded by the wooded hills of Craig Phiobaid and Craig Ghiubhais, the longest of the many fairy-like suspension footbridges on the river spans the Dee at Polhollick, site of an ancient ferry, and half a mile lower down we reach Bridge of Gairn with its handsome single arch over Dee's second longest tributary. The ruins of the old kirk of Glengairn lie just below the bridge. Gairn is approximately 20 miles long. The last 5 miles of its course from Gairnshiel to the Dee are comparatively well-known, but only once (in 1933) have I penetrated to its remote and rugged upper reaches. On that memorable occasion the Deeside Field Club, who since 1920 have helped many hundreds of enthusiasts to explore the riches of the valley, marshalled a fleet of sturdy taxis at Ballater and conveyed a company of over one hundred to lonely Loch Builg, over 13 miles upstream at the summit of the watershed between the Don and Dee basins. Here they were given a real Highland greeting by the laird of Auchernach in Strathdon, who brought along his piper to serenade the 'explorers'. The last house in the Glen is Loch Builg Cottage, a shooters' bothy.

It is at Bridge of Gairn that the Pass of Ballater road emerges from its rocky defile on the north side of Craigendarroch to rejoin the North Deeside road, and a little to the north are the ruins of Abergairn Castle, a link-plan stronghold on the same pattern as Abergeldie. The pass itself was the scene of the Battle of Tullich on 10th February 1654. This was a clash between Cromwellian forces under Colonel Thomas Morgan from Aberdeen and a body of Royalists under Lords Glencairn and Kenmuir. The Roundheads won the day by occupying the northern slopes of Craigendarroch and compelling the Highlanders to withdraw to the open ground west of the pass.

A road on the east bank of the Gairn leads to Morven Lodge on the western slopes of Byron's "Morven of Snows". The mountain is geologically interesting in that, like the Coyles of Muick to the south of it, it is part of a vein of serpentine rock intruding in a granite region and this tends to give it a grassy rather than a heather surface.

The shapely Coyles dominate the lower part of Glenmuick, where the estates of Glenmuick and Birkhall face each other across the winding stream in a delectable vale. Birkhall House on a wooded terrace above the left bank about 3 miles from Ballater has been considerably extended since it was built in 1715.

But the original house, a charming 'ha' hoose' of the period is still entire and its doorway bears the inscription "*17. C.G. R. G. 15*", the initials of its first Gordon laird and his wife. The second Gordon laird, Joseph and his wife were strongly Jacobite in sympathies, and in 1746 Birkhall sheltered two famous Jacobite refugees, the Oliphants of Gask, who concealed their identity by adopting the name Brown. They left items of their personal property in the care of their kindly hostess, Mrs Gordon of Birkhall, and eventually escaped to Sweden. From Gothenburg they communicated the news of their safe arrival, and Mrs Gordon was able to pass on the tidings to their relatives along with the heartful wish, "I trust in Almighty God you'll have the pleasure of seeing them in triumph soon."

In 1885 the future King Edward VII, who had owned Birkhall since his early boyhood, sold it back to Queen Victoria. He had only lived there in one year—1862—but it had been used down the years by many guests of the Queen, including Sir James Clark and Florence Nightingale. It was here in October 1856 that the redoubtable Florence persuaded the Secretary of State for War, Lord Panmure, to set up the Royal Army Medical Corps. Birkhall was the Deeside home in turn of the Prince of Wales (later Edward VIII), the Duke of York (later George VI) and in recent years of Queen Elizabeth the Queen Mother. Her Majesty the Queen, who had spent many happy days of childhood there with Princess Margaret, took the Duke of Edinburgh there to spend part of their honeymoon.

It is the right bank of the Muick, from Ballater to the Loch, where the Capel Mounth pass begins on its mountainous way southward into Angus, that is most familiar to members of the public. It is a lovely road, flooded with light from the south and west, which leads from quiet semi-arable country into an austere treeless amphitheatre in the hills centred by the loch's snow-fed waters. High up on the hill, thickly wooded, opposite Birkhall is Glenmuick House where the laird of Glenmuick estate, Sir Ian Walker-Okeover makes his home.

Nearer Ballater, on the same great wooded ridge of hill, is Braickley, scene of perhaps the most famous of all the Deeside ballads which begins:

> Inverey came down Deeside, whistlin' and playin',
> He was at braw Braickley's gates, ere it was dawin'.
>
> He rappit fu' loudlie, and wi' a great roar,
> Cried "Come down now, Braickley, and open the door!"

As can be imagined it was on no peaceful mission that John Farquharson, the 'Black Colonel' of Inverey, called at Braickley so early in the morning. According to the most familiar version of the ballad, John Gordon of Braickley, realizing that he, and his few retainers, would be vastly outnumbered, was unwilling to accept the challenge but was goaded into action by the taunts of his wife, who, after he had been murdered, entertained the assassins to the great scandal of the neighbourhood, so that

> Frae the head o' the Dee to the banks o' the Spey
> The Gordons may mourn him and ban Inverey.

Close to the public road in Glenmuick near Braickley are the ruins of St Nathalan's Chapel built by the Mackenzies of Glenmuick. Nearer still to Ballater on the west side of the Bridge of Muick is Glenmuick Kirkyard, notable for a rough gravestone which appears to indicate that one John Mitchell lived from 1596 to 1722, making him 126 years old. Here too, at Bridgend of Muick, where the Glenmuick road joins A973, is a memorial seat with a plaque commemorating one of the last public acts by Queen Victoria—her inspection of the Gordon Highlanders in 1899 before their departure to the South African War.

The largest of all the properties neighbouring Balmoral is the estate of Invercauld, which extends all the way from the Gairn's right bank at Bridge of Gairn to the west of Braemar and strikes deeply south up the valley of the Clunie to the west of Ballochbuie Forest. It will be best to deal with it in the next chapter.

VI

THE ROYAL DEE: THE UPPER REACHES

The standard on the Braes o' Mar
Is up and streaming rarely;
The gathering pipe on Lochnagar
Is sounding lang an' sairly,
The Highland men
Frae hill and glen,
In martial hue
Wi' bonnets blue,
Wi' belted plaids,
An' burnished blades,
Are coming late and early.

BETWEEN the North Deeside road and the Dee, halfway from Balmoral to the hamlet of Inver, is a loosely-built cairn within a circle of larch trees. This is the Carn na Cuimhne—'cairn of remembrance'—the rallying point of the Clan Farquharson. As each clansman answered the summons of his chief to warlike service he brought a stone which he laid down close to this cairn. On his return after the campaign he removed a stone from the heap. The stones then left answered to the number of the slain and were added to the cairn.

At the hamlet of Inver the inn is a handsome structure in the neo-Tudor style introduced into Deeside around 1830 from designs produced by the London architect Peter Frederick Roberts. Above Inver the valley narrows with steep wooded slopes on either side and the river foams on a rocky bed. To the north in the vale of the Feardar Burn lies the once-populous Aberarder. In 1834 the school here had ninety-eight pupils. When it was closed a century later there were only two. Three miles farther west, still in the narrow tree-girt valley, the Dee is spanned by the Danzig Shiel suspension bridge leading to the private road to the Falls of Garawalt. Another mile brings us to the narrowest part of the defile and the two bridges of Invercauld—the 1752 bridge closed by the Prince Consort, and, 150 yards above it, the handsome granite bridge he built to replace it. Beneath it the Dee tumbles in miniature rapids over a channel of slaty rock.

From this point, where the main avenue to the Castle of Invercauld leaves the highway, there is a dramatic change in the landscape.

If you have a camera this is where you uncase it, for after putting on record the grand old Invercauld Bridge with its buttresses and gently rising camber, you may be lucky enough to encounter the Invercauld Highland cattle grazing on the sweet haughland that now opens out to the north of the river. You will get a view also of Invercauld House itself on its grassy platform above this pine-studded meadowland. It is really a castle, with imposing central keep from which wings project on three sides. A much altered building, it incorporates parts of the Farquharson stronghold dating back to the sixteenth century, although the house began to take its present shape in the seventeenth century, and paintings survive which show it to have been a typical mansion of that period. From a pediment of one of the dormer windows came the coat of arms of Alexander Farquharson, seventh laird, bearing the initials A. F. and the date 1674, which is now displayed over the present main doorway.

Many families and many clans made history on Upper Deeside, but the Farquharsons have long been the predominant breed. Gone are their ancient overlords the Earls of Mar; gone are the Mackenzies of Dalmore; gone from this valley—though they still flourish on the Don—are the Forbeses. Only the Farquharsons and the Gordons remain of the historic stock. And yet in the beginning the Farquharsons were incomers, descended from the Thanes of Fife through the Shaws of Rothiemurchus on the Spey. A younger son of this family, which is a branch of the Clan Chattan, settled in the Braes of Mar in the fourteenth century. His name was Farquhar and his offspring became known as Farquharsons. One Donald Farquharson wed the heiress of Duncan Stewart of Mar and through this marriage obtained the lands of Invercauld. Their son Findla Mor (Big Findlay) is reckoned the founder of the clan and first Farquharson of Invercauld. His descendant, the sixteenth laird and chief of the clan, Captain Alwyne Arthur Compton Farquharson, holds Invercauld today.

Collateral branches of the family, also descended from Findla

Mor, were the Farquharsons of Inverey, of Monaltrie, of White-house and of Finzean. The Inverey and the Monaltrie lines were strongly Jacobite. As we shall see the Invercauld line held aloof from the Old Cause, save in 1715 when their hands were reluctantly forced, and this perhaps helps to explain their superior staying power.

This staying power has been extremely valuable to Deeside, providing an element of stability in a scene of inexorable change. The present laird is a keen farmer and forester and his imprint is seen in improvements over his vast domain. He and his wife, née Frances Strickland Lovell Oldham of Seattle, Washington, U.S.A., have taken a lead in introducing helpful innovations, both in the management of their sporting estates and in stimulating the tourist industry which is such a vital prop to the economy of the Braes o' Mar.

At Invercauld Castle there are many fascinating heirlooms. These include a richly-carved trinket-box given to Beatrix Garden, the second wife of Findla Mor, by Mary Queen of Scots. The box bears a carving of the crowned double-headed eagle of the Holy Roman Empire, which suggests that it may have been a gift to Queen Mary from a prince of the Holy Roman Empire. Beatrix, called the 'Queen of Song' by Mary Stuart because of her fine voice, also received from that unlucky sovereign a harp with a miniature painting of the Queen on its bow, along with the Royal Arms in gold, and this treasure is now in the Scottish National Museum of Antiquities.

For the next 2 miles the Deeside road, now on the south side of the river, hugs the verge of steep wooded slopes which reach a climax of picturesqueness with the Lion's Face, a cliff on the east side of Craig Choinnich (1764 feet), a hill overlooking Braemar village on the south-east. Just before the road swings southward to enter the village it passes on the right the approach to Braemar Castle on its knoll above the river.

Open to visitors daily in the summer, the appearance of the castle today, with its pepper-pot turrets, is rather different from the original five-storeyed tower house of the L-plan built by John Erskine, seventh earl of Mar of his line, in 1628.

The basic plan, however, is quite unaltered. The castle has a large round stair tower in the re-entrant angle of the L, and the gables of the main house and the wing have each a pair of turrets at their angles—now three storeys high with open battlements, but initially of the usual Scottish type one storey high with pointed roofs. Ostensibly the castle was built by the Earl as a hunting seat for his family—but the fact that it is a strong and massive house-of-fence makes us suspect that he had in mind a counter to the growing power of his feudal vassals, the Farquharsons, in the immediate vicinity.

The test came in 1689 when the Scottish Convention of Estates, about to welcome William of Orange, found itself defied by John Graham of Claverhouse:

> To the Lords of Convention 'twas Claver'se who spoke:
> "Ere the King's crown shall fall there are crowns to be broke;
> So let each cavalier who loves honour and me,
> Come follow the bonnet o' Bonnie Dundee."

The Convention outlawed him and he rode west to raise the clans.

> There are hills beyond Pentlands, and lands beyond Forth;
> If there's Lords in the Lowlands, there's Chiefs in the North;
> There are wild Duniewassals three thousand times three
> Will cry "Heich! for the bonnets o' Bonnie Dundee".

There were certainly wild Duniewassals in the Braes o' Mar and they were led by John Farquharson of Inverey, who might have been kept in check had the government's first instructions, in the panic of Viscount Dundee's rebellion, been carried out. They had ordered the Earl of Mar, who was loyal to them, to occupy Braemar Castle and the surrounding country with a party of 400. But before the order could be carried out the Earl was dead and the whole of the territory was over-run by the Farquharsons and their allies.

The young Master of Forbes from Donside was now ordered to take possession of Braemar Castle with a force of 150 horse and foot, and push on up the valley to Inverey to capture the 'Black Colonel'. In doing so he paused too long at Braemar, and by the time he reached Inverey the bird had flown, though a glimpse was caught of the fleeing clansmen disappearing in a wood. The 'Black Colonel' now watched while the dragoons retreated to Braemar Castle and, setting their horses loose to graze in the vicinity, "very securely laid themselves down to sleep about the house".

This was his chance. With a handful of men he stole up the vale of the Clunie, climbed Craig Choinnich from the far side, and, looking down from its slopes on Braemar Castle, opened musket fire on the sleeping garrison. The result was pandemonium. The horses, terrified by the musket fire, scattered in all directions, and the men of the garrison, after spending anxious hours recapturing and calming the maddened animals, "forsook the house and galloped all their best down the country". As soon as they had gone Farquharson and his men nipped in and burned down the castle.

So complete was the destruction that the castle was not rebuilt for over fifty years. While it remained a burnt-out shell the Earldom of Mar itself went down in ruin. John Erskine, the eleventh Earl, was nicknamed 'Bobbin' John' because of his proclivity for changing sides. In Queen Anne's reign he was Secretary of State for Scotland, and, despite his Jacobite sympathies, when George I came to the throne, he lost no time in offering his services. But George did not trust him, and in September 1714 he was dismissed from office. Almost a year later, on 6th September 1715, he raised the standard of James VIII, the Old Pretender in the Castleton of Braemar—on a spot now marked by two memorials: a plaque on the wall of the Invercauld Arms Hotel, and a stone across the road erected by the Deeside Field Club in 1953.

The Rebellion of Mar's Year, the 1715, was by far the most serious attempt to restore the Stuarts. 'Bobbin' John' succeeded in raising an army of 5,000, but he did not know how to lead it. He hopelessly bungled the Battle of Sheriffmuir and from then his cause was doomed. Yet Deeside today prefers to remember the gallantry of the men who fought under him and the stirring events which preceded the Raising of the Standard. These included the famous hunting party, climaxed by the Jacobite toasts drunk in the "ankers of potent Aquavitae" which had been poured into the Earl of Mar's Punchbowl, a circular rock formation on the left bank of the Quoich Water, a Dee tributary above Braemar. As the standard itself was raised the gold finial surmounting the flagstaff toppled and fell to the ground—presage of disaster.

John Farquharson of Invercauld, unwillingly involved in the debacle, since he was "bounden to attend the Earl" by feudal law, was captured, imprisoned, eventually pardoned and allowed to return home. This had an important bearing on the fate of Braemar Castle. The Mar estates were forfeited on the attainder

The summit plateau of Braeriach

The Pools of Dee

of the Earl and were afterwards purchased, along with Braemar Castle, by the Lords of Dun and Grange. In 1730 they sold the castle to the Farquharsons of Invercauld who have owned it ever since. After the 1745 Rebellion the Farquharsons leased it, still in its desolate burnt-out state, along with 14 acres of ground, to the British War Office as a barracks for troops to keep watch on the still-turbulent Highlands. The roofless turrets were rebuilt, the gables were restored and around the castle the army engineers built a rectangular curtain wall, with a salient symmetrically projecting from each face to form an eight-pointed star, all the flanks of which were pierced for musketry. These remarkable ramparts, which have their counterparts at Corgarff, where the Government took over an even older castle to serve the same purpose for the upper reaches of the Don valley, are among the last things of the kind in Britain and were based on the fortification ideas of the French military engineer, Vauban.

By 1753 the castle was ready for its new role and it remained garrisoned throughout the remainder of the eighteenth century. In the nineteenth century Jacobitism was completely dead, but whisky smuggling was still rife, and between 1827 and 1831 a detachment of the 74th Foot was stationed in the castle to watch over the illicit traffic in the glens. When Braemar Castle reverted to civilian use the turrets and the stair tower were heightened by an additional storey and finished with their present 'gingerbread' battlements.

A fine old iron yett, a pit or dungeon, a wheel stair, interesting old religious paintings in the dining room, and scratched inscriptions on window casements of the drawing room, made by bored English soldiery far from home, are among the attractions of the castle today. There is also a small museum.

Between the castle and the village is the old burial ground of Braemar. Here the most remarkable object is the tombstone of Peter Grant, known as 'Auld Dubrach'—the last of the Jacobites, who died at the ripe old age of 110. Peter was born on the small holding of Dubrach, a little above the Linn of Dee in 1714. He was working as a tailor when the 1745 Rebellion induced him to fight for Bonnie Prince Charlie.

He was promoted sergeant for gallantry in the Battle of Prestonpans, and fought at Culloden as a sergeant-major. Taken prisoner there, he was incarcerated in Carlisle Castle to await trial, but scaled the walls by dead of night, escaped detection and

The Mill of Benholm, last of the water-powered meal mills in Kincardine

Dunnottar Castle

walked all the way back to Braemar. Back at his trade as a tailor he made in 1746 a christening cap for Mary Cumming, the baby daughter of his neighbour. When little Mary grew up he married her. When his father died he took over Dubrach croft and farmed it for twenty years. He then retired and went to live with a son at Letham in Angus. Here the parish minister, whose wife was the daughter of 'Auld Dubrach's' commanding officer in the '45, got up a petition to King George IV, who graciously granted the veteran warrior a pension of a guinea a week. On the strength of this pension 'Auld Dubrach' returned to Braemar, where he died at Auchendryne on 11th February 1824.

No inhabited place in Aberdeenshire is so completely Highland in character as Braemar. It stands at 1,100 feet above sea level and it is difficult to believe that it belongs to the same county that includes the treeless, windswept plain of Buchan. The landscape that we see there today differs much from the primeval wilderness that must have sustained its first inhabitants—particularly in its cultivated fields and magnificent plantations of trees—but even they must have looked on the same soaring profile of guardian hills and on the boulder-strewn, rocky gorge of the Water of Clunie as it gleams and tumbles on its final close reach before emerging into the flat alluvial fan by which it enters the Dee on the scanty haughland in the midst of the mountain ridges which hem it in on every side.

It was from the beginning a place to pause and recruit the larder with handy game, and as such it was patronized by the early kings northward bound via the Cairnwell and Tolmounth passes. There is nothing improbable in the story that King Kenneth II (971–95) had a hunting seat here and started up the first and original 'Braemar Gathering', giving his name to Craig Choinnich; or that Malcolm Canmore (1057–1093) built the first Castle of Kindrochit, though if he did it was probably of earthwork and timber. The oldest buildings that *do* survive are the ruins of the castle at Kindrochit excavated by Dr W. Douglas Simpson in 1925.

As one stands on the bridge over the Clunie which is the central feature of the village, linking its two halves—Castleton on the east and Auchendryne on the west—and faces upstream, one may look down on the grass-covered fragmentary remains of these castles, for there were in fact two of them, both situated on an island site on the east bank of the stream.

The Kindrochit castles were ruinous even in 1618 when John Taylor, the Cockney 'Water Poet', visited Braemar and sang the praises of the Earl of Mar's hunting parties:

> If sport like this can on the Mountains be,
>   Where Phoebus' flames can never melt the snow,
> Then let who list delight in vales below
>   Skie-kissing mountains' pleasures are for me.

If one walks across the road to the other side of the Clunie Bridge and looks downstream one sees the Old Mill on the Clunie. Its great water wheel has gone and it has been converted into a charming holiday cottage by the waterside. This is only one of the initiatives taken by the Farquharsons of Invercauld to add to Braemar's tourist attractions. At the end of the eighteenth century more than half of the inhabitants of Braemar, then a straggling village of thatched hovels, were Roman Catholics living in Auchendryne. The Protestants lived in Castleton, and virtually all, Protestant and Catholic alike, were Gaelic-speakers. Around 1850 the village was rebuilt with handsome houses of stone, in one of which, The Cottage in Castleton Terrace, Robert Louis Stevenson wrote the greater part of *Treasure Island* in the autumn of 1881.

Today with its two large hotels and a great number of boarding houses the village has a winter population of around four hundred. In summer and autumn however seven hundred more people are sleeping here overnight and during the day there are frequently between 4,000 and 5,000 in Braemar at one time. On the day of the Braemar Gathering that total shoots up to 20,000. The number of Catholics in the village has gradually diminished and it is long since the last of the Gaelic-speakers died out.

Just as in the case of Ballater the changing pattern of tourism posed a problem. Seeing that scenery and a glorious past were not in themselves enough Mrs Farquharson of Invercauld founded in 1952 the Braemar Festival.

Extending through July, August and September this provides a sequence of entertainments: drama, music, ballet, talks, film shows and recitals, backed by a permanent exhibition of Scottish crafts and modern Scottish paintings. A former United Presbyterian church on the east bank of the Clunie was acquired by Captain and Mrs Farquharson in 1949 and converted into a festival theatre. Its walls were covered with murals in the Italian primitive style by James Speirs depicting historic incidents—among them Findla Mor bearing the Royal Standard at the battle of Pinkie in 1547, Robert II at Braemar bestowing a pension on Archdeacon John Barbour for his patriotic poem "The Brus", and the Raising of the Jacobite Standard at Braemar in 1715. The former Castleton public hall was acquired and became the Invercauld Galleries, where craftwork and paintings are displayed in a sequence of halls. Mrs Farquharson has also opened a boutique in the village devoted to Scottish fabrics. Craftsmen in wood-carving and deer-horn have also been encouraged to set up work-shops and studios.

From Castleton of Braemar the A93 road strikes southward up the glen of the Clunie to cross over the Cairnwell pass by the corkscrew ascent (now being straightened out), known as the Devil's Elbow, by which it enters Glenshee in Perthshire, passing on the way the chairlifts that are the mecca of East of Scotland skiers. This gives Braemar its most important link with the south, since by this route it is only 34 miles north of Blairgowrie and thus easily accessible to travellers from Perth and Dundee. On the first Saturday of September this mountain highway is dense with traffic. Police with their walkie-talkie radio equipment are stationed near the Fraser Brig, the picturesque two-arched military bridge by which the Clunie was spanned 4 miles above Braemar in 1750, and they control the ceaseless flood of cars and coaches bound for the Braemar Gathering. A second approaching stream is controlled 4 miles east of the village on the road from Aberdeen at Invercauld. The Gathering—a Highland athletic meeting of 59 contests is the grand climax of the Games season in Scotland.

But the present series of gatherings had a very humble begin-ning in 1817 when it started as an annual 'walk' by the members of the Braemar Wrights' Friendly Society. This society had been launched by a few enterprising carpenters and joiners with the object of supporting widows, children and members in distress.

The charitable function of the society remains, but in 1826 the members voted to rename themselves the Braemar Highland Society and in 1832 held their first athletic gathering for prize-money of £5, the events being putting the stone, throwing the hammer, tossing the caber and running—the well-known hill race to the top of Craig Choinnich. The wearing of Highland dress (which had of course been banned by the Act of Proscription of 1747 that had remained the law of the land until 1782) had become all the rage when George IV donned the tartan at Edinburgh in 1822. The Braemar Wrights began wearing it in 1823 and in 1832 the Duke of Leeds, who had taken a nineteen years' lease of Mar Forest, presented every retainer in his service with a full outfit. This example was followed by the Farquharsons and, in 1849, by Queen Victoria, who gave each member on the Balmoral estate a dress of Royal Stuart tartan.

The society became, quite spontaneously, the vehicle for restoring to full vigour all those Highland symbols and institutions which the post-Culloden repression had sought to stifle. The clansmen marched again now arrayed in the tartan of their lairds. Piping and Highland dancing were encouraged and as they returned they brought with them a full freight of tradition.

The Gathering was at first a moveable feast both in space and time. In 1848, when Queen Victoria attended for the first time, it was held at Invercauld. The following year it took place at Braemar Castle. Each of the three lairds (of Balmoral, Invercauld and Mar Forest) played host to the games on numerous occasions before 1906. Five times (in 1859, 1887, 1890, 1898 and 1899) they were held at Balmoral on Queen Victoria's invitation, while it was in 1866, by her special desire, that the prefix Royal was added to the title of the society.

In 1905 a special meeting of the society accepted the offer of a 12-acre site called Moin-a-Gail at the west end of Braemar, made by the Duke of Fife, as a permanent arena of the games. This became the Princess Royal Park, recently renamed the Princess Royal and Duke of Fife Memorial Park, and the Gathering has been held there ever since. Here around 3 p.m. every Gathering day excitement among the 20,000 spectators reaches its peak as the Queen and her party drive in from Balmoral and, after welcome from the Lord Lieutenant of the County and the Gathering officials, take their places in the Royal Pavilion as the treasurer of the society raises the Royal Standard.

Two of the most spectacular features of the Gathering have been discontinued. The hill race up Craig Choinnich was stopped by Queen Victoria after a Balmoral ghillie, Charles Duncan, overstrained himself in winning the contest. The March of the Clansmen—the Balmoral, Duff and Farquharson Highlanders (sometimes accompanied by visiting clans from Atholl and Strathdon)—had to be discontinued after World War II owing to the decline in numbers. But new spectacles have replaced the old. Eleven famous pipe bands march in massed formation round the arena, while among the athletic events the cream of British tug-of-war teams compete and the tossing of the outsize Braemar caber never fails to evoke sympathetic gasps from the ringside.

Skirting the games arena on the west is Chapel Brae, by which one climbs Morrone (2819 feet)—Gaelic, *Mor Shron*, 'Big Nose'. About half way up there is a hill indicator placed there by the Deeside Field Club to identify the Cairngorm peaks which now become so prominent in the west, among them Ben Avon (3729 feet); Ben a Bourd (3860 feet), a mountain which tantalizes skiers on the eastern side of the range with the prospect of ideal pistes on a virtually permanent snowfield; Ben Muichdhui (4296 feet), Scotland's second highest summit; Cairn Gorm (4084 feet) and Braeriach (4248 feet), on whose gravelly summit plateau the Dee takes its rise.

It is perhaps symbolic too that at Lily Bank in Chapel Brae there dwells Mr David Rose, one of the wardens of the Cairngorm Nature Reserve, embracing an area of 62 square miles and including most of the famous peaks. West of Braemar on its way up the valley the road hugs steep slopes down which many mountain rills dash in endless cascades, while the river twists and turns in its much-eroded flood-plain. Two miles above Braemar the conspicuous delta of the Quoich is seen on the left bank. This tributary rises between Ben Avon and Ben a Bourd and is famous for its Linn, a cascade near the Earl of Mar's Punchbowl, mentioned earlier. Between the road and the river a little farther west is another picturesque waterfall, the Linn of Corriemulzie, and a mile above this the Victoria Bridge, on the right of the road, leads across the Dee to Mar Lodge.

The present Mar Lodge was virtually the creation of the Princess Royal, Louise, eldest daughter of Edward VII, but there have been three Mar Lodges. The first, sited just behind the present building on the level plain of Dalmore (Gaelic—Great Plain) was a very plain structure. Dalmore was held by the Mackenzie family from the end of the fifteenth century until, in the eighteenth century, their Jacobite adventures obliged them to part with it and the property was bought by the Earl of Fife. In the middle of the nineteenth century the Fifes built a new mansion on the south side of the Dee, which they called at first Corriemulzie Cottage and then New Mar Lodge. In 1889 the sixth Earl of Fife married the Princess Louise and was created first Duke of Fife in 1900. In the meanwhile—in 1895—New Mar Lodge was destroyed by fire.

It had never been considered a really suitable mansion and has been described as a "shapeless old hunting lodge with verandahs supported by rustic tree-trunks creosoted black". Pictures survive of the Duff Highlanders lined up outside it ready to march to the Braemar Gathering. In time the verandahs became lined with serried ranks of stags' heads—and it is said that when the Duke of Fife was informed that the old house was ablaze his first reaction was: "Save the stags' heads!"

Many of them were no doubt saved and now adorn the Mar Lodge of today. The Princess Royal, with her own hand, drew the first rough sketch of the building. A. Marshall Mackenzie of Aberdeen was employed as architect. Queen Victoria laid the foundation stone and the red-roofed Lodge (in a style unkindly dubbed 'suburban Tudor') was completed in the summer of 1898. Mar Lodge is now a residential hotel.

On the south side of the main road just beyond the Victoria Bridge is the battered stump of a grim arboreal relic, the Gallows Tree of Mar, memento of the times when it served the law of 'pit and gallows' exercised under ancient baronial jurisdiction. The road now swings gently southward in a long curve to pass through Inverey (population 16) a row of cottages which is all that survives of a much larger community that was the castletoun of the 'Black Colonel'. John Farquharson's earlier exploits, the slaying of the Baron of Braickley, for which he was outlawed, the siege of Abergeldie Castle, the firing of Braemar Castle, have been described. But the last chapter remains to tell. After escaping from the redcoats by a gallop on horseback across the steep north side of Craigendarroch, he took part in the Battle of Killiecrankie in 1689 and returned to his Inverey castle (the fragmentary ruins of which still remain). Here he was hunted down. The castle was blown up and, taking to the heather, John Farquharson retreated up the glen of the Ey Burn.

A mile and a quarter up this green valley a footpath descends from the glen road to a recess in the walls of the deep and rocky gorge of the Ey. This was the hide-out, known as the Colonel's Bed, where John Farquharson lay in hiding from his pursuers. Food was brought to him here by a faithful clanswoman immortalized as Annie Bhan—the Fair Annie. The Government troops eventually gave up the hunt and, having scorched the earth with great thoroughness, left the fugitive to his own devices. He died peacefully in his bed in 1698, but one more twist was added to his legend. He had expressed a wish to be buried beside his faithful Annie within the old ruined Chapel of the Seven Maidens at Inverey. This was ignored and his remains were interred in the parish graveyard of St Andrew at Braemar.

The Black Colonel's coffin, however, refused to remain decently below ground. On three successive days, so the story goes, it was firmly "planted" in its grave—only to reappear high and dry and exposed to the atmosphere on the following morning. The recalcitrant coffin was then manhandled to the side of the Dee on which it was towed boatwise upstream with a horse-hair tether and finally interred at Inverey by the side of Annie Bhan. As some were untying the tether to take it away the Colonel's son and heir Patrick spoke up. "Leave it! Leave it!" he admonished them, "My father may wish to rise again."

Inverey was acquired by James Duff, second Earl of Fife in 1798. The Glen has a haunting beauty—tinged with sadness, for its lower stretches are covered with traces of the abandoned holdings from which the old-time crofters were moved in 1846 to make way for deer in a clearance which swept from the country the cattle and sheep that once grazed on its slopes.

Modern Inverey has two claims to fame. On the south side of the road is a memorial to Johann von Lamont (1805–1879), Astronomer Royal of Bavaria, erected by the Deeside Field Club and unveiled by Princess Arthur of Connaught, Duchess of Fife, in 1934. John Lamont was born at Corriemulzie, the son of a forester, and went to school at Inverey. Intended for the priesthood he entered the Scots Benedictine College at Ratisbon, but left it for secular studies at Munich University, where he became a professor of astronomy and built up an international reputation.

One of the spectators at the unveiling of the Lamont memorial was a much-loved local personality—Maggie Gruer (1861–1939), who at Thistle Cottage, Inverey, achieved something like worldwide renown as the climbers' friend. Following her mother, who had also adopted the same role, she provided never-failing hospitality to footsore and weary explorers of the Cairngorms, who knew that once they reached Thistle Cottage they would never be turned away hungry and shelterless.

Her unfailing greeting as she ushered drenched and bedraggled mountaineers to her ingle-neuk was, "Weel, ye'll hae an egg?" The egg usually proved to be a bowl of half a dozen—with oatcakes, fabulous scones and home-churned butter. In her tiny home a seemingly endless succession of wayfarers could be given makeshift beds, and when every cranny in the cottage was occupied there was always the barn at the back of the house—full of clean straw.

Inverey is the last hamlet on Deeside. A mile beyond it the road curves down to the Linn of Dee with its handsome stone bridge built in 1857—and there the public highway ends. Here, at a little under 65 miles from Aberdeen and an altitude of 1,213 feet, the river rushes through a narrow channel between 3 and 4 feet wide cut in the schistose rocks, afterwards opening out into a series of round pools. Here the youthful Byron slipped and was narrowly rescued from a watery grave. The spectacle is still dizzying today.

From the bridge at the Linn salmon may often be seen leaping the cataract below, and with this spectacle Deeside's coach trippers must be content to round off their day while drinking in the fragrance of the pines and the distant view of the Cairngorm peaks to the west. The roads into the wilderness beyond are private but along them the climbers and cyclists may proceed into the hills. Over the bridge the road to Glen Dee passes along the north bank of the river, which, at first tree-shaded, runs in a wide open stretch all the way from White Bridge, a footbridge 3 more miles to the west. At this point Dee emerging from its mountain glen on the north meets its tributary, the Geldie, coming from the peat bogs of the watery col away to the west which lies between it and the Feshie, a tributary of the Spey.

Mention the words Glen Feshie Road to any regional politician or any mountain man in the north-east and you will be met by a spate of controversial oratory. General Wade planned it in 1730, the whole 32 miles of it from Braemar Castle to the Ruthven Barracks at Kingussie. But the road was never made and it is still a hot political issue today. Only today it would have to be a first-class motorway, immensely costly to build, justified largely by heavy tourist traffic—but also as a short route for commercial traffic between east and west. The route through Glen Geldie and Glen Feshie is the least spectacular of the three Cairngorm passes from Dee to Spey. It traverses a vast stretch of desolate moorland, yet the climbers, to whom the Cairngorms are precious precisely because of their solitude, will resist it to the death.

The great slash through the hills from north to south in which Dee makes its upper glen is part of the much more picturesque Lairig Ghru pass. The actual source of the river is a spring under a mossy bank crowned by a small cairn of white quartz stones on the summit plateau of Braeriach, the third highest mountain in Britain.

In his classic work on the Cairngorms the late Sir Henry Alexander, a former Lord Provost of Aberdeen, wrote: "No other river in the country has such a source set at such an elevation and the whole scene is unique in our mountains. The summit plateau of Braeriach in its bigness and bareness exceeds anything in the Cairngorms or in these islands. The stretches of stone and gravel, if they perhaps repel the eye, nonetheless impress the imagination, and if the month be June or early July it is with a start that one comes every now and then upon the lovely cushions of the moss campion pink with flowers, blossoming here on the very edge of the snowfields where almost every other plant has ceased to grow".

Here the Dee sets out on its 85-mile odyssey. It crosses the plateau till it comes to the edge of the Garbh Choire—the 'Rough Corrie', anglicized as Garrachorry—where, tunnelling under a snow-bridge that often lasts the summer long, it rushes over the rocky face and falls in a continuous cascade of 500 feet to the bed of the corrie below. These then are what James Hogg, the Ettrick Shepherd called

> ... the grisly cliffs which guard
>   The infant rills of Highland Dee,
> Where hunter's horn is never heard,
>   Nor bugle of the forest bee:
> 'Mid wastes that dern and dreary lie,
>   One mountain rears its mighty form,
> Disturbs the moon in passing by
>   And smiles above the thunderstorm.

Tributary to the infant Dee, or Garrachory Burn, is another little stream from farther north in the Lairig Ghru pass. This Lairig Burn, sometimes running underground, feeds three tiny lochans called the Pools of Dee. As it descends its glen, Dee passes between the crags of the Devil's Point (3,303 feet), with Cairn

Toul (4,241 feet) behind, and Carn a' Mhaim (3,329 feet), backed by Ben Muichdhui, haunted by his 'Big Grey Man' a monster that has terrified experienced climbers with the sound of giant footsteps. Before it reaches its moorland meeting with the Geldie it crosses over a series of rocky shelves called the Chest of Dee, beneath which are deep and clear pools.

The Cairngorm climbers' normal route to the heart of the hills is by Dee's tributary, the Lui, which enters the river about a mile below the Linn. Here the road leads to Derry Lodge ascending by slopes made majestic by rugged pines, survivors of the Caledonian Forest.

In the Dee valley, with all its royal history and continuing royal associations, Aberdeen and its north-east province has a window into the sublime and untameable immensities of nature. Deeside is a symbol—but it does not stand alone. From their excursions into the stony splendours of the upper valley the sons of the province return to wrest a living from less intractable terrain.

In the deer forests of the province over fifteen thousand stags and hinds—of which about 1,200 stags and 2,500 hinds are shot annually—provide what is probably the most intensive form of land use possible. They provide a double income—from stalking rights and venison sales. These figures come from a recent scientific survey, *Royal Grampian Country*, produced by a team of researchers under Professor Kenneth Walton. This recommended a more intensive development of tourism linked with important conservation measures. However, since this report appeared, two other documents, an economic survey of development potential— the Gaskin Report—and the Wheatley Report on local government (most of whose recommendations have been embodied in a Government White Paper) have stressed that the whole of the north-east province of Scotland must be regarded as a single entity. In this way the special problems of Deeside will fall to be solved as part of a much wider whole.

VII

KINCARDINE: THE LAND OF "SUNSET SONG"

"They went quiet and brave from the lands that they loved, though seldom of that love might they speak, it was not in them to tell in words of the earth that moved and lived and abided, their life and enduring love ... the crofter has gone, the man with the house and steading of his own closer to his heart than the breath of his body." Sunset Song.

THE county of Kincardine is one of the smallest in Scotland, a mere 382 square miles in extent, and over half that area is heather and waste. The population is even smaller in proportion to that of the whole country than the area, a mere 48,819 or less than a hundredth part of the whole. Furthermore 31,067 or nearly two-thirds of its folk live in the burghs or small towns, leaving only 17,752 to inhabit the countryside and till the good earth. They are the remnants of a once much larger number and in 1971 millions of television viewers became aware of these countrymen of the Mearns through the BBC's serial "Sunset Song".

This was a dramatization of the novel *Sunset Song* by Lewis Grassic Gibbon, first published in 1932, a fiery, almost breathless spate of words, depicting a few years in the life of a Kincardine crofting community in the period prior to and including the First World War. One may wonder why such a tale should have come to be acclaimed as the greatest imaginative prose work by a Scot in the present century, why it has taken on a representative character, as much for the urban Scot in the industrial con-urbation of the Clyde as for the Highlander in his remote glen. The answer lies partly in the character of the author and partly in the subject to which he has given a universal relevance. As he reads *Sunset Song* the average Scot feels a stirring of ancestral memories.

Until the nineteenth century Scotland was a very poor, predominantly rural country. As they flooded in to the manufac-turing centres, the coal-fields and the steelworks of the industrial central belt, the Scots who now and for many generations have dwelt there carried with them a sense of disinheritance, of alienation from their true native earth. They were the victims of a population explosion, they were aware that the stony acres from which they came could no longer sustain them. But the ancestral memories of life on the land remained, and they could understand what Robert Louis Stevenson meant when he wrote of "the *real* Scotland—the old land". This sense that there is somehow a superior reality about peasant existence has survived.

In the meanwhile the progress of the agricultural revolution had very greatly increased the numbers who could, with the stubborn loyalty that was bred in the bone, eke a livelihood from the poorer land of the Scottish uplands. Vast areas of moorland and hillside were 'broken in' by small-holding tenants by sheer back-breaking labour. When all was done that could be done, only a precarious life at near subsistence level could be achieved in this way. But, at least until the middle decades of the nineteenth century, the population graph of the rural parishes continued to rise.

When Lewis Grassic Gibbon, whose real name was James Leslie Mitchell, was born on the small-holding of Hill of Seggatt, in the Aberdeenshire parish of Auchterless in the year 1901, the great tide of rural crofting was already on the wane. His father moved into the town of Aberdeen and worked briefly as a carter before securing another small farm—this time at Bloomfield on the upland portion of the Kincardine parish of Arbuthnott. Here young Mitchell spent his often troubled boyhood. The whole environment and the changes that were pressing in upon it forms the subject of *Sunset Song*.

It is now necessary to say something of this unusual boy's temperament and his family circumstances.

He was a rather delicate, sensitive and highly imaginative child. Greatly encouraged by the sympathetic attentions of the schoolmaster of Arbuthnott, he lived in a world of ambitious dreams— no easy thing for a crofter's child. Since he was unable to concentrate on the routine of croft work, a rift appeared between him and his parents. In his first novel *Stained Radiance* he put strong words into the mouth of his heroine to depict it: "Tears were in Thea's eyes, bitter tears, tears of an overmastering, heartbreaking pity. She and her parents were poles apart. . . . In youth they had loved her, thwarted her, misunderstood her. She hated them.

Now all unconscious of the reason, she was weeping because of that tragedy of existence."

Mitchell's youthful unhappiness led him far. Into the details of his career it is impossible to go here. Early work in journalism in Aberdeen and Glasgow ended in breakdown. When he went home to Bloomfield his father urged him, "You'll take a fee!"— that is become a farm servant. Instead he joined the army and then the R.A.F.—as a clerk, and for a decade incubated his ideas. In 1925 he married Rebecca Middleton, who had been a schoolfellow with him at Arbuthnott. When after a hectic apprenticeship to novel-writing and anthropological theory, which had already produced several books, he turned to the Mearns in the flush of his literary maturity it was to perform a great act of reconciliation.

Ignorant then of his line of inner development I had reviewed a number of his books in February 1932, writing: "How will Mr Mitchell develop? It is to be hoped that he will settle down to give us novels of the North-east. After all he must know the countryside of his birth and upbringing best, and the Mearns, unlike the Wessex of Hardy or the Argyll of Neil Munro has not been made to live in a novel, and Mr Mitchell could do it."

To this he replied in a letter to a mutual friend, George Macdonald: "One of these days I'll write the north-east novel he talks about, so Scotch I'll make it that people will tear out leaves to suck in church."

And in the March and April of that year he was writing *Sunset Song* in a white heat of vehemence. Its power owes something to the fact that it was the resolution of an inner conflict, and this conflict is reflected in the soul of his chief character Chris Guthrie, the crofter's child:

> ... two Chrisses there were that fought for her heart and tormented her. You hated the land and the coarse speak of the folk and learning was brave and fine one day and the next you'd waken with the peewits crying across the hills, deep and deep, crying in the heart of you and the smell of the earth in your face, almost you'd cry for that, the beauty and the sweetness of the Scottish land and skies. You saw their faces in the firelight, father's and mother's and the neighbours', before the lamps lit up, tired and kind, faces dear and close to you, you wanted the words they'd known and used, forgotten in the far off youngness of their lives, Scots words to tell to your heart, how they wrung it and held it, the toil of their days and

unendingly their fight. And the next minute that passed from you, you were English, back to the English words so sharp and clean and true—for a while, for a while, till they slid so smooth from your throat you knew they could never say anything that was worth the saying at all.

The visitor to the Mearns can explore for himself the countryside which evoked this passionate outburst. The *Sunset Song* country lies virtually in the heart of the Mearns, where the river Bervie crosses it from west to east. Most of the parish of Arbuthnott, with the exception of two large farms, lies on the north side of the Bervie, which, to quote a former parish minister, "in its winding course, extensive haughs and steep wooded banks, presents at many points scenes of great beauty".

But if one limited one's view to these pleasances of the river valley one would miss their essential counterpart and foil—the 'backlands' of the Reisk to the north. And it is the Reisk that only Gibbon himself can describe: "Across the turnpike the land climbed red and clay and a rough stone road went wandering up to the biggings of Blaweary. *Out of the world and into Blaweary* they said in Kinraddie and faith it was coarse land and lonely up there on the brae, fifty-six acres of it, forby the moor that went on with the brae, high above Blaweary, up to a great flat hilltop where lay a bit loch that nested snipe by hundred. . . ."

"Blaweary" is of course the fictional equivalent of Bloomfield, which can be seen today on the left of the road to the Reisk while the dark little loch is on the shoulder of Bruxie Hill above Hillhead of Pitforthie.

Returning to the B967 road along the north bank of the Bervie, the "turnpike" of *Sunset Song* one may cross it to the Kirk of Arbuthnott on its knoll above the river. The chancel of this church was dedicated in 1242. It has five lancet windows, the three in the gable being fitted with stained glass representing Faith, Hope and Charity by Cottier. They are amusingly satirized in *Sunset Song* as "three bit creatures of queans" in a passage which reflects the salty irreverence of the yokels of the parish.

The second glory of the church is the adjoining aisle, built by Sir Robert Arbuthnott (who succeeded to the family estates in 1471) for the purpose of housing a portable altar. It is a two-storey building of late Scottish Gothic of finely hewn ashlar. Within it there is a feature mentioned in the prelude to *Sunset Song* as "an effigy thing of Cospatrick de Gondeshill, him that killed the gryphon, lying on his back with his arms crossed and a daft-like simper on his face". In reality this full-length recumbent statue of a knight in full armour, helmet and sword, with his feet resting on the figure of a dog, probably represents James Arbuthnott, son of Sir Robert, who died in 1521.

Grassic Gibbon's mythopoetic faculty is illustrated in his story of the above-mentioned Cospatric, the gryphon-slayer, also in the prelude to the novel. The historic counterpart of Cospatric was Sir Hugh le Blond, the ancestor of the Arbuthnott family who have held lands in the parish for over 700 years. This Sir Hugh appears in a ballad first printed in Sir Walter Scott's *Border Minstrelsy*. It tells how Sir Hugh vindicates the Queen of Scotland's honour in the lists by trouncing a villain who had slandered her virtue:

> The Queen then said unto the King:
> "Arbattle's near the sea,
> Give it unto the northern knight
> That this day fought for me."
>
> Then said the King: "Come here Sir Knight
> And drink a glass of wine,
> And if Arbattle's not enough
> To it we'll Fordoun join."

The upper storey of the Arbuthnott Church aisle, reached by a spiral stair and known as the priest's room, was probably the place where between 1471 and 1491 James Sibbald inscribed three very precious and interesting manuscripts—the Arbuthnott Prayer Book, the Arbuthnott Psalter and the Arbuthnott Missal—all at the order and expense of Sir Robert Arbuthnott.

Close to the church is Arbuthnott House, the ancestral home of the family which Sir Hugh le Blond founded. In the Middle Ages there was a strongly fortified castle here, but this was destroyed by fire in 1555 and was never rebuilt. The oldest portion of the existing building is a small wing which used to be described as the bakehouse and bears the date 1588. To this in the seventeenth century was added the present south wing, a plain but handsome three-storey hall-house with dormer windows. Its outstanding feature is a series of magnificently decorated plaster ceilings—in a condition as perfect as the day they were finished in 1650. The remaining portion of the house dates from the nineteenth century.

The Arbuthnott estates were greatly diminished at the end of

Tending disease-free piglets reared in incubators at the Rowett Research Institute, Bucksburn

Baiting lines at Gourdon

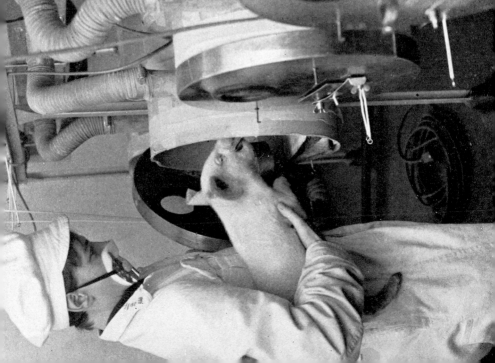

World War I—a fact reflected in *Sunset Song*, where they appear as the lands of Kinraddie and the wartime felling of timber is lamented—but there remain some 2,900 acres and in the past twenty years there has been a marked revival due to the efforts of the fifteenth Viscount Arbuthnott, who was Lord Lieutenant of Kincardine. He brought back the trees by dedicating 200 acres of his lands to forestry and in the same period the decline in population was arrested and numbers once more began to increase.

Never, however, will they return to the old-time peak, and this holds good of every rural area in north-east Scotland. When Grassic Gibbon was a schoolboy Arbuthnott School had a roll of seventy-five. Today it stands at twenty-three. Much more drastic depopulation is to be found in neighbouring parishes. When the BBC film-makers came to produce *Sunset Song* they had to turn to the Mill of Benholm—the sole surviving water-powered meal mill of the traditional type left in the whole of Kincardine—to shoot the scenes featuring Long Rob of the Mill in the novel. Let us consider the case of the film-makers' host on this occasion, the Miller of Benholm, Mr Lindsay Watson.

He was one of those who "went quiet and brave from the lands that they loved"—as *Sunset Song* puts it—not to the first but to the Second World War. He went but returned, wounded in action in the North African desert under Wavell. He had originally come to the Mill of Benholm with his father, another Lindsay Watson, in the year 1929 as a lad of 12. He had attended the school of Benholm—now closed and empty—when it had sixty pupils. Since he came to the parish he has seen thirty homes in this quiet countryside given up and abandoned in the depopulation that follows the death of the crofter way of life—that way of life of which *Sunset Song* is the elegy.

Overlooking the mill from a grassy knoll above the Burn of Benholm—which happens to be the next sizeable stream to the south of the Bervie Water—is the parish church of Benholm with its ancient kirkyard. The church itself was built in 1832 but it has some fascinating treasures salvaged from its pre-Reformation predecessor.

The manse and its beautiful garden sloping to the Benholm Burn is much older than the church, dating from the early eighteenth century, and beside it there stands an intriguing round tower with a conical helmet. It is the entrance to the old-time minister's underground wine cellar.

Fish sales on the quay at Gourdon

Within sight of the Church of Benholm stands ruined Benholm Castle, the old tower of which dates from 1475. Although the parish has seen very heavy depopulation it is pleasant to think that so much survives in it still from the "old Scotland". One of the hardest tasks faced by the BBC in their *Sunset Song* venture was to find a three-storey farmhouse to represent Blaweary—as called for in the script. Just when they were about to give up in despair they discovered Brawliemuir in the parish of Glenbervie. Here was a 'merged farm' and an empty farmhouse of three storeys standing on a hill slope on the very type of land described in the novel—and even more remarkable it happened to be the very farm tenanted for generations by the ancestors of Scotland's national bard—the poet Robert Burns.

For over a century Burns enthusiasts have regarded the Mearns, and the parish of Glenbervie in particular as the 'Fatherland of Burns'. This is because for at least two centuries the poet's paternal ancestors farmed the difficult hill land in the upper vale of the Bervie Water.

In the first half of the eighteenth century the tenants of Brawliemuir (then spelt Brawlinmuir) were James Burnes and his wife Margaret Falconer, the poet's great-grandparents. James died in 1743 at the age of 87, and he and his wife were buried in Glenbervie churchyard alongside the great grand-uncle of the poet, William Burnes and his wife Christian Fotheringham, who tenanted the neighbouring farm of Bogjorgan. The details of their lives were inscribed on flat tombstones which in course of time began to weather away. On three successive occasions Burnsites took steps to preserve the stones, at first raising them on stone supports, then encasing them in a hideous cement envelope and finally in 1968 setting them into the wall of a roofed shelter specially built for the purpose and rededicated with ceremony at an organized pilgrimage on 11th September of that year.

James and Margaret Burnes had a large family, and Brawlinmuir continued to be farmed by the Burneses until 1807. One of their sons, Robert, the poet's grandfather, took the farm of Kinmonth, overlooking the village of Drumlithie and finally moved still farther east to the farm of Clochnahill, on the southern slopes of Carmont Hill, nearer Stonehaven. He had ten children, one of whom, William, born on 11th November 1727, was the father of the poet. Large families mean economic stringency and William, in search of a livelihood moved south to Midlothian and eventually to Ayrshire, the true 'Burns Country' where the poet himself was born.

What is significant I think is that two of Scotland's greatest writers—the 'ploughman poet' and the novelist of the crofters— have these roots in upland Kincardine, not in the fat lands of the fertile Howe, where farming is almost too easy, but in the difficult, 'dour' land of the hill slopes. Truly "from scenes like these Auld Scotia's glory springs".

I have mentioned the village of Drumlithie, a delightful old-world village so haphazard in plan that it looks as if it had been "scattered from the clouds". It lies almost 2 miles east of the ancient parish centre of Glenbervie and grew up in the seven-teenth and eighteenth centuries as a weaving centre. Here is the *Sunset Song* description of it: "There to the left rose Drumlithie ... some called it Skite to torment the folk and they'd get fell angry at that in Skite. No more than a rickle of houses it was, white with sunshine below its steeple that made of Skite the laugh of the Howe, for feint the kirk was near it. Folk said for a joke that every time it came on to rain the Drumlithie folk ran out and took in their steeple, that proud they were of the thing."

The famous steeple is still there. It was built in 1777 to house a belfry and a bell to toll the weaving population to their work at the looms. The handloom weavers of Drumlithie were ruined with the advent of the power loom and the last of them ceased his work over a century ago. But the steeple bell is still used to celebrate local weddings and ring in the New Year on Hogmanay, the present bell-ringer being Mr John Towns who lives nearby in the old narrow High Street. Across the way in the High Street is the little shop of Alexander Murray, tailor, the third of his name and family to carry on the business started by his grand-father, Alexander Murray, a century ago. This may give an inkling of the power of family tradition in the Mearns. Another example takes us back to *Sunset Song* and its author. Grassic Gibbon died in 1935 and his ashes lie in Arbuthnott Kirkyard under a stone which bears the lines from *Sunset Song*: "The kindness of friends, the warmth of toil, the peace of rest". But in the school of Drumlithie today the infants first learn to read under the eye of his full cousin Elizabeth Gibbon McKenzie. A more fortunate 'Chris', she has solved the conflict between learning and the life of the land, for she not only teaches in the village school, she farms the old local holding of Upper Quithel—assisted by her son George McKenzie, the farmer of Nether Cotbank—and finds it possible also to run a hairdressing business in Stonehaven! This illustrates the fact that mechanization has taken the slavery out of farming and, in some lucky instances, enables the folk of farming stock to enjoy the best of both worlds by living still in close contact with "the sweetness of the Scottish land and skies".

Drumlithie lies in the northern tip of the Mearns Howe on a side road leading north and west from the A94 road between Stonehaven and Laurencekirk. The parishes of Arbuthnott and Benholm already described lie on the other or eastern side of that road and between it and A92 the coast road from Stonehaven to Montrose. It is a fact that almost all the interest of the Mearns countryside is to be found off the track of these main highways. So let us continue southwards from Drumlithie along the western rim of the Howe. Two miles west of the village we come to Glenbervie House on a cape of land overlooking the junction of the Bervie Water with a small tributary. This is really a sixteenth-century castle which has been rebuilt in its upper storeys but retains the old plan of a main block with two great round towers at each end. It stands on the site of an earlier manor at which Edward I of England halted on his march to Deeside by the Cryne Corse pass over the Mounth in July 1296. Then and for another century and a half it was the seat of the Melville family whose most famous member, a strong-handed Sheriff of the Mearns, was murdered in a rather gruesome fashion.

Irked by a stream of complaints against his high-handed administration, the Scottish king of the day gave vent to the remark: "Sorrow gin the Shirra were sodden and suppit in bree"—in other words, cooked in his own broth. Overhearing this a group of four local lairds invited the Sheriff to a hunt and proceeded to boil him to death in an outsize kettle and after he had been "sodden" for some time sealed the deed of infamy by each tasting a spoonful of the "bree" or fatal soup.

Today Glenbervie House is the home of Mrs P. Badenoch Nicolson, whose ancestors first acquired it in 1721.

South of Glenbervie lies the parish of Fordoun. Part of it lies in the fertile Howe and reaps rich tribute from its deep red loam, but as one moves north the open fields give way to wooded heights rising up to Strathfinella Hill, a long isolated ridge, which in its turn is separated from the mountains of the Mounth by the Glen of Drumtochty. Through this glen runs the Luther

Water, emerging into the Howe at the ancient Kirkton of Fordoun, while on the higher land on its left bank is the comparatively
modern village of Auchinblae (population 381), a pleasant
holiday resort with a single long main street overlooked by a
hill on the south and rising gently to the rolling country to the
north.

The present Church of Fordoun dates from 1829, but in the
churchyard is the ruin of St Palladius's Chapel, 730 years old.
The patron saint of the parish is now considered to have been
Paldy or Paldoc, a disciple of St Ninian, and Fordoun has always
claimed to be the 'Mother Church' of the Mearns. Much older
than the chapel itself is the mysterious sculptured stone clamped
into the wall of the north gable. It shows a hunting scene with
horsemen, a greyhound and a wild animal, surrounded by
decorative panels and by a serpent.

One guess at the stone's meaning was made by Professor Stuart
of Inchbreck, who took it to be a contemporary monument
recording the death of King Kenneth III in 995 as the result of
the machinations of the Lady Finella, wife of the Mormaer of
the Mearns, who gave her name to Strathfinella Hill. On the
stone, so goes this theory, Finella is represented by the serpent.

There are various versions of Finella's story. She had a grudge
against the King because he had put her son to death, that much is
certain. But according to John of Fordoun, and Hollinshed, she
killed the monarch by a most elaborate ruse. While entertaining
him in the Mormaer's castle—identified as the ruined Green
Castle near Fettercairn at the other side of Strathfinella Hill—
she showed him a brazen image of himself holding in one hand a
golden apple, so artfully devised that if anyone took hold of it
concealed crossbows hidden by the hangings of the room would
discharge their arrows upon him with great force. The King,
invited to accept the apple as a token of esteem, stretched out his
hand and grasped it—with the inevitably fatal result. Mearns
legend, which sees Finella as a witch, goes on to tell how she
fled across the Howe, and met her end in the Den of Finella at St
Cyrus.

Drumtochty Glen is one of the beauty spots of the Mearns.
Forestry Commission plantations fringe it, and on the north side
is Drumtochty Castle, a neo-Gothic pile built early in the nineteenth century by a London banker. In 1885 the Episcopal Church
in Scotland built in the centre of the Glen a new Church of St

Palladius, with a massive statue of the saint, bearded and in bishop's mitre under a canopy on the gable.

Beyond the headwaters of the Luther the glen road continues over water splashes to emerge on the shores of Loch Saugh. On the far side of this lake is Glensaugh, where the Hill Farming Research Organization carries on its work on a farm of 1,000 acres.

Here, indeed, is a portent for the future. Look up at the north-western face of Strathfinella Hill. All around are bleak heather-covered slopes, but on Strafinla Top the heath is broken by three rich green swathes, great bites into the heather, carpeted by lush spring grass and rising up the hill to a height of 800 feet. These are re-seeded areas amounting to over 50 acres on which some of the 950 ewes of the research farm have luxurious grazing. They have been cultivated for the first time in history, sometimes with the aid of great modern tyne-ploughs, sometimes by surface scarifying, so that grass can be sown. It has been estimated that a third of the land surface of Britain consists of mountain, moor-land or heath capable of being used for grazing. Glensaugh shows it can be done.

Beyond Glensaugh the road runs down to Clattering Brig, a little stone bridge over a mountain stream and meets B974 the Cairn a'Mounth pass road from Banchory. It then follows the course of the Devilly Burn, past Finella's ruined castle and the estate of Fasque to the village of Fettercairn—and we are deep in the lush Mearns Howe again.

The parish of Fettercairn is one of the most historic in the county. The most conspicuous object in the village (population 174) is the spectacular freestone archway, turreted and battle-mented, spanning the main street, which was built in 1864 to record for all time the incognito visit of Queen Victoria and Prince Albert in 1861. The inn where they slept is still the chief hostelry of the place and in the square is still the old market cross bearing the date 1670 and the insignia of the Earl of Middleton. But this is perhaps a little deceptive, for it is believed to be the cross of the now-vanished burgh of Kincardine, the original county town, which stood a mile or two to the east and withered away when the court of the sheriffdom was transferred to Stonehaven.

All around, however, are historic mansions. To the north is Fettercairn House, built shortly after the Restoration of 1660 by

John, first Earl of Middleton, who, after a career as a Covenanting general during the Civil War, changed sides and fought for Charles II at Worcester and led various armed adventures during the Commonwealth. As Charles's Lord High Commissioner to the Scots Parliament he was for a time the "first man in the kingdom". Today Fettercairn is owned by Mrs Diana Somervell, a cousin of the Queen. One of her ancestors, Williamina Belsches, who had James Mill the philosopher as her tutor, was wooed by Sir Walter Scott, who made the excuse of excavating Finella's castle in order to visit her at Fettercairn. But instead she married Sir William Forbes, a banker, who brought to Fettercairn two journals by James Boswell and over one hundred letters written by him. These literary treasures were rediscovered in 1930 by Professor Claude Colleer Abbott, purchased by Yale University, and published in the series of Boswell Papers.

To the west is Balbegno Castle, a tower-house built in the decade of the 1560s by John Wood, a relative of Sir Andrew Wood of Largo, a famous Scottish admiral. Above the garden door of the castle is a sculptured bust of the admiral, commemorating his victory in the Firth of Forth when, with two Scots ships, he captured three English warships. The outstanding feature of the castle is the rib-vaulted ceiling in the great hall which dates from 1569 and is divided into sixteen compartments, each containing mural paintings of the arms of the Scottish peers of the day. To the north-east the stately house of Fasque, with its towers and battlements in the English baronial style, was built in 1810 and since 1829 has been the home of the Gladstone family. W. E. Gladstone was a younger son of Sir John Gladstone, first of the Gladstone lairds.

South-west of Fettercairn B966 runs for 4 miles through fertile fields and shady woods to Gannochy Bridge on the North Esk and brings us to the western tip of the county. If we now turn south-east and follow the course of that river to the sea we may make our way north along the Kincardine coast, adding a completely new dimension to the picture. South of Fettercairn lies the parish of Marykirk, a parish so flat and level that one has the optical illusion of a gradual slope. The Luther Water which we last saw in Drumtochty Glen and at Fordoun here returns towards the west after transcribing a wide undulating arc and flows into the North Esk a little below the North Water Bridge where A94 crosses into the county of Angus. East of this stretches a great band of very fertile land filled with rich farms, while to the north between it and the dark conifers of the Forest of Inglismaldie is a moor on which about the end of the eighteenth century there grew the weaving village of Luthermuir. By about 1850 there were 300 handloom weavers here, and it had a population of over 1,000. Today the population is 203, and one weaver, who migrated thither from Laurencekirk, remains to carry on the old tradition.

There are two interesting castles in the parish. Inglismaldie (pronounced Inglismaddie) was built as a turreted tower-house in the seventeenth century by the Carnegies, Earls of Northesk. It was later restored, greatly extended and converted into a modern mansion. Thornton Castle has a much older pedigree and its round tower is claimed to be a thirteenth-century structure. The central portion of the house, linking the square and round towers, carries the date 1662 above the entrance door. After a gap of five and a half centuries the castle returned to the Thornton family, when, in 1893, it was acquired by Sir Thomas Thornton whose present-day descendant is Lady Thornton-Kemsley, wife of the former M.P. for North Angus and Mearns.

At Thornton we are virtually in the centre of the Howe. Less than 2 miles east of it on A94 is Laurencekirk (population 1,389) the burgh I mentioned in Chapter I as being the 'capital' of this red-earth farming paradise.

> From small beginnings Rome of old
>   Became a great imperial city
> 'Twas peopled first, as we are told,
>   By bankrupts, vagabonds, banditti,
> Quoth Thomas, then the time may come
> When Laurencekirk may equal Rome.

The laughing rhyme had its origins in the zeal with which Lord Gardenstone, a Scottish law lord of the eighteenth century, nursed the planned village of Laurencekirk which he had feued out to replace the original Kirkton of St Laurence. In 1779 he had the place erected into a burgh of barony. He built the inn, the 'Gardenstone Arms', still surviving at the north-east end of the little town, and furnished it with a library which intrigued Dr Johnson in 1773. Once famous for weaving and the manufacture of snuff boxes, Laurencekirk today, a straggling town with a High Street over a mile long, is undistinguished in appearance but superb in its situation, overlooked on the east by the Johnston Tower 914 feet up on the summit of the Hill of Garvock. It was built by James Farquhar of Johnston (Lord Gardenstone's successor as laird) and has been Laurencekirk's emblem for 150 years. Beside it is a hill indicator giving a key to the magnificent view across the Howe to the mountains of the Mounth.

The Hill of Garvock is the highest of the long line of hills which separate the Howe from the coastlands of the Mearns, to which, with a fleeting glimpse of the quaint old village of Marykirk close to a bridge over the North Esk, we now turn. A side road along the left bank of the river connects Marykirk (population 126) with the trunk road A92 a little above the Lower Northwater Bridge leading to Montrose, and, turning north, we soon approach the village of St Cyrus, signalled by its very prominent church steeple on a clifftop overlooking what is now a national nature reserve administered by the Nature Conservancy. This wonderful stretch of coastline features a salt marsh at the foot of highly picturesque cliffs. A nature trail has been marked out by the Conservancy, who have issued a guide to its attractions.

The salt marsh with its rich and unusual plant life is one of nature's most recent miracles, for until 1879 it was the actual bed of the river North Esk which all down historic time had turned north along the coast before entering the sea almost opposite the Nether Kirkyard of St Cyrus. In that year an abnormal spate caused the river to break out at the bend where it turned northwards and to enter the sea at that point, considerably shortening its course. The original mouth of the river was then choked by blown sand, and the old course, filled and emptied at each tide from its junction with the new channel, evolved into a salt marsh known locally as 'The Slunks'.

It so happens that the Nether Kirkyard, the most historic spot in St Cyrus, stands right in the centre of the new nature trail on a raised beach where the sea flowed 10,000 years ago at the end of the Ice Age. Backgrounded by a semi-circle of basalt cliffs known as the Steeples is the site of the medieval church of St Cyrus—and very probably also of the Celtic abbey of Ecclesgreig (the Church of Grig) which preceded it. In 1632 a new church was built on the clifftop above, on the site of the present structure, which dates from 1786 and was given its outsize steeple in 1854.

This modern church is famous for its 'dowry brides'. Once a very populous weaving and quarrying centre St Cyrus suffered severe depression early in the nineteenth century. John Orr, a local laird, was touched by the sight of a poor young couple trudging through the snow to be married in the church. He set aside £1,000 in his will, directing that the annual interest from this sum was to be divided into five parts—one to aid indigent old folk and the other four to provide dowries, for the youngest, the oldest, the shortest and the tallest St Cyrus brides of the year. These dowries are still distributed on the last day of each year and form a useful nest egg of the newly-weds of the parish. In the church you may still see the old measuring stand where each bride is measured after the ceremony to see if she is the shortest or tallest. Today the village of St Cyrus has a population of 347, while the parish numbers under a thousand. Net salmon fishing flourishes here.

A fine stretch of rocky coastline punctuated by deep dens by which small streams cut their way to the sea leads north to the small but very characterful fishing port of Johnshaven.

Once the fifth largest fishing village in Scotland with a population of over 1,000 it had dwindled to 625 at the last census, but is kept alive today by lobster fishing, mainly a summer activity.

Gourdon (population 769), some 3 miles north of Johnshaven, is one of the marvels of the Mearns. It claims to be the most prosperous hand-line fishing port in Britain. With Johnshaven men, the Gourdon fishermen were the first in Scotland to adopt the motor boat in preference to the old steam drifter. To see Gourdon harbour today, when over a score of dual-purpose motor fishing vessels are landing their catches, is to feel a great lifting of the heart. When I asked the secretary of the Gourdon Fishermen's Association to explain the present prosperity he had a quick answer: "Our womenfolk!" By their willingness to share the traditional work of the fisher community with the men— each Gourdon fisherman's wife baits the 1,200 hooks of his hand-lines for her husband with mussels day in day out—they have preserved a way of life that has died out elsewhere. Only here can you see the baited lines being wheeled in their 'prams' to the quay-wall. Nor is it merely a quaint old survival. Modern marketing methods and the loyalty of buyers and fish merchants have assured the fishermen of an unfailing demand for their catches because the quality of the fish is so high.

Both Johnshaven and Gourdon lie on steep slopes between A92 and the sea, and on its northward way that road now passes the approach to seventeenth-century Hallgreen Castle and enters the long main street of the ancient royal burgh of Inverbervie. This old town (population 921) lies immediately south of the gorge through which the Bervie Water forces its way from the open haughland of its lower reaches to the sea. The leonine form of Bervie Brow, the hill which bars the river's way when it reaches the coast, ends in a shoulder of rounded cliff which was given the name Craig David, after the landing there on 4th May 1341 of King David II on his return to Scotland from France during the Second War of Independence.

But today the old mercat cross in the square (1737) is Bervie's one visible link with a long past. It has been an industrial town since 1788, when a machine for spinning linen yarn, the first in Scotland, was set up in the Haughs of Bervie.

About a mile above the new Inverbervie Bridge over the river is Allardyce Castle with an elaborate turreted gateway dating from 1662. A92 now passes through the parish of Kinneff at a considerable distance from the coast, where in fact all the real interest lies.

At two points it is worth a visit. The first is the old Kirkton of Kinneff with the old church of 1738 close to the clifftops. Here the visitor's book bears witness to the hundreds of pilgrims who view the memorials within it: to the Reverend James Grainger, parish minister in the Cromwellian era, who buried the regalia of Scotland—crown, sceptre and Sword of State— under his pulpit in the former church on the same site; and to Sir George Ogilvy of Barras, Governor of Dunnottar Castle, who in league with Grainger, denied these "significant baubles" to the Cromwellian occupying power during the "usurpation". How the regalia were smuggled out of the castle during the siege of 1651–2 by Mrs Grainger or her servant girl in a basket of old clothes—or alternatively a basin of dulse (seaweed)—is still a matter of historical debate. But the important thing is that they eluded the grasp of Cromwell and were safely hidden in Kinneff till the Restoration.

Farther north another side road from A92 leads to the clifftop village of Catterline. Nor merely is this an ancient fishing—and smugglers'—haven that has survived to the present day, it has become a haunt of artists in love with its combination of spectacular cliff scenery and traditional fisher life. A motorized salmon coble lands plentiful catches at its tiny pier, while a couple of white-fish boats still use it as their base, marketing their catch at Gourdon. The village perches on top of a great semi-circle of cliffs. Steep paths lead down to the small harbour formed by a former Viscount Arbuthnott early last century and at one time there were twenty small white-fishing craft.

Three more miles northward bring us to the lodge of Dunnottar Castle. The keep of this spectacular stronghold was described in Chapter II. But the visitor today sees far more than this. From the lodge he crosses a grassy plateau till he reaches a point at which the Castle Rock stands grandly before him with ruins covering practically the whole of its flat surface. Then he descends by a narrow path into the chasm of St Ninian's Den and climbs up on the other side to the entry in the solid rock where, as he climbs up the stone stair in its tunnel, he is faced by a fearsome array of gunloops. Once he reaches the top of the stair and emerges into daylight on the summit plateau he can look about him and follow the stages in the castle's centuries-long evolution.

The keep as we know dates from the end of the fourteenth century. Early in the 1500s came the store and stables north-east of the keep; in 1574 the round-towered building known as the Priest's House or Waterton's Lodging; after that the tremendous gatehouse, including the towering seven-storey tenement called Benholm's Lodging; and finally, about 1580, the first part of the palace, the complex of buildings forming a quadrangle on the far, or seaward, side of the rock. These were begun by William, fourth Earl Marischal and continued by the fifth Earl, the founder of Marischal College, who had received the Abbey of Deer from James VI and I as a reward for his part in arranging the King's marriage to Anne of Denmark.

A famous story tells how the Countess Marischal urged Earl George not to accept the abbey, and how she then dreamed that she saw swarms of monks from the abbey, armed with pen-knives, laboriously picking away the Rock of Dunnottar so that it tumbled and fell into the sea.

The Earl died in 1631 and was buried in the Marischal Aisle which he had built in Dunnottar Kirkyard, some distance landward of the castle.

Also in this churchyard is the Covenanters' Stone, which Sir Walter Scott found 'Old Mortality' furbishing and described in the prologue to that novel. It commemorates victims of the atrocity in 1685 when 122 men and 45 women—political internees of their day—were herded indiscriminately in the dungeon known as the Whigs' Vault at Dunnottar Castle and kept in durance vile there for over two months. Those who died of this ordeal were buried here. Under the list of their names is a reference to a text from Revelations: "And they heard a great voice from heaven saying unto them, Come up hither. And they ascended up to heaven in a cloud; and their enemies beheld them."

Some parts of ruined Dunnottar Castle were fully restored by the first Viscountess Cowdray. Among these is the drawing room in the quadrangle range, which has been given a fine heraldic ceiling and, above the fireplace, a memorial to Sir George Ogilvy of Barras and the Cromwellian siege of September 1651–May 1652, already mentioned in connection with the rescue of the regalia.

The A92 road approaches Stonehaven by a superb clifftop, on which is perched the 1914–18 war memorial in the form of a classical ring of pillars. At this point the whole town appears spread out on its bay with the harbour and in the foreground the old town—the little town which was founded by the fifth Earl Marischal early in the seventeenth century. On a quay is the Old Tolbooth, built as the Earl's store, but converted into a courtroom and prison—in which in 1748 three Jacobite episcopalian clergymen were interned. During this period fishermen's wives from the villages along the coast brought their babies to be baptized by the jailed pastors, who extended their hands through the stanchioned windows of the Tolbooth. The building has been restored and, re-opened by the Queen Mother, it is in use as a museum and tea room.

At the end of High Street in the old town stand the mercat cross and eighteenth-century town steeple, along with some finely restored old houses. Along High Street at midnight on Hogmanay (31st December) the young men of the burgh march swinging fire-balls to bring in the New Year.

The Bridge of Stonehaven over the river Carron divides the old town from the new, a planned creation founded by Robert Barclay of Ury in the second half of the eighteenth century. It has a pleasant tree-lined square where the market buildings were erected in 1827 surmounted by a steeple 130 feet high. Today, with its population of 4,505, Stonehaven is not merely a thriving county town but a very popular resort which, at the height of the summer, is thronged with tourists. Indeed from this point northwards the coastlands of Kincardine—despite the bleakness of the countryside traversed by A92—are a magnet to commuters from the city of Aberdeen who continue to snap up bungalows in the succession of old-world fisher havens on the clifftops of a spectacular littoral. Little used by fishing vessels, the harbour is crowded with pleasure craft, and the Stonehaven Yacht Club attracts a fleet of yachts and sailing dinghies.

As the road, passing over the Cowie Water and leaving behind the caravan site and open-air swim pool, climbs out of the town on the north, it overlooks Cowie Village with its tiny harbour and rows of fisher cottages. Near the ruined chapel of St Mary of Cowie there was in the Middle Ages a royal burgh that has vanished without a trace. At Muchalls, farther north, there is a little oasis of fertile land, a truly charming old castle still inhabited, and a clifftop village, anciently known as Stranathro, overlooking one of the most spectacular sequences of cliff scenery in Britain.

Muchalls Castle was built between 1619 and 1627 by the Burnetts of Crathes. It is an L-plan structure with steep slated roofs, turreted and crow-stepped gables and a handsome curtain wall and gateway enclosing a courtyard. You climb a wheel stair for the grand surprise—the great hall with its ceiling of delicate white pargetted plaster work. The ceiling bears six coats of arms, four medallions containing the heads of biblical and classical heroes and three knops with hooks for hanging lamps, all joined by a pattern of straight and curved ribs covered with floral designs in relief. A magnificent overmantel dated 1624 carries the Royal Arms as borne in Scotland following the Union of the Crowns in 1603, with the collar of the Thistle inside the Garter, and surmounted by the Scottish crest.

For 2 miles, between the Burn of Muchalls and the Burn of Elsick to the north, are many famous rock features—May Craig, the Grim Brigs, Dunie Fell, the Old Man of Muchalls and Scart's Craig among them, while a picturesque isolated rock known as the Tillie Tennant is a favourite with landscape painters.

Immediately south of the deep defile by which the Burn of Elsick enters the sea there is the little deserted white-fishing haven of Skateraw. But high above it the clifftop is crowded with houses new and old. The old fisher cottages have been modernized and scheme after scheme of new private enterprise dwellings have been built and occupied by city folk anxious to live with a superb sea view. This community, called Newtonhill, has been doubled in size in ten years.

Upstream on the Burn of Elsick and inland from the A92 road His Grace the Duke of Fife, son of the late Princess Maud and the Earl of Southesk, has made his home at Elsick House, where his ancestors the Bannermans were settled by the end of the fourteenth century.

Between us and Aberdeen on this jagged coast are four more old fishing havens, Downies, Portlethen, Findon and Cove, and all of them are residential meccas. Their survival is highly significant. The Kincardineshire planners, daunted by the cost of making modern roads, water supplies and drainage systems available to these clifftop villages, sought to persuade the dwellers in the old fishing hamlets to move inland to new settlements where new housing schemes had been already serviced. But they dug in their heels and demanded all mod. cons on the spot. They won their case, and today each of these sea-touns is rapidly expanding.

Findon is famous as the home of the 'finnan haddie', a smoked delicacy lauded in Sir Walter Scott's day. In the last century however the factory acts made it mandatory to market only 'Findon haddocks' that had been smoked in modern fish-houses under strictly controlled hygenic rules, and so no 'finnan haddies' have been made in the cottages of Findon for close on a century. Instead a fish-farming enterprise has been set up, but is not yet in full operation.

Beyond Cove the Kincardineshire coast runs to Gregness, Altens and the Bay of Nigg, now within the city of Aberdeen. Under local government reform a much larger slice of Kincardine came within the orbit of the Aberdeen City District—though not without intense local protest, for the three parishes of Nigg, Banchory-Devenick and Maryculter, in the north-eastern tip of the county, petitioned the Government to be included with the rest of Kincardine in the Kincardine and Deeside second-tier authority.

The last two parishes won their case. But Nigg went to the city. The result is the vast new industrial and residential estate at Altens, entirely a post-oil boom development. Even the city dwellers, however, can be glad that Banchory-Devenick and Maryculter remain a lovely wedge of country close to town.

VIII

DON, BOGIE, YTHAN AND UGIE

Ae mile o' Don's worth twa o' Dee
Except for salmon, stone and tree.

THE great undulating shelf of land stretching north from the Dee
to the Moray Firth—a distance of over 40 miles as the crow
flies—is traversed by three eastward-flowing rivers, the Don, the
Ythan and the Ugie, and one which flows northward to join the
Deveron, the Bogie.

By them we can define the five territorial divisions of Aberdeenshire: Mar, the semi-mountainous region between the Don
and Dee; Formartine, the relatively flat easternmost province
between the lower Don and the Ythan; Garioch, sometimes called
the 'meal girnal of Aberdeenshire' in the basin of the Don's most
important north-bank tributaries, the Urie and the Gadie;
Strathbogie, the fertile vale of that stream—and Buchan, the wide
hummocky plain which lies north of the Ythan and east of the
Deveron and runs to the 'outermost edge' of the county at
Kinnaird Head and Buchan-ness.

To a people conditioned to counting wealth in good farming
land, as well as in industrial potential, the Don is a river of far
greater consequence than the Dee. Beauty is in the eye of the
beholder, and I know many who will say that it is also the loveliest
of the two rivers. Eighty miles long and draining a basin of 515
square miles, its uppermost reaches are in rather bleak moorland,
but it soon confines itself in a very beautiful glen in which it
twists and turns, presenting a succession of inviting vistas.

Let us for a change explore it from the top end which can be
easily reached from Crathie on Deeside by A939, the spectacular
old military road via Gairnshiel (mentioned in Chapter V). This
crosses the watershed between Dee and Don at a height of 1,738
feet and descends into the upper Don valley at Colnabaichin.
Turn left here for Corgarff and Cock Bridge, the last hamlet in

The Victoria and Albert Arch at Fettercairn

Pargetted ceiling and sculptured overmantel at Muchalls Castle

the valley, from which A939 suddenly ascends at a frighteningly steep gradient to cross over into Banffshire by the Lecht Pass (often blocked in winter) and with a mountain-top landscape as bleak as the moon. From this terrifying brae one looks back at Corgarff Castle, a stronghold as stern and forbidding as the landscape it centres.

This tall, stark keep-tower, built before 1550, was the scene in 1571 of the burning of the Forbes laird's wife, family and servants by Captain Ker acting on behalf of Sir Adam Gordon of Auchindoun, which is the subject of the ballad "Edom o' Gordon" and of the modern verse play *Towie Castle* by Gordon Bottomley. We shall pass the site of Towie Castle lower down the valley, but at the time of the atrocity it had not yet been built, so here it was that the twenty-seven victims of the Forbes-Gordon feud met their fiery doom.

All the pathos of senseless carnage is in the ballad's image of the daughter of the house who attempted to escape from the blazing castle wrapped in a pair of sheets:

> They row'd her in a pair o' sheets
> And tow'd her owre the wa',
> But on the point o' Edom's spear
> She gat a deadly fa'.
>
> O bonny, bonny was her mouth
> An' cherry were her cheeks,
> And clear, clear was her yellow hair
> Whereon the reid bluid dreeps.
>
> Then wi' his spear he turned her owre;
> O gin her face was wan!
> He said: "You are the first that e'er
> I wist alive again."

The old keep was restored by the Earl of Mar, gave shelter to the Marquess of Montrose in 1645, and was burned again by the Jacobites in 1689. It was commandeered by the Jacobites as an arms store in 1745, and in the snowy month of March 1746, was occupied by a force of 400 Government soldiers who found the Jacobites had just departed. "The fire was still burning in the hearth and no living creature in the place but a poor cat seeking warmth." The castle was then taken over (like Braemar on Deeside) as a barracks for Hanoverian troops. Low wings were

An aerial view of Stonehaven

added to each gable of the tower, and star-shaped ramparts, which still survive, were built to form an outer curtain wall. It remained garrisoned until 1831 as a watch-post against whisky smugglers. The castle has been finely restored by Sir Edmund Stockdale of Delnadamph and the Department of the Environment.

Strathdon, the upper parish of Donside, 20 miles long, is really a misnomer. It is not a strath in the usual sense of the word but a closely-walled winding river valley intersected by the five large glens of the Deskry, the Nochty, the Carvie, the Ernan and the Comrie and many more defiles of smaller tributary burns. The Lonach Hill, the two lower spurs of which project deeply into the valley just west of Inverernan, forms a decisive landmark cutting the Strath in two. In the upper half, between Lonach Hill and Cock Bridge there are comparatively few plantations, but the lower half is richly wooded.

The Lonach gives its name to the Lonach Gathering, held in August near Bellabeg in the lower half of the parish. To this event the Lonach Highlanders still march from Inverernan, providing the kind of spectacle which has vanished from Braemar. Perhaps the loveliest antiquity in the parish is the graceful stone bridge of Poldullie over the Don with a single arch of 70 feet span built in 1715 by John Forbes of Inverernan, who died at Carlisle in the following year—one of the victims of the 1715 Rebellion.

At Bellabeg, where the Nochty joins the Don, is the Doune of Invernochty, a great grassy mound which was the Earl of Mar's motte and bailey castle in the twelfth century before the building of Kildrummy Castle. Here too is the cathedral-like parish church of Strathdon, built in 1851, and recently restored after a defect in the roof drains had resulted in a dangerous cracking of the fabric. A mile or two above Bellabeg is Candacraig House, a composite structure with two round towers, which was finely restored after a fire in 1955.

To the east and north of Strathdon lie the parishes of Towie and Glenbuchat. Towie Castle, a small tower house on the L-plan dating from 1618 has recently been demolished, but Glenbuchat Castle, on a high cape of land at the junction of the glen with the Don valley is under the care of the Department of the Environment and its 'castle park' was acquired by the Deeside Field Club.

It is a Z-plan tower house built by John Gordon of Cairnburrow and his second wife Helen Carnegie in 1590. Over the entrance, with their names and the date appears the motto: "Nothing on earth remains bot fame."

An unusual feature of Glenbuchat Castle is that trompes, or bold squinch arches, are used to carry the two stair turrets instead of the usual corbelling. This device was given the name 'trompe', because of its resemblance to the mouth of a trumpet, by the French architect Philibert de L'Orme in a book published in 1567.

The last Gordon laird of Glenbuchat is known to history as 'Old Glenbucket of the '45'. It is told of George II that during the Jacobite march to Derby he had nightmares from which he awoke screaming, "De great Glenbogget is coming!" John Gordon was 68 when the rising started, but he raised a little army of several hundred men and flung himself into the fray. At Culloden he was in the second line of Prince Charlie's army. After terrible privations as a hunted rebel he escaped to Norway with a price of £1,000 on his head. He died in poverty at Boulogne four years later.

Glenbuchat, one of the most drastically depopulated areas in Scotland, is well worth a visit. Some miles up the glen is the old parish church, disused since 1947, but taken over for preservation as an ancient monument by the county council. It dates from the early eighteenth century and in its spartan simplicity is a model of the old-time Scots parish kirk of the period.

At Bridge of Buchat we are exactly 40 miles west of Aberdeen. For another 3 miles eastward the Donside road hugs the north bank of the river along a close, well-wooded reach, passing the entrance to Glenkindie. Then it leaves the river, and, crossing rolling hills with Glaschul (1,178 feet), and the Peel of Fichlie, another famous motte, on the right, it enters the Den of Kildrummy leading to the castle (described in Chapter II) and the mild and fertile Old Red Sandstone basin which gave it such strategic significance. Besides the ruined castle, now so well cared for by the Department of the Environment, the whole area is worth study. In 1901 a new 'castle' was completed on the far side of the Back Den to the north of the ruin. This is now a hotel, and the defile of the Back Den was converted into a beautiful rock and water garden spanned by what is virtually a replica of the medieval Brig o' Balgownie at Aberdeen. A little to the north-east on a mound near the thirty-fourth milestone are the ruins of the old Kirk of Kildrummy with an Elphinstone Aisle and Easter Sepulchure, and the present church—an oddly shaped building of 1805—at its foot. Not far away are several examples of underground 'Pict's houses'.

Another couple of miles brings us to Toll of Mossat where A97 strikes north for 15 miles to Huntly, the centre and 'capital' of Strathbogie. This road passes through the Rhynie-Lumsden Gap, a passage through the hills formed by the weathering of the softer Old Red Sandstone rock. To the west of it lies the wild and desolate plateau of the Cabrach, guarded by the often snow-capped peak of The Buck (2,368 feet), to the east the lesser ridge of the Correen Hills. Barely 2 miles from Mossat, at a height of 726 feet, this road is straddled by the village of Lumsden, con-jured out of a barren moor in 1825 by a local laird, Harry Leith Lumsden of Clova, and centred by a pleasant village green. Beyond Lumsden the road continues to rise until, just over the watershed, it meets the Burn of Craig, the headwater of the Bogie. One of the two roads which traverse the Cabrach to Dufftown in Banffshire ascends the Den of Craig at this point, passing on the left the secluded ruins of the medieval Church of St Mary of Auchindoir. Probably contemporaneous with the building of Kildrummy Castle in the thirteenth century, it is in the Transitional or Early First Pointed Gothic and has a fine door in the south wall with double arch and bold First Pointed moulding.

At the summit of the Den of Craig, with the stream running below in a lovely wooded defile, stands Craig Castle (briefly referred to in Chapter II). Built by the Gordons of Craig in the second half of the sixteenth century, this L-plan tower-house presents to first view a forbidding cliff-like block of masonry with tiny windows and a battery of fierce gunloops; but when one enters the courtyard flanked by wings of later date one finds much armorial splendour. There is a great hall with a pipers' gallery, ribbed vaulting with sculptured corbel caps and sacred symbolism which identifies this house as one of a group built by Catholic lairds who were involved in the Earls' Rebellion of 1594. To the left of the tower-house is a spectacular gateway of rusticated ashlar work dating from 1726. The modern wings of the castle are still inhabited.

Returning now to the A97 road, one follows the Bogie to the village of Rhynie, the square of which is a spacious village green dominated by the tower of the parish church. Rhynie (population 363) has a history going back to the seventeenth century and was defiantly Jacobite in 1745. To the north of the village rises the

massive cone of Tap o' Noth on whose summit is the second
highest hill fort in Scotland, at an altitude of 1,851 feet.

Druminnor Castle, a couple of miles to the east of Rhynie on
the road to Clatt, was briefly described in Chapter II. Like Craig,
it is also still inhabited, and it is open to the public on Sunday
afternoons, when the famous Happy Room, so called because of
an inscription in fifteenth-century characters attributed to James II
of Scotland, and many other intriguing features, may be examined.

North of Rhynie the hills gradually open out into the Bogie's
widening strath, and at Gartly the A97 road is joined by A979
coming from the east. Diverging 2 miles along this road one may
see Leith Hall, near Kennethmont, another notable show-place,
now administered by the National Trust for Scotland.

This is simply an interesting old family house, but one that has
a peculiar charm. It is approached by a long wooded avenue and
is a mansion of many periods forming four sides of a square with
a central courtyard. The original nucleus, a rectangular tower-
house with twin turrets at each of the gables, was built around
1650 by James Leith. Square pavilions at the corners and low
buildings forming the basis of the other three wings were added
in the eighteenth century. These wings were then heightened, and
the whole composition was completed early in the present century by the addition of a large entrance hall and castellated porch.

The vicissitudes of the Leith and Leith-Hay families have filled
the house and its grounds with romantic features. The name Hay
was added to that of Leith in 1789 on the death of Andrew Hay of
Rannes, a Jacobite and pardoned 'rebel' whose lands were inherited by the Leiths. They also inherited through this connection
many heirlooms including Bonnie Prince Charlie's etui, a green
shagreen writing case given to Andrew Hay by the Prince in
1746. Andrew Hay's official 'pardon' from George III is also
displayed. In the grounds are the Dule Tree from which male-
factors were hanged in the days of heritable jurisdiction, and the
Horse-shoe Tree, in the trunk of which is embedded a horse shoe
cast from the laird's horse as he rode out to the wars. A Chinese
moon gateway leads to a fine walled garden.

If we now turn north to Huntly we can savour at Huntly Castle
a complete contrast, for here is a ruined 'palace house' on a very
grand scale indeed. Huntly, a 'new town' of the eighteenth
century, lies in a little plain entirely surrounded by hills near the
confluence of the Bogie with the Deveron. Laid out around two

long straight streets meeting at right angles in a pleasant square, it owed its existence to the noble house of Gordon and succeeded the ancient Raws of Strathbogie at the gates of the Castle. From the north end of the Square, Castle Street leads to the Gordon Schools, founded by the last Duchess of Gordon in 1839. Here the road continues under an arch formed by the school buildings and becomes a long wooded drive leading to the stately ruins perched on the high right bank of the Deveron. Behind them is the green mound of a Norman motte and the foundations of an L-plan tower house of the middle ages but the 'palace' with its great round tower and oblong main block was first built about 1449, refashioned in a grander style in the middle of the sixteenth century and given its final form between 1597 and 1602.

The oriel-windowed façade of the main front owes something to the Chateau of Blois, of which, during his temporary exile after the Earls' Rebellion, the first Marquess of Huntly was governor. The smaller or staircase tower at the back of the building carries above the main entry what has been called "the most splendid heraldic sequence in the British Isles". Delicately moulded panels form a series that symbolizes divine and human authority: first the arms of the Marquess and his Lady, then the King and Queen, then the Passion of Christ and the Resurrection and finally the figure of St Michael, the warrior archangel, triumphing over the forces of evil. There is another heraldic marvel in the form of a finely sculptured fireplace in the upper hall.

Modern Huntly (population 3,952) is a most attractive holiday resort and market town with a little useful light industry. All around are flourishing farms, typical of Strathbogie, among them Drumdelgie, celebrated in a well-known 'bothy' ballad depicting the hard life of the farm-labourer in the nineteenth century:

> O, ken ye o' Drumdelgie toon
> Where a' the crack lads go?
> Stra'bogie braw in a' her boun's
> A better canna show.

These same "crack lads" or expert farm workers had no easy time of it.

> At sax o'clock the mill's put on,
> To gi'e us a' straight work:
> It taks four o' us to mak' to her
> Till ye could ring our sark [shirt]. . . .

Today at Drumdelgie the slavery of the threshing mill is over and tractors drive the ploughs. The farm servant has become a mechanic and above the sloping fields the leonine form of the Bin Hill is clad from base to summit by conifers planted by the Forestry Commission.

And so with this glimpse of Strathbogie we turn back now to Toll of Mossat to continue our journey down Donside. One of the loveliest close reaches of the Don, finely wooded and over-looked by the hill of Callievar, lies between Mossat and the Bridge of Alford, where the river emerges into another farming basin, the Vale of Alford, made famous by Charles Murray (1864–1941), the author of *Hamewith*, who raised northeast dialect verse to a level of technical perfection that has never been surpassed.

Murray was far more than a superb practitioner of the Aber-deenshire Doric. His work is a touchstone of the difference between the culture of the North-east and the other regions of Scotland. As Dr Nan Shepherd writes in the latest edition of his collected poems, *Hamewith* (A.U.P.), "It is a record of a way of living already altered and of customs and conventions that have vanished. But it is more than a record, it is an affirma-tion of life". In his two greatest poems, "Dockens afore his Peers" and "Fae France", a society is seen in depth. He is com-memorated in the Charles Murray Memorial Park, a fine stretch of natural heathland west of the village of Alford. From there one has a view of the noblest Donside landmark, the Mither Tap of Bennachie.

> Syne on the Mither Tap sae far
>   Wind-cairdit clouds drift by abeen,
> An' wast ower Keig stands Callievar
>   Wi' a' the warl' to me, atween.
> There's braver mountains ower the sea,
>   An' fairer haughs I've kent, but still
> The Vale o' Alford! Bennachie!
>   Yon is the Howe, an' this the Hill!

The scene of a battle on 2nd July 1645, at the height of the Marquess of Montrose's wonderful summer campaign in aid of the otherwise failing cause of Charles I, Alford played a notable part in the farming revolution at the end of the eighteenth cen-tury, and by the time the railway had come in 1859 the hill of Callievar was cultivated up to 950 of its 1480 feet. The railway has gone, but the village it created has continued to expand. South of the village is the recently restored sixteenth-century tower-house of Balfluig. The old parish church of the original Kirkton, a mile and a half west of the present village, has interesting antiquities, while at Montgarrie on the north bank of the Don is another village with an old meal mill.

Alford is just 25 miles west of Aberdeen, to which A944, the most direct road, runs some distance south of the Don through the parishes of Tough, Cluny, Echt and Skene, while a choice of other roads follows the river more closely through the parishes of Tullynessle, Keig, Monymusk, Kemnay and Kintore.

In Tullynessle, north of Montgarrie, is the ruined Z-plan castle of Terpersie, built by William Gordon in 1561. George Gordon the fifth and last laird fought at Culloden for Prince Charles. He was captured in the castle while hiding from the redcoats, after being inadvertently identified by his own children, and executed at Carlisle for his part in the '45.

Keig, to the east of this, is one of the loveliest parishes on Donside, its low-lying half forming the north-eastern angle of the Vale of Alford, while in the upland portion a road snakes in a succession of spectacular curves through the pass known as My Lord's Throat, in honour of the Premier Baron of Scotland, Lord Forbes, whose ancestral seat, Putachie, now called Castle Forbes, stands on the extreme south-western spur of Bennachie, between the road and river. The present castle is modern, having been built to designs by Archibald Simpson in 1815–21.

As it flows east, the Don, emerging from the narrow wooded gorge of My Lord's Throat, spreads itself out in graceful loops over a fertile haugh extending eastward and northward through the parish of Monymusk to Kemnay and Inverurie. Year by year more visitors seek out the 800-years-old parish church of Monymusk in its charming old-world village. When they have seen this they like to go a little farther and savour the mature beauty of Old Paradise woods, planted over two centuries ago by Sir Archibald Grant, a famous 'improver'.

The only Norman church in Aberdeenshire, the Kirk of St Mary of Monymusk was built about 1170 and finely restored in 1929. It consists of a great west tower of red granite but with dressed masonry of sandstone from Kildrummy, a lofty nave and a tiny chancel. The original Culdee monks of Monymusk were replaced in the thirteenth century by a priory of Augustinian canons. At the Reformation part of the priory buildings were incorporated in a castle built by the Forbeses and this in turn, with alterations and additions, became the Monymusk House of today. Here for many years reposed the Monymusk Reliquary or Brecbannoch, now in the Scottish National Museum, a casket containing relics of St Columba which were carried 'before the host' when the armies of the early Scottish kings went into battle.

Now in the parish church is Monymusk Stone, a Pictish sculptured symbol stone dating from around A.D. 800. The outstanding feature of the house is the Great Hall with a heraldic display above the fireplace.

Monymusk's other castle, the sixteenth-century tower-house of Pitfichie is in the course of complete restoration. To the south of Monymusk the parish of Cluny has three castles of considerable interest. One of these, Tillycairn, an L-plan structure dating from 1548 is also in ruin. Massive boulders compose the lower part of the building, while above are richly corbelled cylindrical turrets, crow-stepped gables, tall coped chimneys and a bold embattled parapet.

Between Monymusk and the village of Sauchen on A944 are Cluny Castle and Castle Fraser. The Cluny Castle of today, built for John Gordon of Cluny, fourth of the present dynasty of lairds, between 1836 and 1840, with splendid granite ashlar facing, is one of the best examples of the baronial style of the Victorian Gothic revival, but it conceals within it the relics of ‹ far more picturesque structure—one of the Z-plan masterpieces of I. Bell of Midmar, built between 1600 and 1604. Drawings which survive show it to have been flanked by huge round towers with cap-houses and a fantastic array of corbelled turrets.

It was no doubt this nonpareil among castles which induced the Gordons' near neighbours, the Frasers of Castle Fraser, to call in I. Bell to complete for them the stately Z-plan castle begun for them some years before by Thomas Leiper. To the pre-existing Michael Tower (so-called from a former laird, Michael Fraser) Bell, between 1605 and 1617, added a full storey and a garret, to the round tower at the opposite angle of the building he added three storeys and he also heightened the main block. On the north wall of this block he placed a massive armorial frontispiece carved in deep-red freestone and bearing the Royal Arms above those of the Frasers, while inset at the base on a modest tablet he left the inscription "I. Bell 1617". The finished result is splendid in the extreme. In the eighteenth century it was celebrated in the poem "Don":

> Cast your eyes
> On FRASER'S glorious pile which southward lies,
> Whose fame, whose structure is by none excelled,
> That in our northern climes are yet beheld.
> The sumptuous frontispiece on the north side
> Shines with gilt ornaments of Scythian pride.
> You'll own the fabric raised with skill and art,
> Magnificently built, excels in every part. . . .

The parish of Kemnay has been much battered about by nature and by man. The Ice Age left behind on it the 'kame' or 'kem', the gravelly ridge which gives it its name, and on which the higher part of the village stands, and man has torn a great gash on the flank of the nearby Hill of Paradise to extract Kemnay granite, that magnificent silver-grey stone, which has a light tinge of brown caused by the tints of felspar and contains both black and white mica. Between 1831 and 1900 the production of this building material raised the population of the parish from 616 to nearly 3,000. Today it has sunk back to 1,384. The granite itself is no longer worked, but Kemnay produces instead a synthetic material called Fyfestone, to which the granite dust, available in vast quantities, gives a sparkle and gleam that is much in demand for the facing of buildings. Kemnay village is one of the most pleasing residential centres in the valley and looks out over the Don to a lovely mountain view centred by Bennachie. Kemnay House is an old manor dating from the seventeenth century.

Below Kemnay Don now flows north and east for 4 miles through pleasant wooded defiles to its rendezvous with the Urie at Inverurie, the 'capital' of the Garioch. The historical significance of this ancient royal burgh with its Bass, whereon stood the motte of the Earl of Huntingdon, was mentioned in Chapter II. Today it is a handsome market town of granite with a spacious market place and lovely surroundings. Its present population is 5437 but the pressure for new housing as a result of the North Sea oil boom make it probable that this figure will be doubled in a few years, despite the recent loss of important locomotive works, while its strategic position at the heart of a rich and prosperous farming region, and its existing engineering, papermaking and food processing industries give it great stability.

It stands at the nodal point where the uplands of Mar meet the
open country of northern Aberdeenshire; to the north-west in the
basin of the Urie the Garioch farmlands stretch along the 'back
o' Bennachie' to Insch, under its spectacular hill of Dunnideer,
crowned by an Iron Age fort and the hilltop castle, now a shattered
tower, built for Jocelyn de Balliol around 1260, with the hamlets
of Oyne and Pitcaple between.

Inverurie has its literary associations, the earliest of which is
with Arthur Johnston of Caskieben (1587–1641) the Latin poet
known as 'the Scottish Ovid'. He was born in Caskieben Castle, a
sixteenth-century Z-plan tower-house which still survives as part
of Keith Hall, a splendid Renaissance mansion about a mile east
of the town, built by the first Earl of Kintore in 1690. Then, in the
last century, William Thom the weaver poet settled in Inverurie
during his most productive period and wrote there the verses
which made him for a brief spell a nine days' wonder to literary
London. His best known poem, "The Blind Boy's Pranks", found
a place in Quiller-Couch's *Oxford Book of English Verse*. London
has forgotten Thom, but Inverurie remembers him for lyrics
like "The Wedded Waters":

> Gadie wi' its waters fleet,
> Urie wi' its murmur sweet,
> They hae trysted aye to meet
> Amang the woods o' Logie.

The historic mansion of Logie near Pitcaple (whose castle was
described in Chapter II) is now a country-house hotel. Near here,
too, are castles like Harthill and Westhill, and lovely Lickleyhead,
one of the finest of the Aberdeenshire School, which stands
near Insch at the little hamlet of Premnay. Ruined Leslie Castle
to the north of this is an elaborate Z-plan structure, the last of its
kind, dating from 1660. All this landscape is dominated by the
Bennachie range, and when they feel the pull of home north-east
folk all over the world hum to themselves the lilt—

> O, gin I war whaur Gadie rins,
> Whaur Gadie rins, whaur Gadie rins,
> O, gin I war whaur Gadie rins
> At the back o' Bennachie.

Kintore, some 3 miles south of Inverurie, is largely a ribbon
development on the A96 trunk road, yet it can never forget that

it is an ancient royal burgh. Its graceful Town House was built in the decade from 1737 to 1748 with two quaint external curving flights of stone forestairs and a clock tower with ogival slated roof. The bell in the tower dates from 1702 and originally hung in an oak tree in the parish kirkyard across the way. In this kirkyard is the Elephant Stone, a Pictish symbol stone, while the church itself has a pre-Reformation sacrament house. West of the burgh is the site of a Roman camp and the massive ruin of Hallforest Castle, a keep-tower of the thirteenth century.

At Kintore the Don winds about grassy mounds in a wide valley. On the east side of the river in a secluded vale some 2 miles from the burgh is Balbithan House, an *L*-plan tower house of the seventeenth century which may be visited on application to its owner Mrs M. N. McMurtrie. Balbithan has a peculiar interest and charm due to its special character as a very late example of the genus. It may have been first built as a smaller, more compact tower around 1600 but it was later extended in such a way that it became a tower-house 'spread out'—to such an extent that the limitations of the type are quite transcended. It has angle turrets perched so high on the wallhead that they can no longer serve the usual function of the turret and are purely ornamental. At the re-entrant angle of the *L* there is a stair turret supported on a very tall cone of corbelling which ends on a charming sculptured head.

Below Kintore the river and the main road part company. The road swerves southwards into the Kinellar Basin, a fertile little plain surrounded by low hills, then crosses the southern spur of Tyrebagger Hill into the parish of Newhills now being over-spread by suburbs of Aberdeen. At Clinterty near the village of Blackburn is a school for farm workers. Farther along the road, at Craibstone, is the experimental farm of the North of Scotland College of Agriculture, while near the suburb of Bucksburn is the Rowett Institute for Research on Animal Nutrition.

It was here in the 1920s and 1930s that Lord Boyd Orr initiated the researches that shocked Britain into the realization that a very large number of her people were underfed. Out of them came free milk in schools and the entire fabric of our World War II food policy with all its welfare state implications. Lord Boyd Orr's epoch-making study *Food, Health and Income* was followed by the Rowett Institute's classic series of dietary surveys, which continued into the Second World War and resulted in a food plan based on the nutrition needs of the people, with priority in rationing for mothers and children.

Begun in 1912 with a staff of one, this hive of research has today a staff of over 250, of whom over 100 are scientific officers. Since the end of World War II its sphere of action has been more closely channelled into research on the feeding of livestock rather than of humans, but it still has immense implications for a hungry world.

Let one small example of Rowett research serve to illustrate the immense range of pioneering work that goes on. Pigs were normally slaughtered 185 days after birth to be converted into bacon. But suppose it were possible to rear pigs so free of all the usual diseases, and so efficient in converting food into live weight that they were ready to 'go to market' 30 to 50 days sooner? The Rowett created such a race of 'minimal disease' pigs by means of hysterectomy of the parent sows, which ensured that the baby pigs imbibed no viruses or parasites, either from their mother's milk or by contact with her at birth or after. The foundation stock spent the first fortnight of their lives in incubators. They were then transferred to a normal but disease-free environment and throve exceedingly. Hurdles caused by the first generation of the disease-free pigs having no anti-bodies—which they normally acquire from their mothers—were overcome in subsequent generations born in the usual way.

If we now return to Kintore and follow the Don where it diverges from A96, and runs in great loops to the east hugged by the railway, we may see other significant things. Here the river skirts the parishes of Fintray and Newmachar. On the side road south of the river between Kinaldie and Dyce there is a superb view over the undulating Formartine farmlands with the village of Hatton of Fintray in the foreground. Near here the ancient ruined Church of Dyce, overlooking the gorge of Cothal, has two Pictish sculptured stones built into the east gable.

Dyce where at Aberdeen Airport two helicopter bases keep non-stop contact with the offshore rigs and platforms, has two new industrial estates and forms the tip of a conurbation on the Don from Aberdeen, beginning with Kittybrewster, the city's mart centre, and including Woodside, Bucksburn, Bankhead and Stoneywood. From the gorge of Cothal the Don falls 100 feet over a relatively short distance providing abundant water-power which has been utilized by paper and textile mills for over two hundred

years, while the high land south of the river was exploited for a
series of granite quarries, now worked out.

Dyce has a big bacon factory, a chemical works and a very large
and recent extension to the paper works at Stoneywood. In 1961
its population stood at 1,530 but an increase of 7,500 is predicted
in the Gaskin Report. It is traversed by A947, the main road to
Banff, which diverges from A96 at Bucksburn. Having followed
the Don from its source to its arrival on the outskirts of the city
we may now cross Formartine to the Ythan.

The Ythan estuary is the largest on the Aberdeenshire coast,
yet the river that occupies it is a shrunken giant. Today it is a
mere 40 miles long, in places but a burn meandering among the
reeds—yet a stream that teems with fish to a degree that is
exceptional for its size, a stream that, swollen by the tide, fills a
basin 700 yards across. Prehistory holds the clue to this paradox.
Once the Ythan rolled to meet the Rhine across the plain that is
now the North Sea, replete with the headwaters of the Deveron,
the Bogie, the Shevock and the Urie, each of which now find
another outlet. The estuary it created remains to impress and
delight the visitors who come to Newburgh, many of them to
fish for sea trout. Few of them fail to thrill to the haunting beauty
of this wide, dune-fringed river mouth.

Biologists also make it a mecca, for here is Colterty, the University of Aberdeen's Zoological Field Station, originally a private
bird sanctuary, now equipped with laboratories, lecture rooms
and stores for rings, nets, traps and hides. There is a tiny pier at
Newburgh, though only one cargo vessel, serving a firm of meal
millers, still uses it in place of the schooners and steam vessels
that once frequented the estuary exporting grain and importing
coal, timber, lime and bones.

Across the water on the north bank of the estuary the dunes
pile up to spectacular climax in the little wilderness known as the
Sands of Forvie. Here, buried under the sands is a 'lost' parish,
once good farming land. Dr Johnson marvelled at it in 1773.
The cause of the catastrophe is now well understood. When the
Ythan dwindled in size it left great banks of silt that it was no
longer able to carry beyond the coast. Dunes formed and crept
northwards, over-running the cliffed coastal plateau for several
miles. The process was a gradual one which does not seem to have
reached a critical stage until the end of the Middle Ages, for the
medieval church of Forvie was partially excavated last century

and its pre-Reformation piscina sent to the National Museum of
Antiquities. Then in 1951 Dr Sylvia Landsberg discovered under
the sand the foundations of a village of nineteen circular huts
2,000 years old. The fact seems to be that the original terraced
site was particularly suitable for prehistoric cultivators who grew
barley on the sandy soil. The final overwhelming of Forvie by
sand led to colourful local legend. It was attributed to a curse
uttered by the three daughters of a laird of Forvie unjustly deprived of their heritage:

> If ever maiden's malison
> Did light upon dry land,
> Let naught be found on Forvie's glebes
> But thistle, bent and sand.

Rather more is found, however. The eider duck, the tern and
the grouse nest and innumerable wildfowl settle and breed. The
area is a nature reserve of great beauty and interest. When the
dunes end, great grassy cliffs take over, and one reaches the old
fishing village of Collieston in the parish of Slains, with a pier
and small harbour built in 1894. It is traditionally famed for
'speldins', small fish that are split, salted and dried in the sun. No
speldins are made today and the fishermen have gone, but the
village flourishes with many weekend cottages as a residential
holiday resort. In the eighteenth century Collieston was a hotbed
of smuggling and near the door of the Kirk of Slains, on its
grassy mound to the north of the village, is the grave of Philip
Kennedy, a smuggler who was fatally injured in a scuffle with an
exciseman who was later tried and acquitted of murder in 1798.
A traditional dance, the Lang Reel of Collieston, was danced at
every fisher wedding in the village.

At Collieston we are already in Buchan, but there are features
of inland Formartine which demand notice. The road B9000
running due west of Newburgh will take us to them. In little
more than 5 miles it reaches the village of Pitmedden, just west
of which lies Udny Castle and, on the north side of the road,
Pitmedden House and its Great Garden, one of the show places
maintained by the National Trust for Scotland. The Trust acquired the house and garden from the late Major James Keith,
an expert on farming history, whose memoirs tell of the shaping
of the farmlands he had inherited.

On his own farm of Old Craig in this area there were 8,800

yards of drystone dykes (stone fences), each yard of which contained two or three cartloads of stones collected off the fields by every method from long wooden levers to a portable tripod crane which his father had used for the purpose. One old farmer, describing how he had cleared his land of stones declared: "After a hard day's work, with tired muscles and aching hands I have been unable to enjoy refreshing sleep at night but in a feverish dream repeated the work of the day." Passing through this countryside therefore, one sees green fields that are "a monument to industry comparable only to the slave-built pyramids of Egypt".

But amid this countryside of once-stony fields were the manors of the old lairds. In Chapter III mention was made of the death of 'Bonny John Seton' of Pitmedden in the battle of the Bridge of Dee in 1639. It was his second son Alexander, a Scottish law lord under the title of Lord Pitmedden, who, when he lost the favour of James II and VII, retired to his estate and created the Great Garden, which is entered by a portal bearing the words "FUNDAT 2 MAY 1675". It is contained within a walled square of 475 feet divided in two by a medial wall flanked by pavilions or 'thunder houses' at either end. The eastern half of the square, so excavated as to form a formal garden at a lower level and linked to the western half by a pillared entrance and flights of semi-twin stairs, has now been painstakingly re-created by the Trust on the model of the Charles II garden at Holyroodhouse. It is internally divided into four parterres, one of which consists of a heraldic design based on the Seton coat of arms including the bleeding heart of 'Bonny Sir John'.

Udny Castle to the south was the ancestral seat of the family of Udny of Udny, a line of fourteen Udny lairds dating back to 1426, the last of whom, the late J. H. Udny of Udny, was succeeded by the eleventh Lord Belhaven and Stenton. The keep, a stout rectangular tower 100 feet high, crowned by battlements under a sloping roof and with angle turrets at each of the four corners, was built by three successive lairds and completed in the seventeenth century.

If one pursues B9000 4 miles farther west one comes to the quaint little burgh of Oldmeldrum on A947, the Aberdeen-Banff road, perched on the eastern edge of the Garioch basin with glorious views of Bennachie to the west. Here Barra Castle, a mile and a half to the south-west, Mounie Castle, 3 miles north-west and Meldrum House, now a hotel, are each of interest.

The north wall of Kildrummy Castle seen across the Back Den
The North Sea oil drilling rig Ocean Voyager *berths in Peterhead's vast*
Harbour of Refuge

Barra, an *L*-plan tower-house with massive round towers, and a stair-tower corbelled out to square with a gabled cap-house, bears the dates 1614 and 1618 and received a new wing in 1755 forming a courtyard. Mounie is on the *T*-plan, the main house probably dating from 1590, with a sturdy round tower—also corbelled out to support a cap-house—projecting from the front of the building. This was added about 1637 by Sir Robert Farquhar, Provost of Aberdeen. Built by the Setons and re-acquired by them after Farquhar's day, it houses family portraits and mementoes of Mary Queen of Scots. Meldrum House is a much-altered structure, mainly eighteenth century, but with a medieval core. It lies just north of Oldmeldrum off A947.

Less than a mile north-west of Pitmedden's Great Garden as the crow flies, but a good deal farther by road, is Tolquhon Castle, a handsome ruin under the care of the Department of the Environment. With the exception of the fifteenth-century Preston Tower, Tolquhon, a large quadrangular mansion entered by a gatehouse with two round towers, armorial bearings and quaint figure sculpture, was built between 1584 and 1589 by Thomas Leiper for William Forbes.

This William, a cultured merchant princeling, prepared a stately tomb for himself at the parish kirk of Tarves, 2 miles north of the castle. This, the Tolquhon Aisle, with its portrait statuettes and elaborate decoration, will repay a visit, for Tarves village, centred by a fine square, is a sight in itself.

Little more than a mile north of Tarves, at Raxton, one reaches the main avenue leading to Haddo House, the stately home of the Earls and Marquesses of Aberdeen. In the centre of very lovely wooded grounds, it was built in 1732 to designs by William Adam for the second Earl and is now in the care of the National Trust for Scotland. Queen Victoria visited here in 1857 as the guest of the fourth Earl, her Prime Minister, 'Athenian Aberdeen', who by the end of his life had planted 14 million trees and made vast improvements to his Haddo domain.

In modern times Haddo has achieved a new renown through the Haddo House Choral Society, initiated and conducted by the Marchioness of Aberdeen and Temair. We may consider it in itself a miracle that year by year since 1945, in the heart of rural Formartine, a succession of the masterpieces of world music and drama have been worthily presented by singers and players,

The old Kirk of Gamrie overlooking the village of Gardenstown

A seine-net boat entering the harbour at Macduff

often backed by visiting stars, but drawn overwhelmingly from the native province.

The Haddo estate, much of which is now a publicly-owned countryside park, lies on the south bank of the Ythan. On its north bank, midway between Newburgh and Haddo, is the burgh of Ellon, the population of which shot up from 1455 to 2263 between 1961 and 1971 and is still growing as a commuter satellite of Aberdeen. Yet its church, its square and its castle still stand roughly where they did in the Middle Ages. Its ancient Moot Hill has gone, but Ellon, looking south across the river with its old and new bridges into the sun, is still sheltered from the north by the bold river terrace on which the oldest part of the castle, once the fortalice of Ardgith, has stood for four hundred years. It is now only a fragment, but its situation is superb, for the terrace itself, 190 yards long and 15 yards wide, is upheld by a massive stone retaining wall 18 feet high and the lawn below is nearly 100 yards deep and 90 broad.

Above Ellon the Ythan skirts the Haddo estate below the village of Methlick, while some distance to the north of it is another L-plan castle, the House of Schivas, designed by Thomas Leiper in 1560 for Gilbert Gray, a Catholic laird. In this century it was finely restored by Fenton Wyness for the first Lord Catto of Cairncatto. Yet another Leiper creation in this area is Arnage Castle, 5 miles north of Ellon, a Z-plan structure to which a modern wing has been added.

Upriver from Methlick the Ythan carves its way through the picturesque Braes of Gight, famous as the home of Byron's ancestors, the 'wild' Gordons. Gight Castle, still entire in the days when the poet's father 'Mad Jack Byron', dwelt there with his mother, Catherine Gordon, and gambled away the last of her patrimony, can still be visited. It is a desolate and pitiful ruin— no longer, as it was within living memory, the romantic backdrop to the annual Gight Games, a rural sports meeting at which a highlight was the choosing of the loveliest damsel present to be the Rose of Gight for the year.

Gight Castle, a massive L-plan building, the prototype and first of the four Catholic strongholds of a distinctive type mentioned in Chapter II, was built by the second Gordon laird about 1560. The first laird Sir William had been the third son of George, second Earl of Huntly, by his second wife, Princess Annabella Stuart, daughter of James I of Scotland. The wild Gordons of

Gight—and Byron after them—never forgot this descent from the Scottish kings, but this did not prevent them from high-handed lawlessness, and the story of their dynasty is "crowded with murder and sudden death". Catherine, the poet's mother, was the unlucky thirteenth of this tragic line. In her the old prophecy of Thomas the Rhymer was fulfilled:

> When the herons leave the tree
> The lairds o' Gight shall landless be.

For when she had parted with her last penny to pay her husband's debts the Gight heronry was deserted and the birds crossed the Ythan to settle in Lord Aberdeen's land on the south bank.

Above Gight, the Ythan passes through the lovely vale of Fyvie. Here too there is poetry, beauty and architectural splendour. As the ballad has it:

> There's mony a bonnie lass
> In the Howe o' Auchterless,
> There's mony a bonnie lass in the Garioch, O,
> There's mony a bonnie Jean
> In the toun o' Aiberdeen
> But the flower o' them a' is in Fyvie, O.

In the centre of Fyvie village, just behind the market cross, is a large boulder of white quartz called the Buchan Stone. It marks the boundary between the Earldom of Buchan and the Thanage of Formartine. On the farm of Lewes within sight of the village is the Priory Cross erected in 1868 to mark the site of the ancient Priory of St Mary founded in 1179. But Fyvie's grandest sight is the castle itself, still inhabited and in full and fine preservation. Described by Sir Herbert Maxwell as the "crowning glory of Scottish baronial architecture", it has a south front 150 feet long with a full-sized, angle-turreted tower house at each end and an immense gatehouse tower projecting from the centre. In its present form this was the creation of the first Earl of Dunfermline in the opening years of the seventeenth century, but it conceals within its fabric a battlemented, gatehoused castle which probably dates from around 1400.

Sir Harry Preston, the laird of this period, received the lands of Fyvie as a reward for capturing the English knight Sir Ralph Percy at the battle of Otterburn in 1388. As rebuilt by Lord Dunfermline, Fyvie Castle is a building made for peace not war, its old gunloops and battlements covered over, but two mementoes of sterner days remain—both in the gatehouse. One of them is the yett in the vaulted passage a few feet from the outer door. The other is the meurtriere or 'murder hole' in the great arch four storeys high above the entrance—all ready to provide a rude welcome of molten lead to scald the crowns of would-be invaders. A magnificent wheel stair of stately proportions is the chief glory of the interior.

On the rooftop of Fyvie castle is a grotesque stone figure representing Andrew Lammie, the trumpeter of Fyvie, whose ill-fated love for a rural maiden is the theme of the local ballad "Mill o' Tifty's Annie". Annie was a real person, Agnes Smith, daughter of the miller of nearby Tifty, who with his wife and entire family violently opposed the girl's infatuation for the trumpeter. The lovers were finally parted and the poor girl was beaten by her family.

> Her brother strake her wondrous sore,
>   Baith cruel strokes and many
> And brak' her back at the ha' door
>   For likin' Andrew Lammie.

She died of a broken heart as well as a broken body. In Fyvie churchyard there is a monument with the inscription: "Agnes Smith: Tifty's Annie. Erected by public subscription 1859".

The upper reaches of the Ythan above Fyvie are in the Howe of Auchterless, a rather remote rural glen, but near the point where it flows under a bridge on the A947 road is the castle of Towie-Barclay, a truncated tower house close to a farm. Externally this building has been ruined by being docked of its upper storeys, but inside on the first floor is a most remarkable great hall. Built about 1590 Towie-Barclay was the fourth of the 'family' of castles begun by Gight. The great hall consists of a high rib-vaulted chamber in two bays, with ridge and transverse ribs, diagonal ribs with sculptured corbels and heavy pendant bosses. Above the entrance is a small oratory open to the hall and separated from it only by a parapet. Here a priest might have celebrated mass in full sight of the laird and his retainers in the hall below. Adorned as it is by emblems of Catholic piety, Towie-Barclay, despite its deserted state, has been described by Stewart Cruden as "one of the noblest and most imaginative of all the tower-house interiors".

Three miles farther on A947, having traversed the almost imperceptible watershed between the Ythan and Deveron basins, crosses the Idoch and climbs into the Old Red Sandstone burgh of Turriff (population 2,686).

> Choose ye, choose ye, at the Cross o' Turra,
> Either gang to Aiberdeen or Elgin o' Moray.

Here, 34 miles from Aberdeen and nearly 12 from the county town of Banff, one is at the western tip of Buchan on the edge of a plateau as it dips down to the vale of the Deveron. To the farming and peasant folk of northern Aberdeenshire this is something like the centre of the world. Not for nothing do they say, "Turra, Turra, faur sorra idder?" which being interpreted means "Turriff, Turriff, where else, in sorrow's name, would anybody want to go?" Its importance as a market town is emphasized in the opening lines of a famous 'bothy' ballad:

> Fan I gaed doon tae Turra Market,
> Turra Market for to fee,
> I met in wi' a wealthy farmer
> Frae the Barnyards o' Delgatie.

The town is built of red sandstone from Delgatie. The site of a monastery in the Middle Ages, it was also the scene of the first armed clash of the Great Civil War, in the year 1639, when the Royalists surprised and routed the Covenanters in the raid known as the Trot of Turriff.

In Turriff you are liable to hear joking references to 'the Turra Coo'. This was a white dairy cow 'poinded'—i.e. legally confiscated—from the farm of Lendrum because the farmer, Robert Paterson refused to stamp the insurance cards of his employees "unless they asked him to do so". On 9th December 1913 the cow was put up for auction in Turriff Square. The result was a riot by a crowd of nearly one thousand. Eight men were tried but acquitted for lack of evidence. The cow which had been 'liberated' in the mêlée was returned to Lendrum by farmers who had clubbed together to buy it back, and its portrait was painted for posterity. Today Turriff reflects the prosperity of present-day farming and also has some valuable light industry.

To the north-east of Turriff are two more interesting castles, both approached by side roads leading right off A947.

The nearest is Delgatie, built for the Hays of Erroll by the architect of Craig, Gight and Towie-Barclay, around 1570. It towers, crisply white and gleaming, over the green farmlands, the wing of its L-plan still retaining its open bartizan, while inside the house the turnpike stair, with a span of over 5 feet, leads first to the solar with a magnificent groin-vaulted roof in which the ribs sweep up to a central boss bearing the arms of Gilbert Hay, fourth Earl of Erroll, while the ridge ribs rest on four carved human masks. Two of the rooms above this have painted ceilings exploiting a wonderful vein of Renaissance fantasy.

Craigston Castle, a mile or two farther north, was built between 1604 and 1607 by John Urquhart, the Tutor of Cromarty, and has a tall gatehouse tower somewhat resembling that at Fyvie. Features of the house are seventeenth century carved panels in oak depicting kings, prophets, evangelists and the cardinal virtues, while the library in the long gallery at the top of the house has Urquhart family treasures including the *Genealogy* compiled by Sir Thomas Urquhart, translator of Rabelais, the full title of which is *The True Pedigree and Lineal Descent of the Most Ancient and Honourable Family of the Urquharts in the House of Cromarty from the Creation of the World until the Year of God 1652.*

The streams in this area to the east and north-east of Turriff all run west to join the Deveron on the Aberdeenshire-Banff-shire border. The watershed between them and the headwaters of the eastward-flowing Ugie is an irregular line of low hills, treeless and bare but entirely cultivated, seldom reaching over 500 feet in height. Yet this unpromising land, once an almost continuous succession of barren moorland, is dotted with planned villages or 'new towns' of the eighteenth and early nineteenth century, all 'planted' by improving lairds who vied with one another in creating new settlements.

This is the miracle of Buchan, a miracle that was signed and sealed in the years that followed by an immense labour of land reclamation by crofters and small tenant farmers. Some lines from a poem by Flora Garry in the Buchan dialect illustrate what this meant in human toil. It describes the creation of a farm out of wilderness ·

> It wis jist a skelp o' the muckle furth,
> A sklyter o' roch grun
> Fan granfader's fader bruke it in
> Fae the hedder an' the funn.

Granfader sklatit barn and byre,
Brocht water to the closs,
Pat fail-dykes ben the bare brae face
An' a cairt road to the moss.

Bear with me and I will give you a rough translation: "It was just a chunk of the untilled waste, a splinter of rough ground, when grandfather's father broke it in from the heather and the whin. Grandfather slated barn and byre (cow-shed), brought water to the farmyard, put boundary walls across the bare hillside and made a cart-road to the peat-moss for fuel."

All this followed long after the initial 'planting' of the planned villages. Here is a brief list with the dates of their founding: Cuminestown (founded by Joseph Cumine of Auchry in 1763), New Byth (founded by James Urquhart of Byth in 1764), New Pitsligo (founded by Sir William Forbes in 1787), Strichen (founded by Lord Strichen, a law lord friend of Johnson's Boswell, in 1764), Stuartfield (1772), Fetterangus (1772), Mintlaw (1801), Longside (1801) and New Deer (1803).

Generally speaking what the lairds did was to feu out at very modest rents small parcels of land laid out on either side of the village streets—just sufficient for each settler to build himself a small thatched cottage or 'clay bigging', and with a strip of land behind sufficient to grow food for himself and his family and to pasture a cow. It was hoped that the settlers would augment their incomes by growing flax and weaving linen, or by practising other crafts and trades, while the villages themselves would become market centres for the surrounding farmlands. The immense optimism of these days is typified by the case of Lord Strichen's son, who founded a village called New Leeds in the hope that it would one day rival the Yorkshire mill-town. New Leeds survives today as a tiny hamlet on A92, the Aberdeen-Fraserburgh trunk road.

Cuminestown and New Byth lie on the west side of the watershed, both on high ridges of land with fine views over the surrounding country. A little north of New Byth there is an even finer view from the Hill of Fisherie, which, although only 748 feet high, commands on a clear day a glimpse of the hills of Caithness, 100 miles away across the Moray Firth. To the east is Mormond, the only prominent hill in eastern Buchan, to the west Bennachie, with Lochnagar and the Deeside hills beyond. In the year 1851 the fourth Earl of Fife settled a colony of hundreds of homeless and evicted crofters, the victims of the notorious Highland clearances, on the Hill of Fisherie. It was a hard life for them on poor land, but at least they had once more a place of their own and they 'broke in' the heather with a will.

Almost directly east across the watershed from New Byth, which here rises to an altitude of 628 feet, is New Pitsligo, in some ways the most remarkable of the planned villages. In 1787 the site was a desolate slope on the Hill of Turlundie, cut off from the coast to the north by a vast peat moss, roadless and trackless, and the settlers began by digging the peats out of their back gardens, but the founder spent a fortune laying out miles of roads and planting thousands of trees, and the place grew to be the 'largest village in Scotland'. It has declined since then, but still has a population of over 1,200, some of whom are employed in a big bakery concern while others still work on the peat mosses which surround the village and are now 'harvested' by mechanical diggers, exporting peat to distilleries, some of them as far away as Japan! The village was always a stronghold of Scottish Episcopalianism, and its show place is St John's Church, built by New Pitsligo masons one hundred years ago to plans by G. E. Street.

The village is divided by a burn which forms one of the headwaters of the North Water of Ugie. Several miles farther east, at the foot of Mormond Hill, is Strichen (population 967), also on the North Water of Ugie. It flourishes today as a popular residential centre, with at least one small light industry (netmaking) of its own, while the summit of Mormond is crowned by the futuristic-looking towers of a radar station. Mention Mormond to a folk-song enthusiast and he will immediately think of a well-known Buchan ballad which begins:

> As I gaed doon by Strichen toun
> I heard a fair maid mournin'
> And she was makin' sair complaint
> For her true love ne'er returnin':
> "It's Mormond Braes where heather grows,
> Where oftimes I've been cheery,
> It's Mormond Braes where heather grows,
> And it's there I lost my dearie."

On this western brow of Mormond there still stands forth the figure of the White Horse, formed by the cutting of the turf and its infilling with stones of white quartz. Although many times renewed, the figure is attributed to Captain Alexander

Fraser of the Dragoon Guards, Lord Strichen's grandson, as a memorial to his white charger, shot under him on the battle-field. It is 162 feet long. The White Stag of Mormond, on the eastern flank of the Hill, almost an acre in extent, was laid out in 1870 by another local laird, Cordiner of Cortes.

The North Water of Ugie flows some distance south of Mor-mond and passes under A92, the Aberdeen-Fraserburgh road about three-quarters of a mile east of Fetterangus (population 280) now obviously a place in decline, yet the site of an enter-prising firm which makes snow-ploughs and farm implements for home and export markets. It stood on the old turnpike road and is thus becoming a backwater, while Mintlaw, 2 miles farther south on A92 and a short distance north of the South Water of Ugie, is enjoying a development boom, with its old-time village square centred by a huge traffic roundabout, and a population of over 600.

Of the Ugie's two tributary arms, the South Water is by far the more picturesque. West of Mintlaw is Old Deer, a small village which is the original parish centre. The site of the ancient Celtic monastery where the Book of Deer (see Chapter II) was annotated by the monks is believed to have been the knoll known as Tap Tillery, within a bend of the South Ugie, where the parish church stands today. The famous Rabbling of Deer on 22nd March, 1711, was a riot caused by the Episcopalian opposi-tion to the induction of the Reverend John Gordon, the Pres-byterian nominee to the charge. The Cistercian Abbey of Deer, founded in 1218, as successor to the Celtic monastery, lies a mile farther west in the lovely treegirt Vale of Deer. Dismantled at the Reformation, its ruins are cared for by the Department of the Environment.

On either side of Old Deer, to north and south, lie two great estates, both richly wooded, Pitfour and Aden. It was the Ferguson lairds of Pitfour who founded Mintlaw, Fetterangus, Longside (to the east, where the two arms of the Ugie at last unite) and New Deer (to the west). Pitfour House—a sort of Buckingham Palace in the heart of Buchan—has long vanished, but the great artificial lake of Pitfour and its boathouse, a perfect miniature replica of the Temple of Theseus at Athens, along with many miles of tree-lined roads in central Buchan, survive to attest the vast transformation these 'improving' landowners wrought in the countryside. Their example was infectious and Stuartfield (population 381) was laid out on the Crichie estate, a mile and a quarter south of Old Deer, by John Burnett and named after Captain John Stuart a warrior of Marlborough's campaigns.

When the railway came to Buchan in 1866 it added yet another village to this quiet rural area at Maud, 3 miles west of Old Deer. Because the site was chosen as a junction of lines branching north and east to Fraserburgh and Peterhead, Maud rapidly developed as a market centre, and, although the railway is now defunct, Maud with its cattle mart is still a lively place.

If, now, we move north along the coast from Collieston, we may complete the spectrum of Buchan by adding to it the distinctive contribution of the fisherfolk. On a lonely promontory a little north of that quaint village stands the Old Castle of Slains, today but a shattered tower, companioned by a modern Swedish-type timber holiday lodge built by the Countess of Erroll on the rock where her ancestors held feudal sway in the Middle Ages. Beside it, pointing seaward, are salvaged cannon from *Santa Caterina*, a Spanish galleon, wrecked in the inlet known as St Catherine's Dubb while bringing 'sinews of war' to succour the Catholic Lords' Rebellion in the last decade of the sixteenth century.

As a sequel to the rebellion the old castle was destroyed by dynamite supplied to King James VI by the burgh of Aberdeen. Francis Hay, the ninth Earl of Erroll, then fled into exile in France, and when he returned, pardoned, in 1597, he built a new castle, also on a clifftop, at Bowness on the northern edge of the Bay of Cruden, the next parish to the north. In the subsequent centuries Oldcastle of Slains became a tiny fishing haven.

Two miles north along this rocky coast, punctuated by many caves, we reach Whinnyfold, another such fisher-toun, this time perched on the grassy top of a massive promontory overlooking the deadly fangs of rock called the Skares, or Scaurs, of Cruden. Beyond them for a mile and a half, in a great open semi-circle, stretch the superb sands of the Bay of Cruden, ending in the tiny harbour of Port Erroll and the holiday-resort called Cruden Bay.

Cruden is a parish full of surprises. A couple of miles inland on the upper reaches of the Water of Cruden lies Hatton, a thriving industrial village, 'made' by a bakery founded eighty years ago by Forbes Simmers, when he moved into the village with £60 and a borrowed horse. It now employs over two hundred workpeople. Cruden Bay itself is famous for its golf course, though not so famous as it was at the end of last century when (in 1899) the Great North of Scotland Railway Company built a hotel of 140 rooms which for a time attracted an opulent clientele including numerous millionaires. Both the railway and the hotel have vanished, but at the south end of the golf course is now the landfall of BP's North Sea oil pipeline from the Forties Field over 100 miles offshore. Population is expected to escalate from 600 to around 1734.

Following the Battle of Cruden in 1012 between the Scots and invading Norse a Chapel of St Olav was founded, and near this spot at the Kirk of Cruden in July 1914 Kommander Trygve Gran asked God's blessing on the first flight across the North Sea, from Cruden Bay to Norway. He has many times returned, and in the church today, between the flags of Norway and Scotland, there hangs a model of his plane made by the pupils of Hatton and Port Erroll schools.

Port Erroll, the harbour and fishing quarter of Cruden Bay, is a planned village founded by the nineteenth Earl of Erroll early in the nineteenth century. The local authority seeks to preserve its character and has designated it a conservation area. The new castle of Slains, many times rebuilt over three centuries, is now, like the old castle, a ruin. It overlooks Port Erroll from the north and well repays a visit. It entertained Johnson and Boswell in 1773.

It was from the new castle of Slains that Johnson and Boswell set out on their famous expedition to the Bullers o' Buchan, a mile to the north. This "circular basin of large extent, surrounded with tremendous rocks", as Boswell called it, inspired both the visitors with fascinated dread. Johnson poked his way round the "monstrous cauldron", then insisted on sailing into it by boat through the "high arch in the rock which the tempest has driven out". Today the Bullers (French—*bouilloire*), is also the site of a hamlet to which its residents, like those at Whinnyfold, have stubbornly clung, despite difficulties of water supply and sewage.

The next sea-toun on the north is Longhaven, a tiny hamlet, once also a fisher haven, flanked by rocks which have become a favourite practice-ground for rock climbers, and another mile and a half brings us to Boddam, now rapidly expanding as a dormitory suburb of Peterhead and site of a big new power station under construction. Linked by a bridge with the promontory of Buchan-ness, its old fisher-toun has also been designated for conservation. The Buchan-ness Lighthouse, one of the most spectacular in the north, was built in 1827–8 after a period when there were twenty-three wrecks in four years on this perfidious coast. A malicious little rhyme commemorates the 'salvage scramble' apt to occur after a shipwreck:

> The Anna it came round the coast
> And all the hands on it were lost,
> Except the monkey that climbed the post,
> And the Boddamers hanged the monkey, O!

The explanation of this heartless act is that the rewards of salvage could only be claimed if "no living thing" remained on the shipwreck.

From the lantern balcony at the top of Buchan-ness Lighthouse one has a view of the coast curving north to the huge Harbour of Refuge and the gleaming red granite houses of Peterhead (population 14,160), the largest town in the county after Aberdeen. Now in the throes of intense industrial boom as oil-rig supply bases are developed both in the Harbour of Refuge and at Keith Inch, population is expected to reach 20,000 by 1981. Founded by the Keiths, Earls Marischal, in 1593, the town suffered when in 1715 the last Earl and his brother joined the Jacobites and were dispossessed and exiled.

In exile the true qualities of the last of the Keiths became apparent. The last Earl became the trusted adviser of Frederick the Great of Prussia, and his brother James, a brilliant field marshal, died in Frederick's service at the Battle of Hochkirchen. In 1868 a statue of the Field Marshal, long given a place of honour in Berlin, was presented to Peterhead by William I of Prussia, and now stands in Broad Street in the centre of the town. Near it is the Peterhead Town House designed by John Baxter and dating from 1788.

The most important feature of the town is the harbour, formed by a succession of basins between the mainland and the island of Keith Inch, now linked to the town by its piers. In the latter half of the eighteenth century Peterhead—almost incredibly—became a popular spa through the supposed medicinal qualities of its Wine Well. In the second decade of the nineteenth century it developed a sizeable whaling industry, and in 1820 fifteen whalers were operating. This was followed by the spectacular build-up of herring fishing, reaching its peak in 1907 when 291,713 crans were landed from 420 boats. Fishing is still the major industry,

and is at present enjoying a major boom with landings in some
months higher than those at Aberdeen. Shareholders in family
boats often make big earnings from fortunate voyages. Fish and
food processing is also important.

Keith Inch is the most easterly point of northern Scotland.
North of it the coast curves very gradually north-north-west
through the parishes of St Fergus (where the British Gas Council
pipelines from the Brent and Ninian fields make landfall and
there are massive installations), Crimond and Lonmay.

The river Ugie enters the sea just north of Peterhead and here
are two ruined castles—Ravenscraig and Inverugie, the latter
deserted since the downfall of the Keiths, in fulfilment of Thomas
the Rhymer's prophecy:

> Inverugie by the sea,
> Lordless shall thy landis be;
> Underneath thy cauld hearth-stane,
> The tod shall bring her bairnies hame.

The parish of Crimond gives its name to a famous psalm-tune
to which the metrical version of the twenty-third Psalm was
sung at the Queen's Coronation. On the sea coast is Rattray Head
Lighthouse, built in 1895 to warn shipping of the deadly Rattray
Briggs reef. Before that mariners had to be content with the
cautionary couplet:

> Keep Mormond Hill a handspike high
> And Rattray Briggs ye'll ne'er come nigh.

The desolate dune-fringed Loch of Strathbeg here was once
a bay of the open sea, and near its southern shore was the royal
burgh of Rattray and a castle and small seaport. According to the
Old Statistical Account, in the year 1720 "a furious east wind in a
single night blew a sandhill which had stood near the Castle Hill
into the channel connecting the Loch of Strathbeg with the open
sea. . . . So sudden and destructive had been the storm that a small
ship which was in the harbour discharging slates was trapped inside
and gradually went to pieces."

The Peterhead-Fraserburgh road, A952, runs well to the west
of the loch, but B9003 runs north-east from it to St Combs, the
first of three remarkable fishing villages that lie on this coast
between Rattray Head and Fraserburgh. Across the sands of
Whitelinks Bay from St Combs are the twin communities of

Inverallochy and Cairnbulg, with their low granite cottages standing gable-end to the sea in a continuous line. The two places are now so expanded that they have grown into a single conurbation, divided only by a tiny stream, now imprisoned in a culvert. Yet they cling passionately to their separate identity, and for this reason the large signposts on either side of the approach road are very necessary—since each village has its own separate Main Street, Mid Street and Shore Street.

Each village holds an important Temperance Walk in which the entire community circumambulates the bounds, led by a fishermen's flute band—Inverallochy on Christmas Day, Cairnbulg on New Year's Day and St Combs on Aul 'Eel (Old Yule), 5th January, each year.

Nearby are Inverallochy Castle, a desolate ruin, and Cairnbulg Castle, now restored and the home of the Frasers of Philorth whose ancestors founded Fraserburgh in the sixteenth and early seventeenth century. Now represented by Baroness Saltoun, who is the wife of Captain Alexander Ramsay of Mar, the Frasers came to the area in 1375, when Sir Alexander Fraser married Joanna, daughter of the Earl of Ross and acquired the lands of Philorth. An old rhyme has it that

> While a cock crows in the north
> There'll be a Fraser in Philorth.

However, they had to part with the old castle, then the Manor Place of Philorth, in 1615, to defray the expenses incurred in founding Fraserburgh, and it did not come back into the family until the late Lord Saltoun re-acquired it.

The wide sweep of Fraserburgh Bay lies between Cairnbulg and the burgh which the Frasers founded, and at the centre of it stands another castle, the Castle of Kinnaird, now Kinnaird's Head Lighthouse, dominating the outer tip of Fraserburgh Harbour. Kinnaird Castle was built by Sir Alexander Fraser, eighth of Philorth, in 1570, to watch over the infant burgh which had been founded by charter from Mary Queen of Scots, given to his grandfather. Only the central tower, on a rectangular plan, but much altered, of the castle of 1570 remains. Four floors of the original house survive, but the fifth was removed in 1787 to make way for the lantern-chamber of the lighthouse.

On a shelf of rock between the lighthouse and the sea is a mysterious structure called the Wine Tower. The upper vault of this appears to have been a chapel and it is evidently a sixteenth-century watch tower.

The austerities of Fraserburgh have inspired much poetry, from J. C. Milne's dialect eulogy:

> O Tam, gie me auld Faithlie toon
> Whaur trees are scrunts for miles aroon
> And nae a burn wad slake or droon
> A drunken miller;
> But sands and bents that wear a croon
> O' gowd and siller

to George Bruce's salty praises:

> This is the outermost edge of Buchan.
> Inland the seabirds range,
> The tree's leaf has salt upon it,
> The tree turns to the low stone wall,
> And here a promontory rises towards Norway,
> Irregular to the top of thin grey grass
> Where the spindrift in storm lays its beads.

Fantastic as it may seem, Fraserburgh was for a brief period the seat of a university, built in 1595 with a grant from the Scottish Parliament; but unfortunately its first principal was flung into jail for defying the ecclesiastical policy of James I and VI, and in his absence it decayed and died. The modern town is an attractive place with a sandy lido and a population of over 10,000, sustained by its herring and white fishing industry, food processing plants and a machine-tool factory employing about one thousand workers.

To the west of the town the fishing hamlet of Broadsea leads on to the Phingask Shore, a sandy rock-strewn bay terminated by the village of Sandhaven, with a large deserted harbour, and this built-up area, which has a useful boat-building yard, merges into the older village of Pittulie.

Still farther west is the ancient burgh of Rosehearty, now mainly a dormitory suburb of Fraserburgh, with a swimming pool in its otherwise deserted harbour. The burgh was founded by charter granted to Alexander, second Lord Forbes of Pitsligo, in 1684, and the most interesting antiquities in the vicinity are those associated with his family. These all lie on the hilly road immediately to the south of the town. First there is the ruin of Pitsligo Castle, the old tower of which was built in 1424 by Sir William Forbes. The great vault of its banqueting hall on the first floor is now exposed to view but above this there was a further storey "containing the sleeping apartment for the whole family which had in it 24 beds".

The last Lord Pitsligo, born in 1678, became a Jacobite hero. He opposed the Act of Union in 1707, fought in the 1715 Rebellion, and in 1745, when he might have been excused on the grounds of age, led a band of volunteer cavalry in Prince Charlie's army, being described by Murray of Broughton as "deservedly the most popular man in the country". After Culloden he led for sixteen years the life of a pitiful fugitive, dying at the age of 84, when he was buried in the family vault in the Kirk of Pitsligo, still close to the burgh of Rosehearty where he was adored by everybody.

The old and new Kirks of Pitsligo stand together a little higher up on the road above the castle. The belfry in the ruin of the old church (still visible) was built of carved stones imported from Holland in 1631. The story goes that when they arrived the first Lord Forbes of Pitsligo was ill in bed, but had the stones brought into his bedroom and assembled in his presence. The present kirk was built in 1890, but into it were transferred from the old building a remarkable series of carved panels from the Pitsligo pew—one of the finest examples of Jacobean wood carving in Scotland.

West of Rosehearty we pass from the parish of Pitsligo to the parish of Aberdour and complete our circuit of Aberdeenshire in a blaze of coastal spectacle. Part of this rocky coast is used as a bombing range for navy planes, but beyond this lies one of the most romantic and interesting corners of the Moray Firth. This is reached by the road B9031 to New Aberdour, another of the planned villages of Buchan, laid out by William Gordon in 1798.

There is nothing of special interest here, but a mile to the north on the sea coast of Aberdour Bay is St Drostan's Well, said to be the very spot where this Pictish saint landed from Caithness to Christianize Buchan and eventually to found the Monastery of Deer. Some 150 yards inland from the well, on the right bank of the Dour Burn which gives the parish its name, on a green saddle jutting into the picturesque red sandstone gorge of the stream, stands the ruined medieval parish church.

On the headland to the east of the Bay stands a great Iron Age

The market cross, town steeple and Town House of Banff seen through the Biggar Memorial Fountain

fort dating from A.D. 300, within which the medieval stone castle of Dundarg was afterwards built. On the spine of the promontory Dr Douglas Simpson and Dr F. T. Wainwright conducted excavations unearthing the foundations of a chapel—perhaps a link with St Drostan himself. The medieval castle was originally built in the thirteenth century by the Comyn Earl of Buchan, then laid low by his arch-enemy Robert the Bruce. Thirty years later it was rebuilt in part by Henry de Beaumont, the English-sponsored quisling earl of Buchan, and again slighted by the Scottish Regent, Sir Andrew de Moray. Two centuries later it was re-fortified as a coastal defence in the War of the Rough Wooing. All lies in picturesque ruin now—but a new 'castle' was built on the landward side of the moat.

On the western side of Aberdour Bay a range of cliffs, 300 feet high and riddled with many caves, leads past Strahangles Point and Pennan Head to the village of Pennan, the most picturesque fishing village in the county. The landward approach is by B9031, which suddenly loops down between high green hills to reveal the long row of red sandstone cottages and the tiny pier, concealed to the last moment by a huge overhanging cliff. Nothing in the Cornish riviera could exceed this for spectacle.

This, the most westerly coastal village in Aberdeenshire, dates from the seventeenth century. It acquired its little harbour in 1845 and ten years later there was a fleet of forty boats. Today many of its menfolk serve in fishing fleets off Iceland, off Norway and on the West Coast.

Detail from the elaborate carved Jacobean woodwork in the Parish Kirk of Pitsligo near Rosehearty. It was transferred thither from the Pitsligo Old Church, dating from 1631

IX

THE COUNTY OF BANFF

Banff near the Ocean doth thyself confess
In bulk than Trica or Hypaepe less,
Yet art acknowledged by the neighbouring lands
To be their Regent, and the Boyne commands. . . .

Arthur Johnston

IF they tell you that Banffshire is just a smaller, rougher, poorer edition of Aberdeenshire tacked on to the north-west corner of that county, don't believe it. The County of Banff completes Aberdeen's trio of home counties and glorifies the whole—because it is so different.

This difference is both physical and, yes, spiritual. Physically, the whole county is oriented to the Moray Firth, to which all its rivers run: on the east the quiet, charming and elusive Deveron, a river so shy that it turns away from all towns until it finally surrenders itself to the sea between Banff, the historic county town, and Macduff its modern and commercial twin; on the west the majestic Spey which it shares with Moray, the northern Garden of Scotland.

Perhaps Banffshire can best be defined as a rugged bridge between the austerities of Buchan and the lovely Laich or Lowlands of Moray. Sir Thomas Innes of Learney has pointed out that while in Aberdeen and Elgin there remain, as the result of strenuous efforts, a few old houses, only at Culross in Fife, and Banff in the north, can the tourist and antiquarian see a real olden Scottish town. "Around its sometimes steep but always picturesque streets there are endless quaint but solidly built old houses—not single examples, but in rows."

You reach Banff from the south via A947 after a rather featureless stretch of 11 miles from Turriff. The road curves down from the Buchan plateau to the final sweep of the Deveron—here seen for the first time in the whole journey from Aberdeen—and enters Banff by Banff Bridge, a graceful seven-arched structure, 410 feet long, designed by Smeaton.

The motorist now enters Banff by its Regency south end, a sort of ceremonial introduction. Almost hidden by trees in its parkland to the south is Duff House, that "most ornate of all Georgian baroque mansions" designed for the first Earl of Fife by William Adam. It was built in the years following 1725 and is now being restored by the Department of the Environment.

The public buildings at this end of the town are stately: William Robertson's classical Banff Academy (1838), Collie Lodge like a little Greek temple (1836) and St Mary's Church (1790—though it did not get its fine steeple until 1849). These and the beautiful Trinity and Alvah Church, along with the Fife Arms Hotel (1843) and the Clydesdale Bank, by Archibald Simpson (1836) round off an architectual heritage that is otherwise mainly domestic and of a far earlier period.

The town is built on river terraces at three levels: High Street and Castle Street on top, Low Street half way down and Deveronside alongside the river at the bottom, the three terraces being linked by a series of steep, narrow lanes or streets, sometimes stepped. It has a fragmentary medieval nucleus, a substantial scattering of seventeenth-century structures and whole streets of eighteenth-century houses.

The Banff Castle of today, in Castle Street, was built by Lord Deskford in 1750, but parts of the enceinte wall of its medieval predecessor survive. The two other focal points of the ancient burgh are the Old Kirkyard, with its remnant of the original St Mary's Kirk and the Great Garden south of Low Street, which was the site of a Carmelite Monastery. From the seventeenth century survives No 1 High Shore, with its angle turret and sundial bearing the date 1675. No 5 High Shore, the Market Inn, is the oldest building still in occupation. A stone in the courtyard has the date 1585. In Water Path is Ingleneuk with a pend and charming courtyard dating from 1760. In this street at the Old Manse, now demolished, the Reverend Abernethy Gordon, a kinsman of Byron, entertained the poet as a boy.

Eighteenth-century Banff, the 'Bath of Scotland', was smaller than it is today with a population of 2,860 as against the 3,330 recorded in the 1961 census, but it had a fleet of twenty sailing ships and the seafaring community lived apart in the Seatown, where there are many groups of Georgian houses surviving today.

The local aristocracy lived farther south and there was a

constant routine of gay social events in hunting clubs, card clubs, fortnightly assemblies and picnics. Surviving town mansions of this period include the delightfully idiosyncratic Boyndie House (1740), the more classical Carmelite House (1753) in Low Street and the fine group Nos 1 to 5 High Street, which includes Lord Banff's town house. Artisans' dwellings and shops were equally distinguished. Two characterful groups are on the west side of High Street.

The town steeple with its octagonal sides pierced by oval openings was designed by one of the Adam brothers in 1764 and the severely classical Town House followed in 1796. It is safe to say that far less of historic Banff would have survived if modern industry had not passed the town by. Now, however, it is not being left to chance. Active conservation is pursued by the Banff Preservation Society.

Although Banff has a busy slipway in its otherwise almost deserted harbour quarter, the fishing industry has migrated to the east bank of the Deveron estuary—to the modern burgh of Macduff founded in 1783. Here in the sheltered Moray Firth harbour under the steep green Hill of Doune there is a fleet of thirty-three seine-net boats and the annual value of fish landings exceeds £300,000. Macduff was the darling creation of the second Earl of Fife, who converted a sleepy old fishing village known as Doune into a bustling modern port.

Amid superb rock scenery to the east of Macduff is the Howe of Tarlair with its modern open-air swimming pool. The well which made Tarlair famous as a spa in the nineteenth century, when it was featured in William Alexander's dialect classic *Johnny Gibb o' Gushetneuk* no longer flows—in consequence it is thought of enemy bombing in World War II.

East of Macduff and between it and the Aberdeenshire border at Pennan lies a fantastic coastline. Instead of sloping down to the sea the land rises up to it in waves of green grassy hills pierced by deeply-cut dens each with its tiny stream. The cliffs rise to 536 feet at Gamrie Mhor on the western flank of Gamrie Bay, while on the east of it the massive red sandstone promontory of Troup Head attains 396 feet. Between the two lies Gardenstown, founded by Alexander Garden of Troup in 1720, separated by a minor headland called the Snook from Crovie, an ancient cliff-foot village in which the houses stand two deep in a long line almost overhung by the precipitous cliffwall.

The houses of Gardenstown (population 906) are built on terraces cut in the hillside. Here there dwells an immensely stable and conservative community of the ancient fishing stock. Gardenstown-owned dual-purpose vessels are to be found fishing all round the coast from Mallaig in the west to Aberdeen in the east, and the village—which is a stronghold of the Plymouth Brethren, both Exclusive and Open—is said to be the wealthiest in Scotland.

Overlooking this extraordinary village from the heights of Gamrie Mhor is a famous ruined church:

> Half up the ribs of a bold giant hill,
>   That washes his feet in the sea
> And looks like a king of the watery world,
>   Lo! a patch of greenery.
> Westward and northward the crags rise high
>   To shield it from injury,
> And there looking down on the beautiful bay
>   Is the churchyard of Gamerie.

The ancient parish kirk of St John the Baptist of Gamrie has an almost fabulous origin. It was erected in the year 1004 to commemorate a Norse invasion that ended on the flat summit of that frowning cape with the Battle of the Bleedy Pits, and the skulls of 'three Norse kings' who were victims of the slaughter were built into the walls of the fabric. It remained the parish church of Gamrie until 1830.

Before we pass on to the coastline west of Banff something must be said of the vale of the Deveron. The river is over 60 miles long and rises in the upland fastness of the Cabrach, that moorland wilderness fringed by heather-covered hills and rugged deer-forests between Upper Don and Spey. It passes briefly through Aberdeenshire in the Haugh of Glass south-west of Huntly and skirting that town on the west re-enters Banffshire at Rothiemay, where it turns northward through pleasant wooded defiles to Bridge of Marnoch. Besides Huntly Castle (described in the last chapter) its historic homes include Beldorney in Glass, a Z-plan castle with a massive round tower (circa 1550); the House of Aswanley, a seventeenth-century L-plan structure with a projecting round tower, also in Glass; Kinnairdy Castle at Bridge of Marnoch, a stern L-plan tower-house finely restored by its late owner Sir Thomas Innes; and Forglen, near Turriff, close to which is the ruin of Carnousie, a sixteenth-century Z-plan tower house.

Sweeping north from the outskirts of Turriff, where it is spanned by a fine three-arched bridge of Delgatie sandstone, Deveron flows by Forglen (which has a doorway of 1577 in the modern mansion of 1839) through the estates of Montblairy and Relugas to meet the burn of King Edward by the ruins of Eden Castle, and finally enters picturesque narrows between the Hill of Alvah and the Hill of Montcoffer, where a spectacular single-span bridge crosses a chasm only 17 feet wide over a pool 50 feet deep. This is the last highlight, for now the river, which has spent so much of its course evading rather than seeking the haunts of men, circles a wide flood plain to reach Banff Bridge.

West of Banff runs A98, the main road from Fraserburgh to Inverness. It keeps a little distance from the Moray Firth coast, but a succession of well-sign-posted side roads lead off on the right to the many fishing havens of Banffshire. The first of these is Whitehills, another little sea-town of remarkable character.

"A society quite unique" was how the Reverend Alexander Anderson described Whitehills in 1839, and so it has remained to the present day. Though only 3 miles from Banff its close-knit fisher-family structure is proof against any surrender of individuality. Stake Ness to the west of the village has been chosen as the site of a large nuclear power station, but that too will pass Whitehills by.

From the clifftop of Stake Ness one sees the whole of Whitehills laid out before one under the sheltering bluff of Knock Head, with the white horses of the Moray Firth breakers heaped high by a northerly breeze and throwing spray over the pier head. Today it has a population of over one thousand, most of whom bear the names Watson, Lovie, Adamson, Findlay and Ritchie. This has been so since at least 1727 when a solid and ponderous town-crier's bell (now preserved in a window sill of Trinity Church) had that date carved upon it under the legend "The town of Whitehills". As in so many other North-east fisher havens the use of 'tee names'—additional nicknames—is vitally essential to identify persons of the same surname and Christian name. Today the little port has over twenty seine-net boats, which are all locally manned and owned. The present harbour was built in 1900 and a covered fish market was completed in 1954.

The harbour commissioners are elected at a meeting of ratepayers in the town.

West of Whitehills, in a little glen where the Burn of the Boyne runs down to the sea, is the ruin of Boyne Castle, a courtyard castle built in the last quarter of the sixteenth century in imitation of a medieval stronghold. Its earlier predecessor nearer the coast was the home of Mary Bethune or Beaton, one of Mary Queen of Scots' 'four Maries'—

> Yestreen the Queen had four Maries,
>   This day she'll hae but three:
> There was Mary Beaton and Mary Seaton
> And Mary Carmichael and me.

Six miles west of Banff A98 runs into the burgh of Portsoy (population 1,691), which is really two towns in one. It became a burgh of barony in 1550 but did not spring into prominence until the early eighteenth-century, when Patrick Ogilvie, Lord Boyne, gave it a harbour and developed it for the export of serpentine or 'Portsoy marble'. When this trade declined and the harbour fell into decay, a virtually new town was built on the landward side. In the past decade the town council of Portsoy has carried out a phased restoration of the derelict harbour area. With the aid of grants from the Historic Buildings Council it has restored and modernized many blocks of picturesque old houses, recreating the atmosphere of the old port.

Inland from Portsoy a side-road runs to the quaint old village of Fordyce with a castle dating from 1592. It has angle turrets and a stair tower with a projecting staircase turret and a later plain wing at one side. In the kirkyard, part of the old church survives with a picturesque belfry of 1661 surmounting the ancient porch and session house. Fordyce had a famous academy founded by George Smith, a native of the village, who died on the way home from India with a fortune in 1790. By his will he stipulated that £40 per annum be paid to a schoolmaster who should dwell in Fordyce for the purpose of teaching as many boys of the name of Smith as the residue of his estate could maintain. Fordyce Academy became a great secondary school, but its eccentric situation was against it and it finally perished in the era of comprehensive education.

Still farther inland in rural Banffshire are the village of Cornhill and the small burgh of Aberchirder. Nicknamed 'Foggieloan' from its situation on a former peat moss, Aberchirder, founded in 1764 by Alexander Gordon of Auchintoul, is laid out in the form of three long parallel streets sloping gradually down from a hilltop, with a square a third of the way down Main Street. Its situation is picturesque and from a distance it seems to ride upon a sea of rolling farmland like the crest of a breaking wave.

West of Portsoy the increasing mildness and sweetness of the Moray Firth coast begins to be apparent. In 2 miles one reaches the golden crescent of Sandend Bay (local pronunciation 'Saneyn') with a charming string of cottages and a jetty. Officially it has been a 'port' for two centuries. Beyond this the grim ruin of Findlater Castle stands on its clifftop and then the road runs through gentle woods to Cullen, the gem of the 'Banffshire Riviera', with its spectacular railway viaduct, its colourful old sea town and its delectable stretch of 'singing sands' of dazzling whiteness, on which stand striking stacks of red sandstone rock. A trio of these are known as the Three Kings of Cullen, probably a corruption of the Three Kings of Cologne, i.e., the Three Wise Men. The sands do actually sing, giving out a sound like "woo, woo, woo" when beaten, due it is said to the friction of their uniform spherical grains.

The modern town stands on the clifftop and A98 passes through an arch under the railway framing a view of headland and harbour with gaily painted fisher cottages close-packed with gable-ends to the shore.

The town (population 1,360) was built between 1820–30 to plans by George MacWilliam for the Earl of Seafield to replace Old Cullen, an ancient royal burgh clustered round the old parish church at the gates of Cullen House, a mile and a half inland to the south. The little old pre-Reformation Kirk of Cullen dates from at least 1236. In 1536 a south transept called St Anne's Aisle was added, and in 1543 the church became a collegiate— the last of thirty-eight such churches erected in Scotland between 1342 and 1545. The chancel was lengthened and staffed by a 'college' consisting of a provost, six prebendaries and two singing boys. Two treasures survive from this period, a sacrament house in the north wall and the huge ornate baroque tomb of Alexander Ogilvy who died in 1554. The massive two-storey Seafield Gallery or laird's pew was built in 1602.

Cullen House, home of the Earl of Seafield, dates from 1543 but an east wing was added in 1711 and additions designed by

David Bryce were made in 1859. Its outer face, save for the enlarged windows, is that of a French-inspired chateau of the age of Mary Queen of Scots, but inside it has all the elegance of the age of Queen Anne.

Unfortunately this fine house is no longer open to the public. An attempt to make it a self-supporting place of pilgrimage had to be abandoned. The Earl himself moved to a smaller house in the grounds and there was an auction of many of the famous art treasures amassed by his family. This would have hurt the most renowned of the Ogilvies, James fourth Earl of Findlater and first of Seafield. It was he who, as Lord Chancellor of Scotland at the time of the Union of the Parliaments, prorogued the Scots Estates for the last time with the historic words: "There's ane end o' an auld sang."

Behind Cullen the vale of the Cullen Burn is flanked on the west by the rounded Bin Hill (1,050 feet), which dominates the skyline of the Moray Firth for scores of miles. From the road which crosses the flank of the Bin Hill from the west, glorious with a sea of golden broom, one has a view of all that remains of coastal Banffshire in the wide sweep of Spey Bay: due north at the western end of Cullen Bay high grassy cliff tops run out to Scar Nose, the most northerly point of Banffshire. On the cliff-top here, above a succession of striking rock formations including the Bow Fiddle Rock, with its huge arch perforated by a great circular opening, is the burgh of Portknockie (population 1,100) founded by colonists from Cullen in 1677, in which long straight streets of gaily painted stone cottages run to the cliffs.

On a voters' roll of 1960 Portknockie had 220 Mairs, 124 Woods and 74 Slaters and the first house in the town was built by a Slater nearly 300 years ago. The fine harbour with its two basins was filled with herring drifters until well into the 1930s, but now lies empty save for a few pleasure craft and a children's paddling pond. Much the same story can be told of Findochty 2 miles to the west, with its population of 1,331. There were "port, customs and fishing grounds" at Findochty in 1568, but the present haven was founded in 1716. Two headlands, one crowned by a church, the other by an obelisk, enclose the quiet harbour, over which from the landward side broods the seated statue of a fisherman.

Golf devotees find the Moray Firth courses bracing to a degree.

At Banff there is the splendid Duff House Royal on the haugh-lands of the Deveron. At Cullen there is an ego-boosting course shared with Portknockie. West of Findochty there is the famous course at Strathlene—and this leads on to the remarkable conur-bation, really a 3-mile-long ribbon development embracing the havens of Portessie, Gordonsburgh, Ianstown, Seatown and Buckpool, which make up modern Buckie, the biggest and most active port in the county. The silence that enfolds the harbours of Cullen, Portknockie and Findochty is explained by the centrali-zation of the fishing industry at Buckie.

When the poet Burns visited Buckie in 1787 its two small villages had between them a population of 700 living in thatched but-and-bens. Today there are 7,669 folk. It was the 'fairy tale' of Banffshire fishing development—through undecked Scaffie boats to Fifies and Zulus, with their yacht-like lines, to wooden steam drifters that made this mighty change. Now the drifters have all gone and neat motor-driven dual-purpose boats take their place. There is a fleet of 106 fishing vessels of over 30 feet of keel, although at least half of them are landing their catches at east and west coast ports from North Shields to Ullapool. The Moray Firth fishermen have learned to be extremely mobile.

Architecturally perhaps the most interesting thing in Buckie is St Peter's Roman Catholic Church, built in 1857, with its twin spires—a reminder of the fact that, partly owing to the influence of the old-time Earls and Marquesses of Huntly, and the Gordons of whom they were the chiefs, this corner of Banffshire remained a redoubt of the Catholic religion after the Reformation. In 1617 there were over one thousand Catholics in Banffshire and only fifty in the city of Glasgow!

West of the multiple community that is Buckie there is one more sea-town with a quiet, almost deserted harbour, before we reach the county boundary of Moray at the Burn of Tynet. This is Portgordon (population 910), once a vital commercial port founded by the fourth Duke of Gordon at the end of the eigh-teenth century to export the grain of the rich farmlands of the Enzie in the hinterland. This commercial trade lasted until the end of last century and sixty years ago there were also ninety-four fishing boats. The only fishing still practised is for salmon.

We have now traversed the coast of Banffshire from end to end and may turn south to the interior. The Braes of Enzie, mostly green rolling farmland lying between Portgordon and Keith, the county's central pivot and 'second capital', saw the first serious revival of Catholicism in Scotland after the Reformation. In 1687 the remnant of those faithful to the old religion built at Chapelford on the Burn of Tynet, where there had been a pre-Reformation Chapel of St Ninian, the first Catholic church since the calamities of the sixteenth century. Today the site is marked by a cross in memory of Bishop Nicholson, the first Vicar Apostolic in Scotland. With him are buried the remains of twenty-six priests who laboured in the area.

A barn near the Bridge of Tynet was the next refuge of the Catholic faithful, but it was burned down after the 1745 Rebellion. In 1755 the laird of Tynet offered the use of a building which had been the cottage of a poor woman before being converted into a sheepcot. This long, low, whitewashed structure, with square windows and a slated roof, marked only by a ball of stone on the western gable, survives and is cherished today as the 'Banffshire Bethlehem' of the Catholics.

As we approach Keith from the north-west a vast line of bonded stores, between twenty and thirty of them, holding around one and a half million gallons of whisky, proclaim that we are now in the distillery country. Keith itself has four distilleries. In Banffshire as a whole there are now between twenty-five and thirty, mostly in the upper half of the county. Though they do not employ many men directly they add vastly to the economic wealth of the region, producing by pot still the unique malts which are essential elements in blends that are exported all over the world to boost Britain's dollar earnings by over £100,000,000 per annum.

Keith, on the Isla, Deveron's main tributary, set amid rounded hills, consists of three communities. Old Keith, clustered close to the river, around the Auld Brig built in 1609, was a very ancient place famous for a three-day market held in September. New Keith, on the high moorland plateau to the east of the Isla, was planned and laid out by the second Earl of Seafield in 1750, while Fife-Keith, on the other side of the Isla was founded by the Earl of Fife in 1817. The three townships have grown into one which became a police burgh in 1889 and has today a population of 4,208.

Quite as much of Banffshire by area lies to the south and west of Keith as lies to the north and east of it, but all this area is upland or highland, and very sparsely populated. To the west the railway and one road run through the parish of Boharm and the village of Mulben to Boat o' Bridge on the Spey and thence to Elgin. To the north-west A96, the trunk road crosses a moorland and descends through Speymouth Forest to Fochabers in Moray. To the south-west A920 ascends the upper Isla in lovely Botriphnie parish, through increasingly grand hill scenery by Drummuir and Loch Park to Dufftown, the real capital of malt distilling.

> Rome was built on seven hills,
> Dufftown on its seven stills.

This quaint and delightful small burgh, with a central square from which streets radiate crosswise was founded by the Earl of Fife in 1815 on a high-lying cape of land above the confluence of the Fiddich and the Dullan, highland burns which unite to rush down a wooded defile and empty their waters in the Spey at Craigellachie little over 2 miles to the north-west. Dufftown's coat of arms tells part of its history. Woven into it are the emblems of St Moluag of Lismore, patron saint of the ancient Kirk of Mortlach on the Dullan; that of the Stewart Earls of Atholl, lords of Balvenie, a Dufftown 'suburb' which became a burgh of barony in 1615, and that of the Duffs of Braco, Earls of Fife, the founders of the modern town.

Mortlach Church has a fabulous origin, being said to date from 1006 when Malcolm II defeated the invading Norsemen at this spot, but the Battle Stone in the churchyard is undoubtedly much older than that, and inside the church itself is the Elephant Stone, a Pictish sculptured stone of a still earlier period. Three lancet windows in the chancel gable date back to the thirteenth century. There is also a round-headed medieval doorway and an Easter Sepulchre with the effigy of a knight who is known to have died in 1549. But the loveliest thing about the church is its charming situation in the dell of the Dullan below the town.

Overlooking the Fiddich to the north-west of Dufftown is Balvenie Castle, a courtyard castle of the thirteenth century, which was transformed in the sixteenth century by the Stewart Earls of Atholl, who demolished the south-east front and built in its place a three-storey Renaissance tower-house known as the Atholl Building. It is now a showplace of the Department of the Environment. Dufftown's other castle, Auchindoun, overlooks the Fiddich 3 miles to the south-east from a conspicuous bluff which makes it visible for miles around. Pre-historic earthworks encircle it, and the central tower was built by the master-mason Cochran, ill-starred favourite of James III.

In the sixteenth century it belonged to Adam or 'Edom' Gordon (mentioned in the last chapter) and was destroyed by The Mackintosh, Chief of Clan Chattan, in reprisal for hostile actions. A ballad tells how The Mackintosh was warned of dire consequences:

> Turn, Willie Mackintosh,
> Turn, turn, I bid you!
> If you burn Auchindoun
> Huntly'll head you.

But Willie was not impressed:

> Head me or hang me,
> That winna fley me:
> I'll burn Auchindoun
> Ere the life lea' me.

> Light was the mirk hour
> At the day-dawin';
> Auchindoun was in a lowe
> Ere the cock-crawin'.

Today the life of Dufftown (population 1,557) is in its distilleries and though its passenger rail line is closed it remains the depot of a goods line from Keith with massive grain stores for barley.

From Dufftown Square, with its curious central clock tower, A941 runs north-west to Craigellachie and the burgh of Aberlour on the Spey, its opposite extension to the south-east ascending Glen Fiddich to enter and traverse the Cabrach by a pass between two guardian heights called the Glacks of Balloch. The B9009 road runs southward for 20 miles by Glenrinnes and Glenlivet to Tomintoul, at 1,160 feet the highest village in the Highlands. All this Upper Banffshire country is remote and scenically splendid.

In it we are once more in the upland fastnesses beloved of Queen Victoria. A stone marked "V. R. 24th Sept. 1867" marks the spot at Lynemore on the Glenrinnes road where she stopped for a picnic tea *en route* to Glenfiddich Lodge. Glenlivet, of course, is the home of the most famous whisky in the world, though for over a century it has given its name to a whole family of whiskies. Smith's Glenlivet Distillery, licensed in 1823, is however the only one legally entitled to call itself 'The Glenlivet'; all the others,

and there are over a score, must use the name only in combination
with some qualifying prefix—Glen Grant-Glenlivet, Glenfarclas
Glenlivet, Longmorn-Glenlivet and so on. Besides its renown as
the home country of Scotch—there were once around two hundred
illicit stills in the area—Glenlivet was the site of a famous Roman
Catholic college at Scalan.

Livet is a tributary of Avon, which enters Spey at Ballindalloch
near the south-western tip of the county, the parish of Inveravon.

> The water o' A'an so fair and clear
> Would deceive a man of a hundred year.

Ballindalloch Castle on the holm where the Avon meets the
Spey, the old House of Kilmaichlie higher upstream and the
ruined pile of Drumin at the Livet's confluence are the architectural highlights. Ballindalloch Castle began as a Z-plan tower
house in 1546, with additions in 1602 and extensions in the
eighteenth and nineteenth centuries. Its Macpherson-Grant
lairds built up perhaps the most famous Aberdeen-Angus cattle
herd on record.

Lovely as are its lower reaches, the Avon's middle and upper
glens exceed them in grace and have been claimed to be, from the
point of view of river and mountain scenery, the most perfect in
Scotland. Tomintoul (population 278) is not actually in the glen
itself but high above the river on the barren moorland where it
was laid out in 1779 by the fourth Duke of Gordon. But it is
within very easy reach of the delectable stream and has mellowed
mightily in its 190 years of growth, and it enjoys superb views of
Ben Avon and Ben Muich Dhui to the south.

Banffshire's frontier on the Spey, all the way from Ballindalloch to Boat o' Bridge, is like a window on a softer, sweeter
world. From the picturesque Bridge of Avon at Ballindalloch,
A95 runs along the river's high right bank through cattle-breed-
ing country dotted with distilleries northwards to Charleston of
Aberlour (population 958), a handsome little town with a
pleasant village green and a long main street lined with trees. It
was founded by Charles Grant of Wester Elchies in 1812. With
Ben Rinnes (2,765 feet) to the south-east and Ben Aigan (1,544
feet) dominating the skyline to the north, the Spey here flows in
lordly curves below swelling uplands, and at Queen's View from
Tunnel Brae, on A93 between Aberlour and Craigellachie, it
presents the finest of all its sylvan prospects.

Hardly less picturesque is the scene at Craigellachie itself, where the delicate white tracery of Telford's iron bridge inscribes a gentle arc above the river, leaping from the right bank to the base of the rugged Rock of Craigellachie, a pair of battlemented towers on either side anchoring the fairy-like structure. This famous bridge, built in 1815 and linking Banff and Moray at the pine-clad precipice where in days of old Clan Grant rallied to the defence of Strathspey, is hardly adequate for modern traffic and a new road bridge has been built a little to the north. But it may serve as the terminus of our lightning tour of the county of Banff—a happy ending indeed, amid delectable river scenery, where dippers dart from bank to bank and oyster-catchers nest amid the dazzling shingle or race above the rapid waters uttering their plaintive cries, while the cuckoo calls distantly from the woods of Arndilly.

For administrative purposes—though not for legal or Parliamentary ones—the old county of Banff has been split down the middle, the western portion becoming simply the eastern half of the new Moray District within the Grampian Region of Scotland and the eastern half attached to a district authority called Banff/Buchan. Yet this rather arbitrary share-out cannot unsay the legacy of centuries of history or the consequences of differing social structure. The ancient territory of Banffshire was part of the 'Poor Man's Country', a uniquely characterful peasant farming area including all of Aberdeenshire and the northern half of Kincardine. Its Spartan quality—in stark contrast to the lush indigenous fertility of the Laich of Moray—and its family farming traditions, have moulded the character of its people in a very powerful way. If the city of Aberdeen succeeds in emerging from the age of North Sea oil exploitation with its essential racial traits undamaged and resilient, it may well thank the peasant farming background of its rugged hinterland, so wonderfully transformed by generations of shrewd tillers of a difficult soil.

X

ABERDEEN: THE KEY TO THE PATTERN

Ile toon, boom city,
Texas o' the North—
sombreros instead o' bonnets?
black gowd instead o' siller?

Havers! Frae Fittie
tae Rubislaw yer granite
waas'll halt sic an invasion.
The blunt speak o' Aiberdonian
doddies winna encompass
yon obligatory drawl.

The smell onywye'll tell
ye—nae ile—fish.

Ken Morrice

THE question is often posed: will the impact of the offshore oil industry distort and ultimately undermine the indigenous culture and economy of North-east Scotland? When the supposedly temporary oil boom ends will Aberdeen be left without resource? There are two answers to this: (1) the need for shore-based services and supplies which Aberdeen is now providing to the North Sea oil installations will continue until 2030 at the least, that is for virtually a lifetime, and (2) the 27,000 jobs and 533 new enterprises conjured into being by the oil boom have never been more than a supplement to the city's traditional economic resources.

Go to any corner of the province and you will find that reference back to Aberdeen comes as natural as breathing. To a large extent the reverse is also true. Every other city family has its roots either in north-east farm or fishing havens.

This and the fact that Aberdeen is remote from Scotland's

central belt with its heavy industries, has militated against a self-contained urbanity. Aberdeen had its slums. It still has areas of seedy neglect and human irresponsibility, but the squalor, where it exists, has almost a semi-rural air—not the deep alienation from nature that is to be found in massive industrial conurbations.

It has been said that on the whole the Scots are a nation of small-town and village dwellers, and though perhaps no longer true in the second half of the century, Aberdeen had a sense of small-town intimacy at least until the Second World War. This was exploited by the favourite Aberdeen comedian, Harry Gordon, who in the song written for him by Archie Hyslop portrayed "The Auldest Aiberdonian".

> I'm the auldest man that iver lived in Aiberdeen,
> Oh, lots an' lots o' famous things an' people I hae seen,
> I can min' when Wallace in the city spent an' 'oor,
> I went an' had a drink wi' him inside the Wallace Tower.
>
> Fittie folk, Kitty folk,
> Country folk and city folk,
> Folk fae Constitution Street, and folk fae Rubislaw Den,
> Wallfield, Nellfield, Mannofield an' Cattofield,
> I ken lots o' stories the Professors dinna ken.

Advancing to the footlights in the over-dressed garb of one of his dame parts he would simper and say "Chilly for June!" a popular reference to the occasional summer cold snap Aberdeen endures.

The last word on Aberdeen's climate was probably said by John R. Allan. Explaining how he came to return to the city after some years in 'exile' he remarked: "I stayed away for a long time. I lived in beautiful easy places where I did not have to run to keep warm in summer. But there was something wrong. I began to pine for the want of fresh air. I sat under the magnolia tree in the scented noon and gasped for a south-east wind off Girdleness and the breezes from Rattray Head that blow away the hens and the henhouse too."

William Forsyth, a nineteenth-century editor of the *Aberdeen Journal* put the same thing another way when he wrote of the city:

> And well I wot thy best of wealth
>   The wind of God brings fairly free,
> Thy brave bright eyes and ruddy health,
>   Fair City by the Sea.

For, make no mistake, Aberdeen is bracing. Her "lads o pairts", the poor, bright boys who struggled thither to the universities with a peck of oatmeal to keep away the pangs of hunger while they burned the midnight candle in cramming for a degree found it so. They looked back later and shared the sentiments of Rachel Annand Taylor:

> What marvellous mad hopes were cherished
>   In Aberdeen!
> Oh! that's a city to be born in.
>   The pure air kindles you, and witty
> Your mind goes dancing. To learn scorn in
>   Oh, that's a city.

One of the less impressive consequences of that scorn was the Aberdeen Joke, now I think happily on the way out. No doubt it had its rise, genuinely enough in the extreme frugality of life in the days when economic survival in a difficult land was a sore struggle. Suddenly in the first or second decades of this century the shifts of ruthless hoarding and saving to which their ancestors had been put began to seem comic to Aberdonians themselves. And thus the Aberdeen Joke was born.

As late as 1922 Dr J. F. Tocher, the City Analyst, commented: "Aberdeen is a factory working day and night—especially at night—manufacturing jokes against Aberdeen."

The average Aberdonian, like the average citizen of any other city, is not an intellectual. The most characteristic words on his lips are probably the words "nae bad". His weather is not bad. His temperament, though plodding and deprecating, is not bad either. He has been accused of materialism and Philistinism. But these charges have usually come from his brothers or sisters, poets or prophets or scientists who have been filled with the fires of a divine discontent.

As earlier chapters have made clear Aberdeen has produced many great civil servants, mathematicians, and medicos like the Gregorys. It produced great Empire builders like Sir Robert Williams; it produced the founder of tropical medicine, Sir Patrick Manson; the co-discoverer of insulin, J. J. Macleod; philosophers like Thomas Reid; Concordance-makers like Cruden the Corrector; pioneers of psychology like Alexander Bain; historians like James Gordon and John Spalding, Joseph Robertson and John Hill Burton; missionaries like Robert Laws of Livingstonia. It has had its share of men who travelled far and made fortunes like Sir Alexander MacRobert. But its poets and dreamers have been quite as plentiful as its hard-headed business men.

Anyone who doubts this should take a look at a massive compendium of over 600 pages entitled *The Bards of Bon-Accord 1375-1860*. This takes us back to John Barbour, Archdeacon of Aberdeen, who wrote "The Brus" with its apostrophe to liberty:

> A! Fredome is a noble thing!
> Fredome maiss man to haif liking:
> Fredome all solace to man giffis:
> He levis at ease that freely levis!
> A noble heart man haif nane ease,
> Na ellis nocht that may him please,
> Gif fredome failye . . .

Of course not all the rhyming geese of Aberdeen can be said to have graduated into swans. In the eighteenth century, however, two figures stand out, the one representing the gentility of the Enlightenment, the other the racy vernacular of the national revival, James Beattie (1735-1803) the author of "The Minstrel" and John Skinner (1721-1807) whose "Tullochgorum" was quoted in Chapter IV. Skinner, a Scottish Episcopalian pastor, ministered in Monymusk before settling near Longside in Buchan, and there is a case for linking Monymusk also with the genius of Gawain Douglas, first translator of Virgil's *Aeneid* into memorable verse, for he too lived briefly there.

The two streams of Scots and English poetry have continued down to the present day in modern Aberdeen poets like Alexander Scott, Senior Lecturer in Scottish Literature in Glasgow University; Flora Garry and John C. Milne, who, with George Bruce, were quoted in Chapter VIII; and G. S. Fraser, son of a former town clerk of Aberdeen.

There is also the vast stream of popular ballad lore indigenous to the region. For centuries ballad singing was a vivid element in the rural life of the north-east. Gavin Greig (1856-1914) collected more than two thousand ballads with the airs to which they were sung; 125 of these were published in 1925 in a volume edited by Alexander Keith. The remainder, in the archives of Aberdeen University, are meanwhile under expert study. The late Jeannie Robertson in Aberdeen, who learned the ballads from her mother,

a travelling tinker, sang them in the high traditional style
to the delight of folk-lore researchers.

Lord Byron is not normally listed in the Valhalla of Aberdeen
poets. But in a sense he is the most representative of them all.
Looking back near the end of his life he could write:

> My heart flies to my head
> As *Auld Lang Syne* brings Scotland, one and all,
> Scotch plaids, Scotch snoods, the blue hills and clear streams,
> The Dee, the Don, Balgownie Brig's black wall—
> All my boy feelings, all my gentler dreams.

Owing to its centuries of struggle to subdue a harsh environment, the time which Aberdeen has enjoyed to cultivate the graces
of life has been after all pitifully short. And while its aesthetic
sophistication is not now negligible—its musical life is astonish-
ingly rich and varied and its fine theatre has at least seasons of
serious drama, opera and ballet, while the art gallery and the
civic arts centre organize notable exhibitions—perhaps the greatest
creation of Aberdonians has been the city of Aberdeen itself.

The first visitor's guide to Aberdeen was written in Latin. It
was entitled *Aberdoniae Utriusque Descriptio* and its author was
Parson James Gordon of Rothiemay, who on 16th October 1661
presented to the town council a pen-and-ink drawing "upon ane
meikle cairt of paper", his map of the city "weill done". In re-
compense of this the magistrates voted him a silver cup of 20
ounces with a silk hat for himself and "ane silk gown to his bed-
fellow". In the Latin description of "both the towns of Aberdeen"
which accompanied his map Parson Gordon indulged in a
eulogy of his native city which still has some topical interest.
A somewhat barbarous translation of this was made, from which I
quote:

> Aberdeen exceeds not only the towns of the North of Scotland but
> likewise any city whatsoever of that same latitude for greatness,
> beauty and frequency of trading. The air is temperate and healthful
> about it, and it may be that the citizens owe the acuteness of their
> wits thereunto, and their civil inclinations, the like not easy to be
> found under so northerly a climate, damped for the most part with
> air of a gross consistence. . . .
>
> Many houses have orchards and gardens adjoining; every garden
> has its postern, and these are planted with all sorts of trees which
> the climate will suffer to grow, so that the whole town, to such
> as draw near it . . . looks as if it stood in a garden and little wood.

That was three hundred years ago, but it is a fact that Aberdeen appeals to the visitor today for precisely the same reason. "Where else", said one of them to me, "will you find a town where the main by-pass is lined down the middle with roses? And where will you find another in which trees have been so cherished and intelligently used in urban planning?"

Aberdeen can be taken as a test case of man's ability to live in a city without losing his contact with nature through the surrounding countryside, or polluting and desecrating it. Even here vandalism is not totally absent. The little parish hall at Ardoe by the River Dee 3 miles from the city has had its windows smashed by roving juvenile delinquents from an urban housing scheme. The lower reaches of the River Don are now very seriously polluted by industrial effluent but strenuous efforts are being made to solve the problem.

Aberdonians are aware that the province of which their town is the capital has one priceless asset denied to industrial Britain. Its roads passing through a countryside of great beauty are un-crowded and tension-free. This has been an inducement to the executives of various light industries which have settled in the small towns and villages of the Aberdeen hinterland in the past decade. There are not nearly enough of these to satisfy the North-east of Scotland Development Authority, anxious to offset the continuing drain of population from the farming areas where mechanization of agriculture has displaced great numbers of farm workers.

But so happy are the newcomers that the word will get around. In a Britain where the population pundits forecast a nation of 100 millions by the end of the century, this is one region where the vision of human beings packed like battery hens is still utterly unreal. Not even the advent of a new major factor in the harvesting of North Sea oil, which has already brought an invasion of technicians working on the oil-rigs and led to special housing provision by the local authorities, can alter the basic spaciousness of the North-east environment. For as long as we can foresee there will be room for all in a land where idyllic peace and the joy of timeless nature on the moors and hilltops—or by fantastic rock-fretted coastlines and golden beaches is at everyone's command.

Aberdeen's constellation of satellite counties were drawn into a closer union with the city as a result of the local government reforms which became operative in May 1975. At present the North Sea oil boom has produced certain uncomfortable anomalies: intense demand for land and pressure on housing in the immediate environs of the city of Aberdeen (with £16,000 an acre being paid in favoured localities) while at the same time depopulation continues in the remoter rural districts.

Unemployment has dwindled to negligible proportions in the boom centres, but there is still a need to revitalise the rural economy. The challenge to the new regional and district authorities is one of attempting to spread the new oil-based prosperity more widely over the province.

Down the ages the principal export of Aberdeen and its province—apart from the fruits of the land and the sea—has been brains. This will no doubt continue to be so. But there are still immense problems of land use, of conservation of existing resources, of integration into the economic pattern of Britain as a whole, with Europe and the rest of the world beyond that, which call for the use of North-east brains on the North-east's own territory. The still expanding university and the chain of research institutions devoted to fisheries, soil science, animal nutrition and moorland ecology will help to see that this occurs.

Most Aberdonians can put their hands on their hearts and say simply: "This is a good place to live!" Perhaps the merging of local authorities will also be of benefit to the tourist, if by means of it he can become aware, not merely of the lure of Royal Deeside with its blue hills and clear streams, but also of that necklace of sands and rock-girt fisher havens that enriches the North-east from Spey Bay to the North Esk, of the delectable unfrequented reaches of Don and Deveron, the moors of the Cabrach, the vales of the Ythan and the Ugie and the historic marches "whaur Gadie rins at the back o' Bennachie".

BIBLIOGRAPHY

The Region as a Whole

Alison, James (editor), *Poetry of North-east Scotland* (Heinemann Educational 1976).

Allan, John R., *The North-east Lowlands of Scotland* (Robert Hale 1952). This shrewd picture of the characteristics of the region and its people can be supplemented by the same author's *The Seasons Return: Impressions of Farming Life* (Hale 1955) and *Farmer's Boy* (Methuen 1935).

Cruden, Stewart, *The Scottish Castle* (Nelson 1960).

Gaskin, Maxwell (editor), *North-east Scotland: A Study of its Development Potential* (H.M.S.O. 1969).

Graham, Cuthbert (editor), *North-east Muse Anthology* (Aberdeen Journals 1978).

Gray, Sir Alexander, *Selected Poems* (Maclellan, Glasgow, N.D.).

Hamilton, Henry (editor), *Third Statistical Account of Scotland: County of Aberdeen* (Collins 1960).

Keith, Alexander (editor), *Last Leaves of Traditional Ballads and Ballad Airs Collected in Aberdeenshire by the late Gavin Greig* (The Buchan Club, Aberdeen 1925).

Keith, James, *Fifty Years of Farming* (Faber 1954).

O'Dell, A. C. and Mackintosh, J. (editors), *The North-east of Scotland* (British Association, Aberdeen)—a scientific survey.

Simpson, W. Douglas, *The Province of Mar* (Aberdeen University Studies No. 121, 1944) and *The Earldom of Mar* (A. U. Studies No. 124, 1949). Also invaluable are the same author's *The Ancient Stones of Scotland* (Hale 1968) and *Portrait of the Highlands* (Hale 1969).

Spalding, John, *Memorialls of the Trubles in Scotland and in England A.D. 1624–A.D. 1645* (The Spalding Club, Aberdeen 1850). A contemporary historical classic of great interest and charm.

Aberdeen City

Fraser, G. M., *Historical Aberdeen* (Smith, Aberdeen 1905) and *The Bridge of Dee* (Smith, Aberdeen 1913).

Fraser, G. S., *Home Town Elegy* (Nicholson & Watson 1944).

Gordon, James, *New and Old Aberdeen* (maps) and *Description of Both Towns of Aberdeen 1661* (The Spalding Club, Aberdeen).

Johnston, Margaret, *Ninety Wonderful Years 1869–1959* The biography of Sir Thomas Mitchell (G. & W. Fraser, Aberdeen 1960).

Keith, Alexander, *A Thousand Years of Aberdeen* (Aberdeen University Press). The latest comprehensive and detailed history of the city.

Linklater, Eric, *White Maa's Saga* (Cape 1929). Novel which pictures student life in Aberdeen in 1920s.

Mackenzie, Hugh, *The Third Statistical Account of Scotland: The City of Aberdeen* (Oliver and Boyd 1953).

Robbie, William, *Aberdeen, Its Traditions and History* (Wyllie, Aberdeen 1873).

Robertson, Joseph, *The Book of Bon-Accord* (Simpkin, Marshall 1839). A historical classic of wit and charm.

Taylor, Rachel Annand, *The End of Fiammetta* (Richards Press).

Trail, Katherine E., *The Story of Old Aberdeen* (Wyllie, Aberdeen 1929).

Walker, William, *The Bards of Bon-Accord* (Edmond and Spark, Aberdeen 1887).

Wyness, Fenton, *City by the Grey North Sea: Aberdeen* (A. P. Reid & Son, Aberdeen 1963). This thorough, well-illustrated history has since been supplemented by the same author's *Spots from the Leopard: Stories of Aberdeen and the North-east* (Impulse Books, Aberdeen 1971).

Deeside

Alexander, Sir Henry, *The Cairngorms* (Scottish Mountaineering Club 1928).

Bremner, Alexander, *The Physical Geology of the Dee and Don Valleys* (Aberdeen University Press 1921).

Brown, Ivor, *Balmoral: The History of a Home* (Collins 1966).

Braemar Gathering, Book of the—annual issues 1925–71 (Herald Press, Arbroath).

Deeside Field, The: First series 8 vols. 1922–37. Second series, 8 vols. 1953–70 (The Deeside Field Club, Aberdeen).

Fraser, G. M., *The Old Deeside Road* (Aberdeen University Press 1921). Reprinted 1980 (Robin Callander).

Henderson, John A., *Annals of Lower Deeside* (Wyllie, Aberdeen 1892) and *A History of the Parish of Banchory-Devenick* (Wyllie 1890).

Humphrey, Frank Pope, *The Queen at Balmoral* (Fisher Unwin 1893).

Mackintosh, John, *History of the Valley of the Dee* (Taylor and Henderson, Aberdeen 1895).

McConnochie, A. I., *Deeside* (Wyllie, Aberdeen 1893) and *Lochnagar* (Wyllie, 1891).

Michie, J. G., *Deeside Tales* (Wyllie 1908) and *History of Logie Coldstone* (Wyllie 1896).

Nethersole-Thompson, D. and Watson, A., *The Cairngorms* (Scottish Mountaineering Club 1974).

Robertson, Joseph—real author of *The New Deeside Guide* by James Brown (Lewis Smith, Aberdeen 1843).

Shepherd, Nan, *The Living Mountain* (Aberdeen University Press 1977), a fine study of the Cairngorms, and three novels all published by Constable—*The Quarry Wood* (1928), *The Weatherhouse* (1933) and *A Pass in the Grampians* (1934).

Smith, Robert, *Grampian Ways* (Melven, Perth 1980).

Victoria, Queen, *Leaves from the Journal of Our Life in the Highlands 1848–1861* (Smith, Elder 1868) and *More Leaves from the Journal of Life in the Highlands 1862–1882* (Smith, Elder 1884).

Stirton, John, *Crathie and Braemar:* A History of the United Parish (Milne and Hutchison, Aberdeen 1925).

Walton, Kenneth (editor), *Royal Grampian Country*, a Survey (Department of Geography, Aberdeen University 1969).

Watt, V. J. Buchan, *The Book of Banchory* (Oliver and Boyd 1947).

Wyness, Fenton: *Royal Valley: The Story of the Aberdeenshire Dee* (A. P. Reid and Son, Aberdeen 1968). Invaluable up-to-date history and reference book.

Kincardineshire

Gibbon, Lewis Grassic, *A Scots Quair: Sunset Song, Cloud Howe,*

Grey Granite (Hutchinson 1966); *A Scots Hairst*, Essays and Short Stories edited by Ian S. Munro (Hutchinson 1967).

Kinnear, G. H. *Kincardineshire* (Cambridge 1901).

Munro, Ian S., *Leslie Mitchell: Lewis Grassic Gibbon* (Oliver and Boyd 1966).

Simpson, W. Douglas: *Dunnottar Castle* (Wyllie, Aberdeen 1966).

Donside and Buchan

Alexander, William: *Johnny Gibb of Gushetneuk* (Heritage Press, Towie Barclay Castle, Turriff 1979). A classic first published in 1871.

Bruce, George, *Collected Poems* (Edinburgh University Press 1971).

Carter, Ian, Farm Life in North-east Scotland, 1840–1914: The Poor Man's Country (John Donald, Edinburgh 1979). A sociological study which goes far to explain the peasant culture of the North-east.

Findlay, J. T., *A History of Peterhead* (Scrogie, Peterhead 1933).

Garry, Flora: *Bennygoak and Other Poems* (Rainbow Books, Aberdeen 1975).

McConnochie, A. I., *Donside* (Jolly, Aberdeen 1901).

Milne, John C., *Poems* (Aberdeen University Press 1964).

Murray, Charles, *Hamewith*, the Complete Poems of Charles Murray (published for the Charles Murray Memorial Trust by Aberdeen University Press 1979). First published in 1900 *Hamewith* remains a best-selling classic.

Pratt, J. B., *Buchan* (Heritage Press, Towie Barclay Castle, Turriff, 1978). First published in 1859.

Simpson, W. Douglas, *Craigievar Castle* (National Trust for Scotland 1966), *The Book of Glenbuchat* (Third Spalding Club, Aberdeen 1942), *Huntly Castle* (H.M.S.O. 1960), *The Castle of Kildrummy* (Wyllie, Aberdeen 1923).

Stirling, A. M. W., *Fyvie Castle* (John Murray 1928).

Toulmin, David, *Hard Shining Corn* (Impulse Books, Aberdeen 1972), *Straw into Gold* (Impulse 1973), *Blown Seed, A Novel* (Paul Harris, Edinburgh 1976 and Pan Books 1977), *Harvest Home* (Harris 1978).

Banffshire

Barclay, William, *Banffshire* (Cambridge 1922).

Blair, John L. and Peter D. Sharp, *Royal and Ancient Banff* (Banff Preservation Society 1967).

INDEX